Labor Market Politics and the Great War

Labor Market Politics and the Great War

The Department of Labor, the States, and the First U.S. Employment Service, 1907–1933

WILLIAM J. BREEN

THE KENT STATE UNIVERSITY PRESS
Kent, Ohio, and London, England

© 1997 by The Kent State University Press, Kent, Ohio 44242
All rights reserved
Library of Congress Catalog Card Number 96-36067
ISBN 0-87338-559-4
Manufactured in the United States of America

Library of Congress Cataloging-in Publication Data

Breen, W. J. (William J.)
    Larbor market politics and the Great War : the Department of Labor, the states, and
the first U.S. Employment Service, 1907–1933 / William J. Breen.
    p. cm.
    Includes bibliographical references and index.
    ISBN 0-87338-559-4 (cloth : alk. paper) ∞
    1. Labor policy—United States—United States—History—20th century. 2. Labor
policy—United States—States—History—20th century. 3. World War, 1914–1918—
United States. 4. Reconstruction (1914–1939)—United States 5. United States. Dept.
of Labor—History. 6. United States Employment Service—History. I. Title.
HD 8072.B726 1997
331.12'042'097309041—dc20   96-36067
                                                        CIP

British Library Cataloging-in-Publication Data are available.

Contents

In memory of

BERNADETTE CATHERINE FITZGERALD

born Bridgeport, Connecticut, August 9, 1916

died New Milford, Connecticut, February 5, 1990

Acknowledgments

At the end of the protracted labor associated with the writing of this book, it seems appropriate to look back and thank the many individuals who have assisted me along the way.

All historians are dependent on archivists and librarians. This project relied heavily on the essential preparatory work done by archivists, particularly those located at the National Archives in Washington, D.C., and at a number of state archives. They were extremely prompt in responding to my inquiries from Australia and helpful in providing me with access to the appropriate records on my various research trips. I gratefully acknowledge that assistance. Without their patient labors, historical scholarship would wither.

The librarians in the Borchardt Library at La Trobe University, particularly those associated with the Inter-Library Loan Service, deserve special mention. Their ability to locate obscure references and to get them to La Trobe via the Inter-Library Loan Service system was of wonderful assistance to me throughout the research.

I am particularly grateful to the Australian Research Council for funding a number of trips to the United States that enabled me to do the basic archival research for this project. La Trobe University also afforded me generous leave and research support for this project. Without such assistance, this kind of scholarly project would be impossible.

I consider myself fortunate to be a member of the School of History at La Trobe University. Over the past twenty-five years, the school has provided a stimulating intellectual and collegial environment. I would particularly like to acknowledge the support and friendship of my colleague

John Salmond, with whom, for a quarter of a century, I have taught and discussed U.S. history. He also found time, in a busy schedule, to read and comment on an earlier draft of this manuscript.

Research and writing are difficult and lonely tasks. I doubt that this book would have been finished without the support of my family—both immediate and extended. The children have lived with the first U.S. Employment Service for a long time, although mostly without having to put up with the details. For my wife, Johanna, however, it was a different story: she listened patiently while I tried to sort out my ideas and ruthlessly blue-penciled early drafts. For that labor of love, as for many others, I am profoundly grateful.

This book is dedicated to Johanna's aunt and godmother, Bernadette Catherine Fitzgerald, who offered hospitality and friendship in Dallas, Texas, a long time ago when I needed both. She contributed more to both Johanna's and my own happiness than perhaps she ever knew. This book is dedicated, with love, to her memory.

Introduction

By the end of World War I, the first U.S. Employment Service (USES) had acquired far-reaching powers over the domestic labor market and controlled the distribution of unskilled labor to major war industries throughout the United States. Located within the Department of Labor, the USES had been little more than a paper organization before the United States entered the war. However, by mid-1918, in a labor market that had begun to register a serious labor shortage, the embryonic employment service was transformed into one of the major wartime administrative agencies of the federal government. Throughout 1918 the number of workers registering each month at USES offices climbed dramatically. In January only 82,353 registered; by November the figure had jumped to 744,712. This steep increase in registrations paralleled a similar increase in notifications from employers seeking labor. In January employers made notifications of only 80,002 vacancies; by November the figure was 1,724,943. Between January and November 1918, 3,675,858 workers registered at USES offices and employers made notifications of 7,895,675 vacancies. From the late spring of 1918, it was clear that the demand for labor was beginning to outstrip the supply. By midsummer, the American war effort faced a crisis in the labor market.[1] The reponse of the Wilson administration to that emerging wartime crisis is the focus of this study.

In the United States, the prewar labor market was characterized by considerable unemployment and irregularity of employment, enormous labor turnover, significant geographical mobility of labor, and the presence of a "labor reserve" fed by internal migration and immigration. The bulk of the industrial labor force was composed of unskilled or semiskilled workers. A system of direct employment, in which employers advertised in newspapers and hired directly at the factory gate, was characteristic of prewar American industry. There also existed a chaotic network of employment offices connecting workers and employers that was operated by commercial, philanthropic, union, employer, and other agencies. However, the overwhelming majority were private, competitive, fee-charging offices. Although neither the various states nor the federal government played a major role in the labor market prior to 1917, the dislocations caused by American intervention in the war created a growing pressure for large-scale state intervention.

A number of individual states had begun to experiment with free, public employment offices in the two decades before the outbreak of the war. Although these only handled a minute fraction of the total business, by early 1917 almost half the states of the Union operated such offices in direct competition with the fee-charging, private agencies. Insofar as the national government was involved in the labor market, it was through the U.S. Department of Labor, which, in the immediate prewar period, had begun to project itself in a very limited way into employment office work. However, public employment offices, both state and federal, serviced only a tiny proportion of the total market. The wartime crisis created tremendous demand for labor, and the federal government, through the Department of Labor, began to move toward regulating the national labor market. Although the labor market was never completely regulated, the direction in which policy was moving was clear and had the war lasted longer, much more intrusive state controls would have been implemented.

On the surface, the story of the USES can be read as one further example of a general process already familiar in Europe. Wartime demands appeared to lead inexorably to a more centralized, bureaucratic national administration and to greater state intervention in the economy.[2] Wartime crisis and state expansion seemed to go hand in hand. American involvement in World War I was the catalyst that projected the national government into labor market regulation. Without that crisis, it is difficult to envisage such a rapid expansion of the role of the national government in the labor market.[3] However, the move toward centralized state control over the wartime labor market masked a fundamental division within the administration over what the nature of that centralization should be. Was the centralized labor market to be administered on nationalist or federalist principles? That division was of fundamental importance in explaining the outcome of this episode of state intervention in the economy.

State building in the United States has been a slow and convoluted process. In recent years scholars have begun to explore why the American state developed so much later than did the major European states. Stephen Skowronek, in 1982, described the nineteenth-century American state as one composed of courts and parties that loosely held America together but that lacked any real national administrative capacities. The United States, in the nineteenth century, was an anomaly among Western states, having a "combination of extremes—a highly developed democratic politics without a concentrated governing capacity."[4] There was, by European standards, no strong central administrative state in the United States. This situation began to change around the turn of the century, but the process of state building proved long and tortuous. It was not until the Great Depression and World War II that the American state could be said to possess national adminstrative capacities. The story of the USES in the World War I era is one aspect of this wider development: it was an ambitious attempt to expand the power of the state over the labor market. In an immediate sense, this attempt proved to be unsuccessful, because it was not until 1933, in response to another crisis, that Congress finally established the USES as a permanent part of the state administration. However, the failure of the first USES is instructive: it illustrates some of the problems hindering the expansion of the American state in the early twentieth century.

Until the 1960s, historians usually associated the growth of the American state with a series of reform movements, when periodic swings in the national mood allowed reformers or "progressives" to unite men of good will in successful efforts to enlarge the range of state responsibilities. Any expansion of state responsibilities was considered to be reformist on the rather simplistic assumption that the state could identify the public interest and would always promote it. Based on a loose cyclical theory of change, this theory lost credibility under the weight of research demonstrating that a clear division between reform and nonreform periods was too simplistic: no such clear pattern of state growth was discernible.[5]

This "progressive" perspective on state building was supplanted by one that drew heavily on constructs from political science and sociology. The role of interest groups and elites was emphasized. In this version, in the late nineteenth century the railroads created a unified national economy which, in turn, spawned a host of special interest groups that were anxious to use the state to further their ambitions. This process usually entailed some expansion of the role of government in society and the creation of appropriate administrative machinery to match that enlarged role. In this pluralist model, the state was pictured as a more or less neutral umpire responding to a variety of societal pressures mounted by different organized groups. This model assumed that the public interest could be readily defined and that interest group pressure decided whether or not the state acted in the public interest.

An older Marxist interpretation suggested, instead, that the state was the instrument of the ruling class and functioned to ensure that the interests of capital always prevailed. New Left, neo-Marxist scholars, aware that the weight of historical evidence undermined such a crudely instrumental approach, began to develop more sophisticated models. One group espoused a corporatist or corporate liberal approach that suggested that farsighted corporate leaders influenced the state to enact welfare measures in order to deflect rising working class militance. Again, the lack of sufficient empirical evidence to support such large assertions and the tendency of the approach to lead "to notions of conspiracy that rested upon unbelievable premises" made the theory ultimately unpersuasive.[6]

Another approach rejected the idea that the state was merely a reflection of societal interests—whether of interest groups, the capitalist ruling class, or farsighted corporate leaders—and suggested, instead, that the state acted autonomously. The social scientists and historians who have promoted this more state-centered concept have divided over whether the state acts autonomously or only potentially or relatively autonomously.[7] However, in spite of this division, there is agreement that state policy is not a simple reflection of societal interests but, rather, that the state itself plays a considerable role in shaping events and outcomes. Statemaking is seen as an ongoing process of struggle in which "the state becomes a battleground on which conflicting classes and contending bureaucrats simultaneously compete for power."[8] As Ellis Hawley suggested in 1988, it seemed likely that "a more satisfactory answer" to the problem posed by the growth of the American state "can be had if pride of place in the story is given to state institutions as they are operated by public officials."[9] In this book I endeavor to follow that advice by looking in detail at the attempt made by public officials to expand the role of the state to cover a quite new activity, namely, labor market regulation. A detailed sifting of the available evidence indicates the crucial importance of the state itself in promoting that expansion and the relative unimportance of wider societal interest groups in the process. In this particular instance of wartime crisis, the state did appear to act autonomously.

In the debate over the growth of the American state there has been a curious lack of attention paid to the role played by federalism. Scholars have been at pains to outline the influence of the separation of powers—the divided nature of sovereignty embedded in the U.S. Constitution—and the consequent difficulty in getting common policies agreed to among the executive, the judicial, and the legislative branches. However there has been little effort to explore the influence of the federal-state division on the growth of the state. In the early years of the twentieth century, the states were powerful influences on and competitors with the national government and, in the case of labor market initiatives, they made the initial experiments with public employment exchanges and developed some institutional and administrative expertise in the area. The existence of such expertise in the states proved to be a formidable barrier to the national government's expansion even in wartime. In addition to obstructing the expansion of the central state, the federal structure also influenced the shape of federal policy. Not just the separation of powers among the executive, the legislature and the judiciary, but the existence of a complex federal structure retarded the growth of the American state.

To understand the way in which the federal structure influenced government manpower policy, it is necessary to understand the administrative struggle that took place within wartime Washington. A wartime manpower policy emerged haltingly.[10] A variety of alternative policies contended for support within the wartime administration and it was not until mid-1918 that the steady contraction of the labor market forced government officials to agree on a common policy involving a centralized labor market under USES auspices. That agreement was only temporary. The struggle within the administration had begun before America entered the war and would resume after the armistice. Congress played a very minor role in this conflict during the war period, although it reasserted its authority in the immediate aftermath of the war. The outcome was not fore-ordained, but the Department of Labor was clearly disadvantaged in the struggle by its lack of "administrative capacity."[11]

The administrative struggle in Washington over the wartime labor market was not waged by faceless bureaucrats. The ambitions and tactics of individual administrators were crucially important. Some of these individuals were not well known in wartime Washington and their contribution has been overshadowed by such well-known figures as Herbert Hoover at the Food Administration, Harry Garfield in the Fuel Administration, Bernard Baruch at the War Industries Board, and William Howard Taft and Frank P. Walsh on the National War Labor Board. However, the administrators connected with the USES made just as important a contribution to the American war effort. Individuals such as William Bauchop Wilson, secretary of labor; Louis Freeland Post, the able and ambitious assistant secretary of labor; Felix Frankfurter, chairman of the War Labor Policies Board; and Fred Croxton, head of the Ohio state employment service, the Ohio state council of defense, and the Ohio food administration, all made substantial contributions to the development of American labor policy. Indeed, the determination and administrative skill of these individuals shaped the final policy. However, such administrative struggles have attracted little attention: as Louis Galambos has remarked, "historians have been slow to grapple with the emergence of America's bureaucratic state."[12]

The current dialogue between historians and social scientists concerning the relationship between the state and the development of knowledge is linked to some aspects of the development of labor policy in World War I.[13] One of the issues raised in that literature is whether policy tends to be knowledge driven or whether policy precedes knowledge and creates a demand for it. The history of the wartime expansion of state control over the labor market appears to be a clear example of knowlege being policy driven. The debate, which raged for the first year of American involvement in the war, concerning whether or not the labor market was registering a shortage of labor or whether it was a matter of maldistribution of labor, could not be resolved because of a lack of adequate, up-to-date information on the labor market. The decision to expand the powers of the USES and to move toward centralized labor market controls in mid-1918 was therefore taken in the absence of adequate knowledge and was guided by informed guesswork. However, once taken, that decision generated enormous pressure to create adequate flows of statistical information on the labor market on which to base the new centralized policy. This was part of a wider movement, reflected in different parts of the wartime administration, to develop a more sophisticated knowlege base on which to base policy. In the wartime crisis, policy preceded knowledge but the implementation of that policy generated great pressure to develop an adequate knowledge base.

The creation of a system of representative advisory committees designed to assist the USES at national, state, and local levels appears, on the surface, to be an example of private sector penetration of the state. From a neocorporatist or corporate liberal perspective, this development could be perceived as an example of organized private groups using the state to stabilize a capitalist system drifting into crisis. Both employers and labor were represented on the advisory structure, which was designed to strengthen the USES, overcome potential opposition, and stabilize the labor market. However, appearances were deceptive; the pressure to create this new advisory structure came entirely from within the state itself, not from either businessmen or organized labor. Both business and labor organizations shared a common distrust of the state that made them wary of becoming enmeshed in its operations. Even within the state itself there were bitter divisions over the introduction of the system. Officials from the Department of Labor, for example, were adamantly opposed to the new system because they interpreted it as a dilution of their control over the USES. However, despite the differences among state administrators, it remains true that the initiative for the development came from within the state itself.

Other themes are touched upon. The increasing professionalism that was evident in many aspects of American society in the prewar period had an important influence on the way in which the USES developed. In 1913, the American Association of Public Employment Offices (AAPEO), a professional association representing all those working in public employment offices, was formed. No doubt reflecting the fact that most employment professionals worked in employment offices funded by the various states, the AAPEO tended to favor a federalist rather than a nationalist policy for the embryonic USES. As a professional association, it gave to the advocates of a federalist USES, who were geographically scattered, a measure of cohesion, a sense of direction, and a degree of political leverage that was to prove extremely valuable in blocking the nationalist ambitions of those in charge of the Department of Labor.

Voluntarism is an important aspect of wartime labor policy. Both the Public Service Reserve and the Boys' Working Reserve, which were eventually absorbed by the USES, exemplify wartime voluntarism. The establishment, in 1918, of community labor boards also reflects the same theme. It was an interesting experiment in the sharing of responsibility between Washington and the local community with parallels in other wartime administrative experiments.

In addition to the broad reform thrust implied by the attempt to regulate the labor market, the first USES also reflected other aspects of the progressive reform movement of the prewar era. Those in charge of the USES during the war tried to promote some modest, progressive reforms through administrative rather than legislative action: equal representation of labor with management was a cardinal feature of the advisory structure that the USES eventually created; representation of women, both in the

Washington office and in the states, was another; the attempt to establish special offices for juveniles and the handicapped was also part of this reformist thrust.

The dismantling of the USES in 1919 has usually been seen as just one more example of the reactionary mood that gripped American society in the immediate aftermath of the war. Congress refused to fund the service and it was cut back to a skeletal organization and remained such until the Great Depression. Yet a close examination of the episode suggests that the cutback had as much to do with the continuing internal struggle between nationalists and federalists over the structure of the USES, coupled with the political misjudgment of Department of Labor officials, as with the parsimony and ideological conservatism of Congress. Congress had always been wary and distrustful of the pretensions and union sympathies of the Department of Labor, but the failure, until it was too late, of the department's senior officials to recognize the need to secure united support for the USES was a political blunder that could not be reversed. Those officials, unwittingly, sabotaged their own ambitions to have the USES play a large and permanent role in the organization of the labor market in the postwar era.

The history of the first USES is a tale of an attempt at state building in the United States that failed. That failure was not foreordained: ambition and chance both played a part in the final outcome. Had the war lasted longer, the outcome might have been very different. As it was, the armistice came just as the reorganized USES was beginning to gain public support and to demonstrate its potential to respond to the mounting crisis in the labor market. The newly created community labor boards had the potential to give the USES real support at the local level among both business and labor interests, and the increased emphasis on shifting labor out of nonessential, local industries rather than moving labor over long distances was an important step toward resolving the spiraling labor shortage. Even another six months would have given the federalist principles embodied in the recently reorganized USES a chance to become so firmly entrenched that Department of Labor officials might not have thought it wise to challenge them. These things did not happen and the USES, in fact, reverted to a paper organization throughout the 1920s. A major effort to expand the role and function of the state in the pre–New Deal period lapsed.

Little is known about the first USES. A few studies of the organization were published before the New Deal but were written either by individuals who were involved in the first USES or by their contemporaries. Most of these related to the political argument about the structure of the USES and were quite polemical in intent. Then for fifty years, the first USES virtually dropped out of historical memory and certainly out of the historical research agenda. The destruction of the central records of the organization doubtless contributed to this lack of interest.[14] It is only in the past decade that historical interest in the early-twentieth-century labor market and in the first USES has revived. The recent publication of Udo Sautter's *Three Cheers for the Unemployed: Government and Unemployment Before the New Deal* (1991), which deals with the first USES in the context of a broader study of government responses to unemployment, is a welcome addition to our understanding of how that body operated. By chance, it also complements this study. Sautter's book deals mainly with the prewar period and with the 1920s and looks only glancingly at the wartime USES. Unfortunately, by slighting the wartime experience, Sautter has missed the significance of the federal-national struggle over the USES and has, consequently, underestimated the effect of the war itself on postwar developments. The American experience of World War I was relatively brief, but it left an enduring mark on the politics of the labor market.

The Prewar Labor Market

CHAPTER ONE

State Initiatives and National Ambitions

Origins of the U.S. Employment Service

U nemployment was a chronic, although curiously neglected, aspect of American industrial society in the late nineteenth and early twentieth centuries. However, by the end of the first decade of the twentieth century, traditional explanations of the causes of unemployment, which had stressed the moral failings of individuals, were being seriously questioned. For the first time, both the full extent of unemployment in the community and the impersonal nature of the forces causing it began to be clarified.[1] A detailed analysis of the 1900 census figures on unemployment, published in 1915, showed that six and a half million working people, or nearly 25 percent of the work force, were unemployed for some part of the year: 50 percent of that group were unemployed for between one and three months, almost 40 percent for between four and six months, and over 10 percent for between seven and twelve months. More detailed surveys reinforced these findings.[2] This increased awareness of the alarming extent of unemployment, coupled with a growing perception that most of it was caused by structural rather than personal deficiencies, began to focus attention on the issue.

From the turn of the century on, a number of legislators, reform groups, and social scientists had begun to probe the phenomenon of unemployment and to suggest remedies that might, at least, alleviate the sufferings of the unemployed. An increasing number of articles about unemployment began to appear in journals and magazines. In the more industrialized states, legislatures began to pass workers' compensation laws and minimum hours legislation and to establish widows' pensions. In 1906, the creation of the American Association for Labor Legislation (AALL) in New York, composed of government officials, journalists, academics, and a few businessmen and labor leaders, was another indication of changing public attitudes. Although the formal purpose of the AALL was to encourage the study of labor conditions, it soon became the leading pressure group advocating social legislation, particulary measures relating to unemployment. In December 1914, in response to the economic downturn of that year, the AALL issued a pamphlet entitled *A Practical Program for the Prevention of Unemployment in America,* which specifically attributed the evil of unemployment to "our present method of industrial organization."[3]

The pamphlet provided a useful summary of reformist thought on the problem of unemployment in the immediate prewar era. It proposed four different approaches to the problem: (1) the use of public works to alleviate unemployment; (2) the regularization of industry; (3) unemployment insurance; and (4) the development of public employment exchanges. The idea of using public works as a means of minimizing the extent of unemployment during economic downturns had been advocated since the mid–nineteenth century, although with very little practical application prior to World War I. The regularization of industry referred to proposals for encouraging private enterprise to smooth out the ups and downs of the business cycle by consciously spreading the total work load more evenly over the twelve months of the year. This solution depended on employer initiative, but, although popular with reformers in the prewar era, it had only minimal support among employers. The idea of unemployment insurance had been imported from Europe shortly before the turn of the century and received a great fillip when, in 1911, Great Britain established a state-operated system of unemployment insurance featuring contributions from employers, employees, and the state. Despite this concrete example, the concept gathered little political support in the United States. The most popular of the prewar solutions to unemployment was the public employment exchange.[4]

Two key publicists for the public employment office in the prewar era were Frances Kellor and William Morris Leiserson. Frances Kellor attended graduate school in sociology at the University of Chicago. She then moved to New York in 1902 to do research on that city's employment offices. The project expanded to cover Boston, Philadelphia, and Chicago as well. In November 1904 she published *Out of Work,* one of the first studies to analyze unemployment as a social problem. The book was very critical of existing private employment agencies and "advanced a program of change that relied primarily on scientific knowledge, state intervention, and government centralization." She wanted the state to establish agencies that would assist individuals to find respectable employment. In a revised and expanded edition of the work, issued in 1914, Kellor emphasized the need for greater state intervention and regulation of the economy in order to do something about chronic unemployment. It was a plea for a state-supervised labor market.[5]

William M. Leiserson, a former student of John R. Commons at the University of Wisconsin, became one of the pioneer students of the labor market when, in 1909, he was invited to become the special investigator on unemployment for the Wainwright Commission investigating unemployment in New York State. As part of his duties, he traveled to Europe in 1910 to study the methods being used to deal with unemployment in England, Belgium, Switzerland, France, and Germany. Like most others interested in the unemployment problem, Leiserson was much influenced by the work of the Englishman William H. Beveridge, who had published his famous work *Unemployment: A Problem of Industry* the previous year. Beveridge was an advocate of the employment exchange and became the first director of the new British national system of government-supported employment exchanges established in Britain in 1909.[6] The report of the Wainwright Commission in 1911 reflected the influence of Beveridge on Leiserson: unemployment was seen primarily as a structural problem related to the malfunctioning of the labor market that could be remedied by the establishment of a statewide system of free, public employment offices. This landmark study brought recognition to Leiserson and formed the basis of his Ph.D. in political economy from Columbia University.

Although the New York State legislature showed little interest in the recommendations of the Wainwright Commission, Leiserson was invited to put his ideas into practice in Wisconsin and there established a model network of public employment offices.[7] He received a further opportunity to publicize his ideas after being appointed an investigator for the Commission on Industrial Relations, which was created in 1912.[8] By the outbreak of the First World War the idea was gaining ground among reformers and government adminstrators that an efficiently operating labor market could dramatically reduce unemployment through its ability to connect "the jobless man and the manless job."

The problem of connecting workers and work in this period was exacerbated by the enormous labor turnover that was common throughout industry. Workers, particularly the unskilled, were badly treated and poorly paid. As a consequence, they felt no loyalty to their employers and could be induced to change jobs for very small advances in wages or betterment of conditions. A contemporary student of the labor market remarked that "fully half of our labor passes through our industries rather than into them."[9] One careful survey of labor turnover concluded that, on average, labor turnover in large factories was approximately 100 percent per annum in the immediate prewar period.[10] Although coping with this turnover was a problem for industry before the war, large-scale immigration nevertheless produced a surplus of labor, which meant that replacements could usually be hired at the factory gate. Once America was involved in the war, however, the constant labor turnover became a much more serious matter. One Bureau of Labor Statistics investigation of twelve plants in the San Francisco area, for example, revealed a turnover of 224 percent in 1917 and 1918.[11] This constant labor turnover made it virtually impossible for the USES to estimate with any precision the real extent of the emerging labor shortage confronting the nation.

The problem of labor turnover was further compounded by the multitude of private employment offices operating in the labor market. Private offices constituted the major distributing mechanism for labor. The Commission on Industrial Relations, which was established by Congress in 1912, estimated that there were between 3,000 and 5,000 private, fee-charging employment agencies operating in the United States in the immediate prewar period. Although some were operated honestly, many were not. The most frequent complaints registered related to fees that were out of all proportion to the services rendered, to discrimination in the charges made for the same jobs, to men being sent to places where there were no jobs, and to collusion with foremen to maintain artificially high turnover rates. The most frequent abuse was misrepresentation of the terms and conditions of employment. Although thirty-one states had made some effort to regulate the activities of private employment agencies operating within their borders, these efforts had "with few exceptions . . . proved futile." The final report of the Commission on Industrial Relations asserted that the private employment business "as a whole reeks with fraud, extortion, and flagrant abuses of every kind."[12] Apart from the obvious injustices involved, the dominance of private employment offices made the possibility of greater efficiency in conecting workers and jobs a virtual impossibility. The situation seemed to demand some kind of state intervention in the labor market.

Both state and federal governments had begun to take an interest in the operation of the labor market in the period immediately prior to World War I and both had begun to experiment with publicly funded employment offices. Some of the states had even begun experimenting with free employment exchanges before the turn of the century. In 1890, the Ohio state legislature established state-funded employment agencies in the five largest cities in that state. Other states gradually followed the Ohio example until, by early 1917, twenty states were operating one or more free employment offices. However, most of those states funded only one or two such offices, which were usually located in the major industrial city. These offices had little or no impact on the overall labor market, which continued to be dominated by the private agencies. New York City alone, for example, had over 600 private agencies.

In the main, the state employment offices were poorly funded, staffed by untrained personnel, badly administered, and served relatively few workers or employers. Most of their clients were casual and unskilled laborers, and the majority of positions they had to offer were short-term.[13] Positions in the state employment offices were regarded as patronage jobs and there was a high turnover in personnel. Union men were suspicious of state employment offices, fearing they might be used "as strike-breaking agencies, or to lower wage rates." Employers, for their part, worried that such offices might be used "to fill their shops with union men and labor agitators."[14] Prior to World War I, state intervention in the area of employment exchange work in the United States seemed to be a failure.[15]

However, there were indications of change in a number of states. Massachusetts pioneered the development of an adequate record-keeping system that other states began to adopt. Wisconsin developed the idea of advisory committees attached to each office to be composed of employers and employees "to advise in the management as well as to insure impartiality in labor disputes." In 1914, in Cleveland, Ohio, the state-city labor exchange established specialized vocational guidance and protection bureaus for children and immigrants. In the same year, the Ohio Industrial Commission began an extensive reorganization of the state employment offices in an effort to improve their performance.[16] In the period 1914–17, a number of important northern states had begun to give some attention to improving the efficiency of their fledgling public employment offices.

If the states were first in the field of public employment offices in the prewar era, the national government, through the Department of Labor, had also begun to respond to the need. The Department of Labor had been formally established by Congress in March 1913, its purpose, spelled out in the organic act, being "to foster, promote, and develop the welfare of the wage earners of the United States, to improve their working conditions, and to advance their opportunities for profitable employment." The American Federation of Labor had agitated for more than a decade to establish such an independent, cabinet-level Department of Labor and was delighted by President Woodrow Wilson's choice of William B. Wilson, a former official of the United Mine Workers, as the first secretary of labor.[17]

As initially constituted, the new department was a heterogeneous collection of four bureaus drawn from other departments: the Bureau of Immigration, the Bureau of Naturalization, the Bureau of Labor Statistics, and the Children's Bureau. Two of these bureaus—Immigration and Labor Statistics—were of long standing and were semi-independent because their heads were appointed by and responsible to the President. The Bureau of Immigration dwarfed the other bureaus in the department: in the early years it absorbed 70 percent of the department's funds and 80 percent of its personnel. However, none of the four original bureaus was directly involved in the labor problems facing industrial workers. During his administration as secretary, William B. Wilson attempted to remedy this situation by creating three new agencies: the Women's Bureau, the Division of Conciliation, and the U.S. Employment Service. This expansion of functions took place in spite of the critical and often hostile attitude of Congress which refused to grant departmental requests for funds to support such expansion.[18] This parsimonious attitude on the part of Congress reflected the department's lack of political influence and the low esteem in which it was held.

In 1907, Congress had taken a first, halting step to promote the role of the national government in public employment work by establishing a Division of Information within the Bureau of Immigration and Naturalization. At that time, the bureau was located in the Department of Commerce and Labor. The purpose of the new division was to relieve the concentration of immigrants in the large port cities by publicizing information on employment opportunities in other parts of the country. Both private employment agencies and organized labor were very suspicious of the new agency. The division relied on the mails to solicit employment information throughout the United States and was unable to monitor local placements. In 1908, it unwittingly aided some employers to obtain strikebreakers, and this reinforced union suspicions. In 1913, when the Bureau of Immigration was incorporated in the newly established Department of Labor, the secretary of labor tried to mollify the unions by emphasizing that the division would neither direct "cheap alien labor" to areas that already had sufficient labor nor supply workers to any factories where strikes were in process.[19]

The outbreak of war in Europe in 1914 gave the Department of Labor an unexpected opportunity to enlarge its limited employment functions. The Division of Information responded to the crisis by expanding its employment office role to cater not only to immigrants but to all workers. In order to do this, it reassigned officers from the Bureau of Immigration, who had little to do because of the drop in immigration caused by the war, to employment duties. There was no formal congressional authorization for this change of function. William B. Wilson simply chose to interpret the statute establishing his department as providing a sufficiently broad mandate to authorize the establishment of a national employment service.

The first secretary of labor was very sympathetic to union complaints. Born in Scotland in 1862, William Bauchop Wilson had migrated to the United States with his parents in 1870 and began working in the Pennsylvania coal mines at age nine. He became involved in union activities and was an officer of the Knights of Labor in the 1880s. In 1890 he was one of the founders of the United Mine Workers of America (UMWA) and served on its general executive board from 1890 to 1894. From 1900 to 1908 he served as the international secretary-treasurer of the UMWA. In 1906 he was elected to Congress on the Democratic ticket and was reelected twice. A staunch defender of the interests of labor in the House of Representatives, he was made chairman of the Committee on Labor in 1911 with the backing of the American Federation of Labor and successfully guided through Congress a bill creating an independent Department of Labor. In February 1915, the newly elected president of the United States, Woodrow Wilson, selected him as the first secretary of the newly created Department of Labor. Of medium build, ruddy complexion, and blue eyes, Wilson remained a genial, if rather austere, Presbyterian throughout his life. He had a reputation for honesty and loyalty that he had earned while leading the miners through a series of major strikes around the turn of the century. His loyalty to the union movement would eventually be an impediment to his desire to promote a national system of public employment exchanges.

Secretary Wilson's right-hand man in the new department was Louis Freeland Post, the first assistant secretary of labor. Appointed in March 1913 at the age of sixty-four, Post remained in the position for eight years during the formative years of the new Department of Labor. Although admitted to the New York bar in 1870, Post became increasingly absorbed in newspaper writing, editing, and ideas. He became a friend of Henry George in the early 1880s and was thereafter the leading advocate of the Georgist "Single Tax" philosophy. In 1898, together with his wife, he founded and edited the *Public*, a liberal weekly that also espoused the single tax philosophy. He was an advocate of various liberal causes: prior to his appointment as assistant secretary, he had written *The Ethics of Democracy, Ethical Principles of Marriage and Divorce, Social Service,* and *The Single Tax.* At a more practical level, as a member of the Chicago school board, he had championed academic freedom and supported the right of teachers to organize. As assistant secretary he attracted great notoriety in 1919–20 for of his courageous and principled stand against the deportation of "radical" aliens during the great Red Scare. As assistant secretary he fought to establish the Department of Labor as a truly independent entity, not merely as an adjunct of the union movement.

Post and Secretary of Labor William B. Wilson worked well together: Post "was the idealist, the intellectual, the man of ideas, an admirable complement to Wilson, the practical man, experienced in the rough and tumble ways of trade unionism."[20] Post always remained very loyal to Secretary Wilson, and the latter was quite dependent on Post's advice and on his adminstrative abilities. Post was, with Wilson's blessing, the "guiding spirit" behind the creation of a national employment service in the Department of Labor.[21] This rather unlikely partnership provided direction to the Department of Labor during the first eight years of its existence.

In the second half of 1914 the Division of Information began to expand rapidly. In 1913, it operated only one employment office, called a "distribution agency," in New York City. By mid-1914, it had set in motion a project to divide the United States into eighteen "distribution zones," each with a branch office and subbranch offices in major cities as required.[22] By mid-1916, the number of zones had increased to twenty, each with its own branch office, and there were sixty-two subbranch offices making a total of eighty-two separate offices.[23] In effect, the department had created the United States Employment Service (the term first came to be used in 1915) out of the old Immigration Service. This association meant that all the officers of the new USES were completely untrained in employment work, and most regarded

their time with it as a purely temporary, wartime interlude. This close association with the Immigration Service was eventually to prove a major handicap for the new, national employment organization.

Although it existed on paper as a national organization, the new employment service had virtually no funds to promote its work and depended
heavily on securing liaison agreements with other federal and state bodies
in order to project a genuinely national presence. One proposal aimed to
utilize the facilities of the 60,000 post offices throughout the country. Local postmasters were to keep two boxes of file cards—one to register unemployed workers, the other to list vacant jobs submitted by employers. The
file cards would be available to both employers and workers for their pe-
rusal, and it was confidently asserted that, with such a system in operation,
no worker need "be out of work over 24 hours."[24] It was an impractical
proposal that was never implemented. An agreement was eventually reached
whereby local postmasters were expected only to display notices concerning employment opportunities sent out by the Department of Labor. These
were mainly concerned with seasonal work on farms.[25] However, the original proposal drew much criticism from employment experts and reinforced
their view that the Department of Labor lacked the necessary knowledge to
operate a successful national employment service.

In the immediate prewar period, the increasing concern over both the operation of the labor market and the role of public employment offices in
relieving unemployment culminated, in Chicago in December 1913, in the
formation of a specialized professional association, the American Association of Public Employment Offices (AAPEO). William L. Leiserson, one
of the foremost students of the labor market, who was at the time deputy
industrial commissioner of Wisconsin in charge of the state employment
offices, was the leading spirit in forming this association.[26] Representatives
from public employment offices in nine states and three Canadian prov-
inces attended the initial conference, which adopted a constitution for the
new association. Its aims were "to improve the work of public employment
offices, to secure co-operation and closer connection between them, to promote uniform methods, interchange information and reports, and to secure a proper distribution of labor through the country."[27] Membership
was restricted to those engaged in public employment work.

The early meetings of the AAPEO addressed a broad range of issues. The
very first meeting of the association established a committee on standardization to examine the possibility of developing uniform record-keeping

Second Annual Meeting of the American Association of Public Employment Offices (AAPEO), Indianapolis, September 24, 1914. Founded in 1913, the AAPEO was an important forum for those who favored a federalist rather than a nationalist U.S. Employment Service. In the front row, third from left, is William M. Leiserson, secretary-treasurer, 1913–16; also in the front row, fourth from left, is Fred C. Croxton, president, 1913–14. *Courtesy of the State Historical Society of Wisconsin.*

methods. Everyone agreed that statistics from existing employment offices were virtually useless for comparative purposes because there was no agreement on what the different figures actually meant. Some offices registered every applicant, others only those for whom positions were available; some reregistered individuals who reapplied, others did not; some offices reported positions as filled if they sent an applicant to the position, others only if the applicant actually got the job.[28] There was agreement on the desirability of promoting coordinated, statewide employment systems; most public employment offices within individual states had been operating completely independently of each other. There was also a broad consensus on the desirability of jointly funded state-city employment offices, toward which the municipality would make some contribution, usually office space and utilities, while the state would pay for the salaries of employees and other major expenses. Members felt that the direct involvement of the municipality would contribute to the successful operation of the local office.

Three key issues that were discussed at length and on which a consensus was eventually reached were the potentially explosive issue of the role of the employment office during a strike, the issue of advisory committees, and the relationship between public and private employment agencies. While there was agreement that the role of the public employment office was to serve both employer and employee in an impartial and businesslike manner, the question of how to do this once a strike or a lockout had been declared remained a difficult one. The association eventually went on record as favoring the British system in which jobs at factories where a strike or lockout was in progress were advertised and the employment office then notified applicants of the existence of an industrial dispute but left the final decision on whether or not to apply up to the individual. A number of states had already adopted this practice.[29]

There was also agreement that each state, and preferably each local public employment office, should have an advisory committee composed of an equal number of representatives from both organized labor and employer groups. These committees would oversee the operation of each office and offer guidance on general policy matters. It was anticipated that such committees would ensure the impartiality of the offices and serve to overcome any suspicion or hostility on the part of management or labor. The Wisconsin employment system had pioneered in this development, as it had in the adoption of the British policy relating to strikes.[30]

Another issue that evoked considerable discussion was the question of the attitude that should be adopted toward private employment agencies.

There was universal agreement that many of the private agencies duped unemployed workers. Although a number of states required private employment offices to obtain special licenses, this practice had not proved very effective in controlling abuses.[31] Some members of the AAPEO opposed this regulatory approach and wanted to concentrate on building up the public employment offices so that they would, over time, drive out most of the private agencies by providing better service at no cost. However, a sizable body of opinion was in favor of more drastic action. At the second annual meeting of the association in Indianapolis, in September 1914, a resolution was adopted favoring the elimination, through federal and state legislation, of all private employment agencies.[32] The question of the role of the private employment agencies, however, remained a contentious issue for the rest of the decade.

The most politically sensitive issue facing the association, and one that was to dog it until 1933, concerned the relationship between the national government and the various state governments in employment work. The fundamental issue was whether there should be a centralized employment system operated by the national government and, presumably, located in the Department of Labor, which would be largely independent of the states, or a federal system with complementary but quite distinct roles for federal, state, and municipal governments. The matter was discussed at the first meeting of the association, in 1913, and a resolution was passed urging the newly organized Commission on Industrial Relations to study the general question and to make some recommendation. The 1914 meeting gave tentative approval to a preliminary plan proposed by the commission, which favored a federal organization based on state employment offices.[33] William Leiserson, who had been elected secretary-treasurer of the AAPEO, also served as assistant director of research for the Industrial Relations Commission during 1914–15 and vigorously promoted the concept of a federal employment service based on the states, with the national government playing the role of supervisor rather than that of a major actor. Early in 1915, Leiserson thought that his views had prevailed, but, in the end, the commission refused to make a firm recommendation to Congress.[34]

The Department of Labor adamantly opposed the proposal for a state-centered, federal employment service in which it would have only a supervisory role. Officials recognized that a nationwide, centralized employment service, operated through the department and quite independent of the state employment offices, offered a rare opportunity to expand the visibility and influence of the newest and least significant federal department. Although hampered by a lack of funds, they lost no opportunity to assert the desirability of this kind of centralized, independent system. However, until Congress could be convinced to fund such a system, it was necessary for the Department of Labor to secure maximum cooperation from the state employment offices.

In August 1915, Secretary Wilson called a conference in San Francisco of executive officers of the Labor Department and representatives of the states and municipalities engaged in employment work. Although the professed aim of the conference was to discuss how to achieve better cooperation among all three agencies, Secretary Wilson made clear that he believed that the "ideal" kind of organization would be a highly centralized, independent national system that would cooperate with, but remain separate from, state employment offices.[35] Five months later, in hearings before a congressional committee, Secretary Wilson elaborated on this theme: he wanted his own employment offices in all the larger cities, regardless of the existence of state offices and, in addition, in any large towns that had no public employment offices. It was clear that the Department of Labor would not be content with a supervisory and coordinating role in employment work.[36] At the same hearings, Royal Meeker, the commissioner of labor statistics in the Department of Labor, stated his belief that, eventually, "we will come to an out-and-out Federal [i.e., centralized] system."[37] Because it did not have the funds to develop such a centralized national system, the Department of Labor was willing to cooperate with the state offices for the time being. Such cooperation, however, included the right to bypass the state and local authorities whenever it desired.[38]

There was considerable criticism of the attitude of the Department of Labor.[39] At the July 1916 meeting of the American Association of Public Employment Offices, William Leiserson ridiculed the idea of the federal government "establishing employment offices, like post offices, throughout the country, or making the post offices do the work of employment bureaus." He thought the idea of the federal government establishing employment offices to compete with or duplicate the work of the approximately one hundred state and municipal offices was "absurd." Moreover, he believed that the department's proposed scheme for federal-state cooperation, which, in practice, involved state and federal employment offices competing against each other, was administratively unworkable. There had to be a clear definition of roles: the state and municipalities should be in charge of actual placement work, with the federal government in charge of broader policy issues.

Leiserson went on to articulate the main principles of the federalist position, which most members of the AAPEO supported. He believed that there was an important role for the Department of Labor in any properly organized national employment system but that this did not include the actual operation of any employment offices. The key function of the department would be to assist the states to develop and improve the functioning of their own employment offices. Another important function would be to gather and distribute information on the labor market based not on vague estimates of demand but on the actual number of workers requested by employers and the actual number of employees registered for work. Another function would be to license and regulate the private employment offices engaged in the interstate shipment of labor. Leiserson also believed that any proposed national employment system ought to have an advisory council to consider all important policy decisions and administrative regulations before they were adopted.[40] Both the federalist position articulated by Leiserson and the nationalist position adopted by the Department of Labor shared a common commitment to a vastly expanded role for government in the labor market. Beyond that general proposition, however, there was no agreement.

In the immediate prewar period a number of legislative attempts to define the role of the national and state governments in employment work were made. In 1914, two bills introduced in Congress proposed federal intervention in the labor market. One bill sought to establish a three-tier, federal-state-municipal cooperative structure; the other called for the utilization of the post offices throughout the country as employment offices. Action on a compromise measure was delayed partly in order to give the Commission on Industrial Relations, which had announced that it was investigating the subject, an opportunity to develop proposals for appropriate legislation.[41] In the end, Congress adjourned before taking any action. In the next Congress, John I. Nolan, a Republican from California, reintroduced an amended version of the earlier bill, which had the support of the Department of Labor, but it never came to a vote.[42] In April 1917, Nolan brought the bill forward again, and a parallel measure was introduced in the Senate. However, President Wilson's war message deflected the attention of the legislators to more urgent matters.

In its 1916 annual report, the Department of Labor had publicly indicated its support for the Nolan bill. One year later, in the 1917 annual report, the department published the full text of the bill and, with some minor amendments, recommended it to Congress for enactment.[43] The ambiguity in the language of the proposed bill reflected the ideological divisions among its supporters: the bill permitted the establishment of independent USES offices in the various states but also authorized assistance to, and cooperation with, state and municipal labor exchanges. In addition, it explicitly mentioned the use of post offices, omitted any reference to advisory committees, and indicated that the Department of Labor would adhere to its stated policy of not sending men when strikes were in progress. Under such an umbrella, the USES could develop in either a federalist or a nationalist direction.

Neither employer associations nor organized labor had taken much interest in the early proposals for a national employment system. In fact, Leiserson felt that there was "considerable opposition to the movement that rarely comes out in the open." He believed that this came from both "the strongly organized employers' associations and from highly organized skilled trades." Each body had its own reasons. Many employers' associations had organized their own employment agencies, which were used to discriminate against union labor, and they did not want them supplanted. On the other hand, the stronger unions operated unofficial employment services for their members through their business agents and felt that the development of public employment agencies might weaken their own organizations.[44] The traditional suspicion of state intervention in industrial matters that permeated the American Federation of Labor reinforced union misgivings about the proposed scheme.[45]

With both employers and organized labor adopting a neutral stance, the struggle over the development of a national system of public employment offices was left largely to the organized groups directly interested: the bureaucrats in the Department of Labor, and the employment professionals in the state-funded employment offices who had recently formed their own association, the American Association of Public Employment Offices. By late 1916, both groups had articulated different, if partially overlapping, versions of a desirable national system. Neither group was strong enough to get legislation through Congress. Although lacking funds, the Department of Labor had seized the opportunity created by the drop in immigration associated with the war in Europe to establish a national employment service on its own terms using officials in the Immigration Service. Those officials would eventually have to return to immigration work, but, in the meantime, if the USES could demonstrate its value to the workingmen and employers of the country, Congress would, presumably, be obliged to continue it. For the new and insignificant Department of Labor the European war had created a rare opportunity to expand its role. The Secretary of Labor seized it.

1917

Labor
Market
Politics
in Wartime

CHAPTER TWO

Federalist Aspirations in the States

American entry into the European war in April 1917 precipitated an intense struggle between the rival proponents of a federalist or a centralist USES. The federalist cause received some initial support in the summer and fall of 1917 from a remarkable demonstration of the efficiency of the Ohio employment service, which also served to underline the fact that existing employment expertise was concentrated in the states and not in the Department of Labor's embryonic USES. Both sides sought support for their position within the wartime administration in Washington. However, in spite of intense lobbying in support of the federalist cause, the Department of Labor was able to retain exclusive control over the USES and even to expand the organization by temporarily transferring Immigration Service officers to employment work. By the winter of 1917–18, the effort to create a federalist USES seemed to have been thwarted.

The potential of existing state employment services to organize the wartime labor market was very clearly demonstrated in Ohio immediately after Congress declared war. The key figure in Ohio was Fred C. Croxton. Forty-six years of age, with an LL.B. and an LL.M from George Washington University, Croxton had been appointed chief statistician for the U.S. Immigration Bureau in 1907. Three years later, he switched to the Bureau of Labor Statistics to supervise the preparation of its extensive series of industrial and social reports. In 1913, the newly established Ohio Industrial Commission invited him to take charge of industrial mediation and statistical work for that state. While in that post he was also instrumental in reorganizing the Ohio public employment offices. A foundation member of the

AAPEO, he was elected the first president of that organization in 1913–14. In 1916, he accepted the position of social service director of the Ohio Institute for Public Efficiency, a private, nonprofit corporation that had been founded in 1913 to offer technical advice to the state and city governments in Ohio and to promote "scientific principles of social welfare." An active Methodist, the recording secretary of the Ohio Sunday School Association, a trustee of the Cleveland Girls' Bureau, and involved in a variety of social causes, Croxton found the prospect of such socially useful work irresistible.[1]

When America became involved in the war, Croxton immediately seized the opportunity to build on his earlier initiatives in promoting a state-regulated labor market by expanding the existing Ohio free employment service.[2] The governor approved Croxton's proposal and within a month fourteen new employment offices had been opened throughout Ohio. More-over, at the governor's insistence, Croxton was placed in charge of all twenty-one state offices, which now covered every important industrial and agri-cultural center in the state.[3] The Ohio Institute loaned his services to the state for the duration of the war, and the wartime mobilization of civilian labor within Ohio became primarily Croxton's responsibility.

The principles on which Croxton relied in both the expansion and the operation of the Ohio employment offices were those that had guided his reorganization of these offices a few years earlier. He insisted that the com-munities in which the new offices were to be established should become involved in their operation by furnishing appropriate quarters and office equipment. In appointing new office supervisors he insisted that the indi-viduals chosen be acceptable to both management and labor. He demanded that all workers, union and nonunion, be treated alike by the state system. To preserve the neutrality of the state employment offices, he adopted the British policy on strikes: if requested by employers, the Ohio offices adver-tised the positions of striking workers but advised applicants of the indus-trial dispute. Croxton also took steps to introduce more uniform adminis-trative and record-keeping practices in all the offices. To oversee the expansion, he appointed four field secretaries to travel throughout the state to organize the new offices and select personnel.[4]

In addition to expanding the number of offices in the state and insisting on uniformity of policy and administrative procedures among them, Croxton took the additional step required to make the Ohio offices operate as an integrated, statewide system. He established a central office in Columbus, which acted as a clearinghouse for all twenty-one offices throughout the state. This was the first time that any state had attempted to do this. All branch offices having positions that they could not fill or applicants they could not place communicated such information to the head office on a form letter each day. The head office then consolidated this information in a daily circular sent to all other offices. Individual offices then contacted each other directly about positions. This became very cumbersome after a short time, and a more efficient system that placed greater reliance on the telephone was installed. With this mechanism established, Croxton was able to monitor the entire labor market within the state.[5]

The most impressive example of the efficiency of the centralized Ohio state system was associated with the construction of the army cantonment at Chillicothe, in the southern section of the state. Croxton's first step was to request an agreement from the construction management that all workers at the site would be hired through the state employment service. This request was only reluctantly granted. He then committed the Ohio employment service to deliver the men as they were needed to the camp site and to draw them from all over the state so that no one geographical area was stripped of labor.

Demand for labor at the camp site was erratic: in the first week, about 300 men were shipped; in the second week, about 1,500. In the third week, because of a shortage of building materials, only 500 men were needed. In the fourth week, 1,300 men were requested and supplied. Demand continued to increase, and in the following three weeks the employment service supplied 2,500, 2,800 and 3,500 men. Over a twelve-week period, the state employment service supplied over 17,000 men to Chillicothe with the skills that were requested and in the numbers demanded.[6] Between May and December, almost 25,000 men were supplied. The men supplied were not all unskilled laborers: as a contemporary noted, the majority were "carpenters, plumbers, electricians, pipe-fitters, painters, tinners, bricklayers and laborers," and the Ohio employment service also supplied "the full complement of accountants, payroll auditors, clerks and checkers, civil engineers, stenographers and typists."[7] When the work was nearing completion, Croxton set the reverse procedure in motion by establishing a temporary employment office at the camp site to assist the men in finding work elsewhere in the state. It was an orderly procedure that benefited both employers and employees. There was no indiscriminate newspaper advertising, the cantonment got the labor in the quantities and at the times it was required, no work days were lost by workmen, and there was minimum disruption to the state economy in that no town or city was asked to contribute more than its proportion of the total labor required.

The building of the Chillicothe cantonment was an impressive illustration of the potentialities of an integrated system of employment offices. Croxton had insisted upon detailed weekly statements of the actual demand for labor, including the specific skills required, rather than relying on generalized projections of labor needs. He had prevented indiscriminate newspaper advertisements for labor that was not actually needed at a specific time. By applying a careful system of quotas to each employment office across the state, Croxton ensured that no particular locality was stripped of its labor in order to supply the Chillicothe camp. Ohio became an exemplar of what a centralized, well-organized state employment system could accomplish. Federalists trumpeted its achievements.[8]

If Ohio demonstrated the potential value of properly organized public employment offices, it was the American Association of Public Employment Offices (AAPEO), the newly organized professional association, that attempted to translate the relevant lessons from that experience into national policy. Shortly before President Wilson's war message to Congress, the executive of the AAPEO wrote to the Council of National Defense, the preparedness body created by Congress in 1916, offering the services of the organization in the mobilization of the nation's "manpower," drawing attention to the work of the state and city employment offices in twenty-six states and stressing the need for "one central federal system" that would establish some degree of supervision over the total labor market. The letter drew attention to the resolutions passed at the previous three annual meetings of the AAPEO requesting the federal government to establish such a national bureau and mentioned the AAPEO's support for the Nolan bill that had come before the recent session of Congress. The letter urged the Council of National Defense to press Congress to enact legislation establishing such a national employment system.[9]

Three months later, the AAPEO adopted a more aggressive stand. In June 1917, meeting in Chicago, the committee on standardization, established by the AAPEO the previous year to encourage more uniform record-keeping practices among the various public employment offices, unanimously passed a resolution urging Congress immediately to establish "a National Bureau of Employment Offices under the United States Department of Labor." The resolution made clear that the proposed national bureau was to operate on federalist, not centralist, assumptions.

The proposed "National Bureau" was to assist state employment offices where they existed, encourage backward states to establish such offices, and promote uniformity in record keeping and office procedures. The state was to be the basic unit of administration, while the federal government was to match money spent by the states on employment office work. The national office would also establish clearinghouses among groups of states as necessary. The standardization committee also proposed the establishment of a national advisory committee, to consist of the director of the National Bureau together with the director of each state employment system. Finally, the National Bureau was to be given authority "to license, supervise, and regulate all private employment agencies doing an interstate business."[10] The committee's recommendations went considerably beyond the rather ambiguous principles embodied in the Nolan bill.

The AAPEO had clearly staked out its position: it wanted a federal employment system that retained existing state control of employment offices but that incorporated both a supervisory and a financial role for the federal government via the Department of Labor. The federal government itself was not to become involved in the detailed operation of such employment offices; insofar as it was involved, it would be to establish regional or zone offices for the coordination of the interstate movement of workers. It was to be a federal rather than a national employment service.[11]

If the AAPEO was determined that the USES should be organized on clearly federalist principles, officials in the Department of Labor had not abandoned their aspirations for a purely nationalist organization. In mid-July, a three-man AAPEO committee, consisting of Charles B. Barnes, president of the AAPEO and director of the state employment system of New York, Fred C. Croxton of Ohio, a former president of the AAPEO, and W. G. Ashton, the commissioner of labor in Oklahoma, went to Washington to present the proposals approved at the June meeting of the standardization committee to the Department of Labor. The committee met with Assistant Secretary Louis Post, but its proposals "did not seem particularly to meet with his favor." Post talked about an anticipated congressional appropriation of $750,000 for "the development of a National Employment Bureau." Croxton was disappointed at the outcome of the meeting: "I feel that they are not on the right track and I very much fear that we cannot get the work changed into a workable plan if it is started on the plan suggested by Mr. Post."[12] At the end of July 1917, it appeared that the Department of Labor was determined to ignore the advice of the employment experts of the country.

It was in the Council of National Defense organization that the most significant developments occurred over the summer. The Committee on

Labor of the Advisory Commission, chaired by Samuel Gompers, had been concerned about the issue for some time. In early June, it had established a special Subcommittee on Coordination of Employment Agencies to discuss the development of an emergency system of federal and state employment bureaus.[13] In the first week of July the subcommittee recommended the establishment of a supervisory Emergency Service Board having representation from "Government departments, trade unions, universities and professional societies, women and employers." The meeting felt that such a board, if given adequate powers, would be strong enough to impose some order on the labor mobilization. In the eyes of many of the employment experts it would also be strong enough to override the ambitions of the Department of Labor. A further conference was arranged for the following week to prepare a formal resolution to go to Gompers' Committee on Labor for endorsement before being forwarded to the Council of National Defense.[14]

At the conference held on July 10, which lasted for four hours, the Department of Labor was as adamantly opposed to this initiative as it was to the AAPEO proposal.[15] Secretary Wilson, alluding to the employment work already being done by the Department of Labor, thought that "the creation of an Emergency Service Board" would "result in duplication rather than in the elimination of it."[16] The AFL representatives were rather opposed to the proposal, as were some of the representatives from the other government departments. The proposal lacked support and was referred back to the Subcommittee on the Coordination of Employment Offices of the Committee on Labor.[17] The Department of Labor, with the assistance of the AFL representatives, had successfully blocked this particular initiative. The proposal to create a wartime labor board under CND auspices was stalemated.

However, the supporters of some form of Emergency Service Board were not deterred. Negotiations began immediately on a revised measure. By mid-August 1917, Secretary Wilson had indicated his general approval of a compromise proposal.[18] It seemed, at last, that some agreement might be possible between the groups in the Council of National Defense and the Department of Labor. The new proposal called for a five-member board appointed by the Council of National Defense that would include representatives of the Department of Labor, the AFL, technical and professional labor (presumably through the Intercollegiate Intelligence Bureau), and employers (through some representatives chosen by employers' associations). The board was expected to concentrate only on war work and "not undertake any work that would be carried on in times of peace by any government department." It was to be, essentially, a high-level coordinating board with advisory powers only, which would act as a central funnel for exchanging information on the likely wartime demand for labor and the available supply.[19] It was a step toward centralization but a modest one; there was no mention of the exact role to be played by the Department of Labor's employment service or of its relationship with the states.

Initially, the proposal had the support of organized labor. Both Samuel Gompers, president of the American Federation of Labor and chairman of the Committee on Labor of the Advisory Commission of the Council of National Defense, and his close friend and adviser James W. Sullivan were happy enough with the proposal for a "War Labor Service Board." In fact, Sullivan made it clear that he wanted the proposal passed immediately by the CND and details about the exact composition of the proposed board discussed later rather than risk delay. Sullivan believed that the proposal would benefit the Department of Labor and would "not interfere with or attempt to parallel its [employment] activities." Given the nature of the emergency, he felt that any wartime national employment system would have to encompass more than just the existing employment service located in the Department of Labor.[20] Although Sullivan did not believe that an actual shortage of labor existed in the United States, he did acknowledge the existence of an acute imbalance between supply and demand, "with no adequate public attempt at solution of this problem."[21] His proposed "War Labor Service Board" would at least centralize information on the existing supply and the projected demand for labor during the wartime emergency.

Although the proposal had received Secretary Wilson's tentative approval, it met with bitter opposition from Assistant Secretary of Labor Louis Post. In a memorandum to Secretary Wilson, dated August 29, Post strongly attacked the proposal. He believed that the duties of the proposed "War Labor Service Board" clearly overlapped the functions of the U.S. Employment Service. The overall effect of such a board, he felt, would be to undercut the functions and powers of the Department of Labor. The proposal "would merely establish an unnecessary administrative machinery, having its source of power in the Council of National Defense, which is already adequately connected with the Department of Labor by the membership in the Council of the Secretary of Labor." Post urged Secretary Wilson not to become enmeshed in the proposal: "Such committee as the Secretary himself may establish purely for advisory purposes, is the only outside alliance that in my judgement is practically necessary or administratively desirable."[22] Post was adamantly opposed to making any concession.

In spite of the opposition of Post, the proposal went forward. At a meeting of the Advisory Commission of the Council of National Defense on September 6, the director, Walter S. Gifford, presented a resolution prepared by Gompers, who was unavoidably absent. The resolution, which had been endorsed by Secretary Wilson, urged that the Council of National Defense create a War Labor Board composed of representatives of the Department of Labor, the AFL, the special war boards (War Industries Board, U.S. Shipping Board, Aircraft Production Board, etc.), employers, and technical and professional labor. The commission unanimously adopted the resolution and forwarded it to the Council of National Defense itself for final decision.[23] After a long struggle over the summer, it looked as if the Department of Labor would accept this compromise proposal and permit some degree of centralization of the wartime labor program under the umbrella of the Council of National Defense.

At its meeting on September 26, the Council of National Defense failed by one vote to reach a unanimous decision and decided to defer any action on the proposal.[24] Secretary Houston's lone dissenting vote was a protest against yet another advisory board rather than a protest against centralization.[25] After a summer of frustration, a compromise agreement had seemed tantalizingly close. That possibility abruptly receded with the September meeting of the Council of National Defense.

While lobbying for a federalist USES among wartime administrators in Washington, AAPEO officials had not lost sight of the need for formal congressional authorization to establish the organization on a permanent basis. The AAPEO had been pressing for legislation since the summer of 1916. In September 1917, the annual meeting of the association unanimously endorsed a draft bill embodying the resolutions approved by its committee on standardization. This draft bill provided for a federalist employment service located in the Department of Labor whose function would be to encourage, through a system of matching grants, the creation of employment offices in all the states, promote improved administrative methods for all offices in the system, and license all private employment offices engaged in interstate transfers.[26] The text of the draft bill had been shaped by Professor Henry R. Seager and Thomas I. Parkinson, both of Columbia University, with the assistance of Charles B. Barnes, the New York State director of employment and the chairman of the AAPEO.[27]

For a brief period it seemed that this proposed bill might be acceptable to all parties. Although it differed quite significantly from the original Nolan bill, the Department of Labor had responded positively and "with some suggestions [it had] been adopted by the Department as being the kind of bill necessary." Barnes believed that the Executive Committee of the American Federation of Labor was also in favor of some such national system.[28] However, it was felt that the introduction of the bill in the very last days of the current session of Congress "was tactically unwise," and thus no immediate action was taken.[29] The next session of Congress was not scheduled to begin until early December 1917.[30]

Barnes used the delay to secure the assistance of the American Association for Labor Legislation (AALL) both to finalize the text of the bill and to help in securing its passage through Congress.[31] John Andrews, the secretary-treasurer of the AALL, arranged to have the bill introduced simultaneously in both houses by Senator Joseph T. Robinson (D-Ark.) and Representative Edward Keating (D-Colo.) on Friday, December 7.[32] In correspondence with Senator Robinson, Andrews urged that the bill be introduced as a war emergency measure and outlined the widespread support it enjoyed: Charles Clayton, who was in charge of the war emergency division of the USES, had helped draft the bill; the Legislative Drafting Bureau had added "the finishing touches"; Grant Hamilton, the legislative representative of the AFL, had stated that the bill was "in conformity with action at their recent annual convention and all right"; the AAPEO had endorsed it; and both Dr. Henry R. Seager, secretary of the Shipbuilding Labor Adjustment Board of the Emergency Fleet Corporation, U.S. Shipping Board, and Professor L. C. Marshall, head of the Industrial Service Section of the Council of National Defense, were "heartily in favor of it as a war emergency need."[33] Andrews also anticipated that Marshall would be able to obtain an official administration endorsement of the bill as an emergency war measure and wide publicity for it "within a few days."[34] However, in spite of this auspicious beginning, the anticipated unanimous support for the measure failed to materialize and it stalled in Congress. Samuel Gompers was responsible for this unexpected development. The sixty-seven-year-old longtime president of the AFL had read in a newspaper that the bill had been introduced in Congress and that it "had the approval of the Department of Labor and the American Federation of Labor." Aware that the AFL had not specifically endorsed the bill and discovering that Louis Post opposed it even though Charles Clayton, Post's trusted assistant, had helped draft the measure, Gompers decided to stifle the Robinson-Keating bill although "avoiding a public denunciation" of it. He organized a conference of about twenty interested individuals to discuss the proposed legislation. At the conference he declared his opposition to the bill because it infringed on the powers of the Department of Labor and managed to engineer the appointment of a committee to draft a revised version.

However, Gompers' stratagem misfired. He had appointed his close associate, James W. Sullivan to chair the committee, which included John B. Andrews and Leon C. Marshall.[35] Charles Clayton, who had represented Post at the first conference, signaled the hardening attitude of the Department of Labor toward the proposed legislation when he declined to be appointed to the committee "on the grounds that the Secretary had proposed a bill in his annual report."[36] A week later the committee presented a revised draft bill that provided for the appointment of a labor director with great powers together with an advisory board of seven members made up of representatives of the Labor, War, Navy, and Agriculture departments, the Shipping Board, the American Federation of Labor, and the U.S. Chamber of Commerce. This advisory board was to have the power "to name and control" the director of the proposed national employment service during the war period "and for one year thereafter." Gompers subsequently declared that the bill was "in the judgement of the labor men and some others . . . not any better than the bill which Mr. Andrews had prepared."[37] In fact, it was a return to the original proposal of the Council of National Defense made some months earlier.

Although Gompers felt that both the proposed bills usurped the authority of the Department of Labor, his trusted lieutenant J. W. Sullivan strongly supported the Robinson-Keating bill and the proposed amendments establishing a representative advisory board.[38] Sullivan obviously felt that the proposals embodied in the draft legislation were not unreasonable and would secure sufficient support to get the bill through Congress and thus establish the USES on a secure and permanent basis. Sullivan's support for the bill left Gompers in a difficult position.

Assistant Secretary Post was bitterly opposed both to the Robinson-Keating bill and to the proposed revision of it. At the second conference, he declared that both bills were "unnecessary during the war, now that appropriations for the already established employment service are in hand."[39] Obviously, Post had decided that any legislation passed by Congress at that time was likely to contain provisions diluting the authority of the Department of Labor over such a national employment service. The special funds granted by the President had strengthened Post's hand and he decided to gamble on creating a national service first and seeking congressional approval later. It would be more difficult to dislodge the Department of Labor from control of an established national service than to dislodge it from an embryonic one.

The outcome of the conference was a victory for the Department of Labor. Gompers declared that nothing further should be done until the secretary of labor returned from his trip out west on the President's Mediation Commission.[40] Although he had succeeded in stifling the Andrews bill, Gompers had been unable to find any common ground on which to construct an alternative proposal that would command broad support. Even within the AFL there was no consensus on an appropriate bill. The issue was stalemated and the opportunity to establish the USES on a formal legislative basis passed.

Shortly after Secretary Wilson returned to Washington at the end of December 1917, he was appointed war labor administrator by President Wilson. This meant that the Department of Labor would have a decisive role in shaping the new wartime labor administration. The appointment was "a stunning defeat for the administrative radicals" who had been advocating the establishment of a completely independent wartime labor administration and it was followed, shortly thereafter, by the President's refusal to establish a comprehensive munitions administration, on the English model, to oversee the entire war production program. Instead, he strengthened the existing War Industries Board and appointed Bernard Baruch to chair it. By his actions, President Wilson effectively blocked the growing pressure for a drastic administrative reorganization of the whole war program that had developed in the fall and early winter. However, neither Baruch nor Secretary Wilson were given any substantial power: "both decisions left the two administrations . . . to find their way through an organizational context largely unaffected by the presidential pronouncements."[41] Although the appointment of the secretary of labor as war labor administrator obviously strengthened the position of the Department of Labor, it had the unanticipated effect of offering the federalist cause one further opportunity to present its case.

In mid-January, the secretary of labor, in his new role as war labor administrator, appointed an Advisory Council of seven members representing capital, labor, and the general public to assist him in the task of devising an appropriate administrative structure and necessary national policies for the wartime labor administration.[42] Professor Leon C. Marshall, dean of

William Bauchop Wilson was the first secretary of labor (1913–21) and was also appointed by President Woodrow Wilson as war labor administrator during World War I. *RG 165 WW, 443-B4, National Archives.*

the School of Economics at the University of Chicago and in charge of the Industrial Service Section of the Council of National Defense, was appointed as economist to the new council and served as its executive secretary. The Advisory Council remained in session until March 4, when it delivered its final report, which, in effect, mapped out the structure of the wartime labor administration.[43] The deliberations of the Advisory Council gave those who supported the AAPEO model for a national employment service an unexpected further opportunity to present their case.

Part of the Advisory Council's role was to investigate and make recommendations concerning the role of the U.S. Employment Service. On February 6, after consulting and unanimously accepting the advice of a group of employment experts, the Advisory Council presented a memorandum to Secretary Wilson proposing a drastic reorganization of the U.S. Employment Service. In effect, the memorandum resurrected the AAPEO model for the national employment service that had been rejected in December.[44] It recommended "a system which uses the state as the administrative unit with federal supervision and aid." Federal offices were to be established only in those states that had no employment offices. A system of federal grants was to ensure that the system operated "on uniform policies and with standardized machinery." There was to be a national advisory board. The directors of existing state employment services, "wherever practical," were to be appointed to act "in the dual capacity of director of the state system and federal director for that state." Finally, the memorandum urged that Congress "be called upon to approve the general plan and make reasonable assurance of its continuity."[45] Although well aware of Louis Post's attitude, the members of the advisory council were hopeful that Secretary Wilson would accept their recommendations.[46]

On February 21, Secretary Wilson formally replied to the Advisory Council concerning the organization of the employment service. While agreeing that "the ultimate objective should be to make the state the administrative unit, with Federal supervision and aid," he declared that the demands of the wartime emergency could not wait on "the slow processes of legislative action in forty-eight states." Secretary Wilson rejected outright the proposed national advisory board. Nor was he prepared to accept a proposal made by the Advisory Council to restructure the internal organization of the USES. No mention was made of any legislative proposals.[47] The following day, Secretary Wilson directed that Assistant Secretary Post would remain in charge of the administration of the USES.[48] With victory seemingly within their grasp, both in December and again in February, the advocates of a state-based U.S. Employment Service had been unexpectedly but decisively defeated. The centralists in the Department of Labor had triumphed.

The first year of American involvement in the war had witnessed a series of bitter setbacks for the advocates of a U.S. Employment Service structured on federalist principles. Although the federalist case had been strengthened by the Ohio example of what a well-organized state system of employment offices could accomplish, senior Department of Labor officials remained unimpressed. The initial effort to get the Department of Labor to accept the AAPEO model had been rebuffed. The subsequent attempts to circumvent the department by establishing a supervisory War Service Board appointed by the Council of National Defense had also been narrowly defeated. A final, unexpected opportunity to win over Secretary Wilson to the AAPEO vision in February also came to nothing. It was with bitter feelings that the AAPEO supporters watched the pell-mell expansion of the USES in the first half of 1918. The federalists had been narrowly defeated, and the centralists in the Department of Labor were clearly in control of the USES by early 1918. However, only the most optimistic of the department's administrators could have imagined that the ideological struggle was over.

CHAPTER THREE

Nationalist Initiatives in the Department of Labor

Throughout the summer and fall of 1917, Department of Labor officials had worked to expand the embryonic USES in spite of a lack of funds and congressional indifference to their requests for assistance. Although politically weak, the department had managed to rebuff efforts to dislodge it from the position it claimed as the appropriate body to regulate the wartime labor market, and it continued to project itself aggressively in a number of different ways onto the national stage. Departmental officials hoped that, if they could hang on, eventually events would begin to move in their favor. Finally, in the winter of 1917–18, their patience was rewarded.

The initial strategy adopted by the Department of Labor in its efforts to project itself as the appropriate body to regulate the labor market was to promote cooperative agreements with other departments and wartime agencies. By late summer 1917, the department had reached tentative agreements with the Post Office Department, the Department of Agriculture, the Civil Service Commission, and the State Councils Section of the Council of National Defense, which coordinated all state councils of defense throughout the country.

Although starved of funds and lacking a clear mandate to establish a national employment service, department officials used these cooperative agreements to promote the visibility of the USES. Under the proposed agreement with the Post Office Department all fourth-class post offices were to operate as labor exchange agencies linked to the USES. The state councils of defense were to promote the establishment of labor exchanges in smaller towns and cities, which would also cooperate with the USES.

The U.S. Civil Service Commission, "with about 3000 agencies throughout the country devoted to examining and recruiting employees into the national service," agreed to cooperate with the USES as did the Office of Farm Management in the Department of Agriculture, which had county and local machinery dealing with food production and conservation. At the apex of this nationwide network of local employment offices was the machinery of the USES, which by July 1917 "had 88 offices operating in 27 different states."[1]

While anxious to secure the cooperation of other departments and agencies, Department of Labor officials fought tenaciously to retain maximum independence for their embryonic national employment service. Although initially prepared to grant cooperating bodies some degree of control over the USES in return for their support, these officials soon recognized the dangers in this approach and moved quietly to reassert departmental control. This process was reflected in the changes made to the successive versions of the draft cooperative agreement that the Department of Labor circulated to other agencies over the summer and fall. The most important change concerned the powers of the proposed national supervisory "consulting committee on emergency labor" which was originally to be composed of persons designated by the secretary of labor, the secretary of agriculture, the Civil Service Commission, and the State Councils Section of the Council of National Defense. This representative committee was charged with "general supervisory powers over the organization and operation" of the proposed nationwide exchange system. However, the functions of this committee were steadily whittled down over the summer. At the same time, the proposed agreement became more specific on details for the establishment of representative advisory committees at the state level to oversee state employment exchanges.[2] In effect, the Department of Labor pushed the advisory committee concept back to the state level, thereby ensuring that any national advisory committee would have no real power. Department officials were determined to maintain maximum freedom of operation.

In the early months of American involvement in the war, it was the problem of farm labor rather than industrial labor that overshadowed all discussions. However, for the Department of Labor to attempt to supply agricultural labor was to risk a direct confrontation with the Department of Agriculture. Initially, relations between the two departments were relatively harmonious. The difficulties of meeting the peculiar demands of agriculture, with its scattered and very seasonal labor needs, had been addressed well before America's entry into the war. In 1914, largely through the work of the AAPEO, the National Farm Labor Exchange had been established to ensure an adequate supply of harvest hands in the midwestern grain states. This organization consisted of representatives from the U.S. Department of Labor, the U.S. Department of Agriculture, and a labor official from each participating state in the grain belt. It aimed to facilitate the movement of harvest hands between the various states.[3] This organization had been moderately successful in meeting the heavy seasonal demand.

On April 27, 1917, Secretary Wilson and Secretary of Agriculture David Houston signed a "Memorandum of Understanding" concerning cooperation between their respective departments in securing agricultural labor. The memorandum specified that the Department of Agriculture would use its own organization, in cooperation with the respective state agricultural institutions and other state bodies, to establish the likely demand for farm labor, the wage rate, and the availability of such labor in each local area. If the labor supply was insufficient, then the Department of Labor would be invited "to use its best endeavors to supply such numbers of farm laborers upon the request of the Department of Agriculture as such Department's investigations may reveal to be needed."[4] The role assigned to the Department of Labor was that of a minor adjunct to the Department of Agriculture. Attempts by the Department of Labor over the summer to expand its peripheral role in supplying agricultural labor were resisted.[5]

Although rebuffed by the Department of Agriculture, the bureaucrats in the Department of Labor seized another opportunity to attempt to project the department into the agricultural labor market. This involved the establishment of the Boys' Working Reserve. It was estimated that there were between five and six million boys between ages sixteen and twenty-one in the United States and that at least "two million boys are either idle, or change their occupation for the summer months."[6] A number of states had begun to make moves to tap this potential source of labor for the farms and, on April 20, 1917, Secretary Wilson invited William E. Hall, a corporation executive and the nonsalaried president of the Boys Clubs of America, to take charge of the wartime mobilization of boys.[7]

On May 7, a notification concerning the United States Boys' Working Reserve was sent to all states, announcing the appointment of William E. Hall as national director, the appointment of a representative National Advisory Council to assist him, and the establishment of a National Committee to be composed of the state governors, or their representatives, and the leaders of the "great national boy organizations." Each state was invited to nominate a state director.[8]

The general aims and policy of the Boys' Reserve were clear. Boys had to be at least sixteen years of age and physically fit. No boy was to be permitted to work more than eight hours in any one day. The farmers were to pay for the boys' labor, although the actual rate would vary "since different kinds of work, different localities, and increasing experience command different compensation." The boys were to be organized into squads of not more than twenty-five and assigned to farms. The Reserve did not wish to disturb any existing state or municipal organization designed for a similar purpose but, "in the interest of unity and national efficiency," requested that boys enrolled in such organizations also enroll in the Boys' Working Reserve.[9] The national director summed up this policy at a conference in June: "The Reserve believes in a policy of decentralization—that is, it desires the State organizations to work out their own destiny with as little interference as to policy or organization rules as is possible."[10]

By midsummer 1917 a number of states had developed quite impressive Reserve organizations. Most states relied on school superintendents to promote the project. In late June, Massachusetts reported that there were camps in nearly every county of the state, each catering for between twenty and twenty-five boys. The state organization relied on school superintendents as "the connecting link between the State officers and the farms and camps."[11] In Wisconsin, high school principals had been asked to register the boys and to act as supervisors for those sent to local farms: "Reports from county schools [in Wisconsin] showed that eighty-five per cent of boys are at work on farms or in industry." In Connecticut, universities and high schools allowed students leaves of absence for agricultural work and even credited a certain amount of such labor toward academic grades. New Jersey also used the school system to enroll and place boys, and the county superintendents and school principals supervised the operation.[12]

Finance for the Reserve came from private sources. The national director served without pay for patriotic reasons. In September 1917, Hall noted: "The Young Men's Christian Association and the Boys' Club Federation have loaned to the Reserve capable assistants, and their salaries have been paid by such organizations."[13] It was an organization operated on a shoestring. The Boys' Working Reserve had enabled the Department of Labor to project itself into the important agricultural labor market in every state in the union even though Congress had not appropriated any funds for such expansion. It had been a very successful initiative.

In early summer 1918, the Department of Labor received unexpected support in its struggle to control the wartime labor market in the form of an offer to establish a voluntary organization to assist in mobilizing skilled labor. In June, a group of four individuals, including William Hall, the recently appointed director of the Boys' Working Reserve, met in Washington to discuss the problem of how best to connect technical and skilled labor with government needs. In addition to Hall, the group included John T. Pratt and Nathan A. Smyth, both lawyers with business interests from New York City, and I. W. Litchfield, a graduate of the Massachusetts Institute of Technology and manager of the Acme Harvester Company of Chicago. This meeting eventually led to the formation of the U.S. Public Service Reserve, a volunteer organization for mobilizing skilled labor, which offered its services to the Department of Labor. The offer was accepted and Hall was placed in charge of the new body. The aim of this Reserve was to encourage technically trained professionals, especially engineers, and highly skilled tradesmen to offer their services to the government. By enrolling in the Reserve, each individual signified his willingness to transfer into government service if and when he was needed. All offers of service were centralized and indexed by skill and geographical location and made available to the government on demand.

The Public Service Reserve began enrolling in early August and within a month it had over 11,500 men, including 7,500 engineers, on its lists. Reporting to the president in January 1918, Secretary of Labor William B. Wilson noted that approximately 26,000 technically trained men had been enrolled and classified: "Of these about 12,000 are engineers or other highly trained specialists." The Reserve supplied the Ordnance Bureau with individuals capable of "designing heavy gun carriages, for work on the most minute instruments of precision, and for almost everything else within this scope." The Medical Corps was supplied with food and drug experts, the Treasury Department with lawyers, the Department of Agriculture with engineers and chemists, and the Shipping Board with production engineers. In addition, "textile workers, leather men, metallurgists, sheet metal workers, experts on aluminum, chemists and many others have been furnished."[14] The Reserve was also able to supply large groups of individuals with quite specialized work experience: it recruited 2,500 men for the Ordnance Department to act as inspectors of ordnance material, 472 structural steel workers for the erection of radio towers in France for the Navy, and several thousand skilled motor mechanics for the Aviation Corps.[15]

Because most of the work was done by volunteers, the cost of the Reserve to the Department of Labor was negligible. Louis Post, assistant secretary of labor, seized this opportunity. In the fall of 1917, he took steps to enlarge the scope of the Reserve by creating a nationwide field organization: with the cooperation of the state councils of defense, the Reserve appointed directors in each state and, eventually, county and local Reserve officers. These individuals were linked closely with the the USES offices in the states. By the time of the armistice in November 1918, there were approximately 14,000 county and local Reserve enrollment officers scattered across the country; of that number, 2,000 were skilled tradesmen who had been appointed at the suggestion of the local unions. All these men donated their services for patriotic reasons as dollar-a-year men. In effect, Post had been able to capitalize on the widespread voluntarist sentiment in the community and harness it to support the fledgling USES. By late 1917, in spite of the refusal of Congress to appropriate funds for the purpose, the Department of Labor had created a nationwide employment machinery that was, at least on paper, an impressive organization and one that clearly could not be ignored.[16]

A major impediment to the ambitions of Department of Labor officials was the uncooperative attitude of Congress. Shortly after the United States entered the war, Secretary Wilson asked Congress for a supplemental appropriation of $750,000 to expand the existing U.S. Employment Service, and for authority to establish it as an independent administrative entity within the Department of Labor directly responsible to the secretary.[17] Technically, the USES was within the Bureau of Immigration, one of four separate bureaus within the Department of Labor, and was not directly under the control of the secretary of labor. Congress delayed action on the request. It was not until late September 1917 that a special conference between the Senate and House appropriations committees finally agreed on an appropriation of $250,000 for the expansion of the USES. This was a dramatic reduction of the $750,000 that the secretary of labor had originally requested in April and served as a warning signal that the Department of Labor had few friends in Congress. No action was taken on the request to establish the USES as an independent body.

Assistant Secretary Louis F. Post, however, was not easily deterred. Left in charge of the Department of Labor during the last three months of 1917 while Secretary Wilson was absent on a special presidential assignment, Post resolved to bypass Congress. He decided that the 1913 organic act

Louis Freeland Post, assistant secretary of labor (1913–21), energetically promoted a nation-alist rather than a federalist U.S. Employment Service. *Courtesy of the Prints and Photographs Division, Library of Congress.*

creating the Department of Labor conferred sufficient powers on the department to effect any necessary internal transfers without requiring specific congressional authorization. This meant that he could make the necessary internal administrative changes that would make the USES completely independent of the Bureau of Immigration and its chief, Commissioner Anthony Caminetti, who, Post felt, had been obstructing the expansion of the USES.

On October 13, 1917, Post divided the existing U.S. Employment Service into two quite separate divisions. The first, designated the war emergency service, was to be completely independent of the Bureau of Immigration and was to report directly to the secretary of labor. It was to be funded out of the new congressional appropriation and was to concentrate almost exclusively on meeting the labor needs of the shipbuilding industry. The second branch of the USES, the regular service, would continue to be operated by the Division of Information under the jurisdiction of the Bureau of Immigration and would continue to be funded through that bureau's appropriation. It was an awkward administrative makeshift but it did transfer at least partial control over the operation of the USES from the Bureau of Immigration to the Office of the Secretary.[18]

To overcome the niggardly congressional funding for the department's employment work, Post lobbied senior officials in the wartime administration. These efforts were rewarded when, in late November, President Wilson asked him for advice on whether funds should be made available to expand the USES.[19] He immediately submitted a lengthy memorandum outlining the gravity of the labor situation, particularly in the shipbuilding industry, and the urgent need for funds to expand the employment service of the department.[20] Following a further request from President Wilson for details on finances, Post submitted a proposal for a deficiency appropriation of $825,000 for the remainder of the fiscal year 1917–18, and an appropriation of $2,000,000 for the 1918–19 fiscal year.[21] On December 5, 1917, President Wilson allocated $825,000 from his National Security and Defense Fund to the Department of Labor in order "to defray expenses in connection with the work of distribution of productive labor throughout the United States."[22]

Post's lobbying had been extremely successful. He had bypassed congressional opposition and now had the funds he needed for a vastly expanded national employment service that would be directly responsible to the secretary of labor. Post moved quickly to capitalize on his good fortune. On December 13, he issued a departmental order transferring the entire U.S.

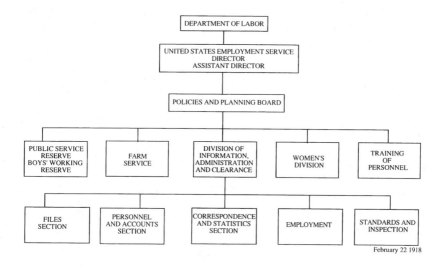

U.S. Employment Service, February 1918. Source: *Report of Director-General, USES* (August 1, 1918), 678.

Employment Service from the Bureau of Immigration to the Office of the Secretary. All employment work would henceforth be directly managed by Post himself. Moreover, "All officers, clerks and employees of the Bureau of Immigration and the Immigration Service found to be experienced in the work of the U.S. Employment Service" were transferred to that service.[23] With unfettered control of an expanded USES, Post now felt that the Department of Labor would play a prominent and powerful role in the wartime administration.

By Christmas 1917, the first phase of the wartime struggle over the organization of the national employment service was over. Skillfully led by Assistant Secretary Post, the Department of Labor had managed to ward off challenges to its position and had secured sufficient funds to permit a vast expansion of the employment service under terms and conditions decided solely by the secretary himself. In addition, cooperative agreements had been made with the Department of Agriculture, the Shipping Board, a number of state employment agencies, and the State Councils Section of the Council of National Defense. The voluntarist spirit in the community had been harnessed to the department's ambitions through the Boys' Working Reserve and the Public Service Reserve. In all this, Post had managed to retain unhampered freedom of action for the USES. Although he had lost the battle for legislative enactment, he appeared to have won the administrative struggle.

The opponents of Post's vision of a powerful, centralized employment service operated solely by the Department of Labor were in some disarray. Strong in individual states, particularly those with established state employment services, they remained unable to influence events in Washington. Their professional association and mouthpiece, the AAPEO, had demonstrated some capacity as a pressure group and, indeed, in the fall had almost mustered sufficient support for legislation embodying its views. However, the Department of Labor's vision of a centralized, rather than a cooperative, federal employment service appeared to have triumphed.

On his return to Washington at the end of December 1917, Secretary Wilson endorsed Post's actions. On January 3, 1918, he issued a departmental order formally establishing the United States Employment Service as a separate administrative unit directly under the control and supervision of the Office of the Secretary. The service was to be managed by a director and two assistant directors, one in charge of field work and quasi-official bodies, the other to oversee administrative work. There were to be seven separate divisions of the organization: a Division of Information, Administration, and Clearance, a Woman's Division, a Reserves Division (both the Public Service Reserve and the Boys' Working Reserve), a Farm Service Division, a Division of Investigation, a Statistical Division, and a Division of Service Offices.[24] In effect, Secretary Wilson promulgated the organizational structure suggested by Post in late December with only very minor amendments.[25] In addition, the USES formally took over 146 officers and clerks who had been engaged in employment work under the Bureau of Immigration and paid them directly from USES funds.[26] Provision was made for an internal policies board to oversee the operation of the USES, which was to consist of the director, the assistant director, and the heads of the various divisions of the USES. In fact, this body never functioned.[27]

Post's victory, however, was not complete. Secretary Wilson decided to appoint John B. Densmore of Montana, the first solicitor of the Department of Labor, as the director of the reorganized USES. Forty years earlier, Densmore's father, at that time the Iowa superintendent of the water supply system of the Illinois Central Railroad, had given William B. Wilson a job as a fireman after he had been blacklisted by the Pennsylvania coal operators for union activities and was unable to get work. Wilson lived with the Densmore family for a time and this enabled him to support his family

NATIONALIST INITIATIVES 45

PUBLIC EMPLOYMENT OFFICES IN THE UNITED STATES
1890-1921

YEAR	TOTAL OFFICES	CITIES WITH OFFICES	STATES WITH OFFICES
1890	5	5	1
1900	15	13	7
1910	55	53	21
1917 (early)	96	88	26
1917 (late)	181	152	42*
1918 (Oct.)	773	605	49
1921 (Oct.)	174	160	35*

* Includes District of Columbia

Source: Adapted from Shelby M. Harrison et al., *Public Employment Offices: Their Purpose, Structure, and Methods,* 624.

until he was able to return to work in Pennsylvania. He did not forget the kindness. Densmore had force and drive but no experience in employment work. Moreover, his appointment was a bitter blow to Assistant Secretary Post, who had anticipated that Charles Clayton, his personal secretary whom he had placed in charge of the USES in 1917, would be appointed director. Post disliked Densmore intensely and nearly resigned over the issue.[28] Friction between the two men was to hamper the development of the USES in the first half of 1918.

Now adequately financed, the USES expanded rapidly. Federal offices were opened as soon as possible in most of the states. At the beginning of February there were approximately fifty-five USES offices in the various states; by the end of March, this figure had more than doubled.[29] The offices varied a good deal in size. In New York City, for example, the office employed around forty people, but most USES offices employed only two, or sometimes three, men. The larger city offices had separate women's sections to handle female labor.[30] By the end of April 1918, the USES had 262 offices in operation: this total consisted of 119 state or municipal offices cooperating with and partly financed by the USES, and 143 offices solely financed and controlled by the USES.[31]

The Washington office of the USES expanded dramatically. In May, the USES moved out of its crowded quarters in the Department of Labor building into the Hotel Gordon, which had been recently vacated by the Food Administration. It occupied all five floors of that building and, for the first time, the Public Service Reserve was located on the same premises. By the end of April the USES had more than 1,000 people on its payroll: 196 in the central Washington office and 813 in the field service. The volume of business had expanded dramatically: the correspondence handled by the central office rose from about 200 letters per day at the beginning of 1918 to approximately 5,000 per day by the end of April."[32]

The rapid expansion of the USES brought it into increasing conflict with existing state employment services and highlighted the desirability of cooperative agreements between the USES and the individual states. A few such agreements had been made although the details varied a good deal. In May 1918, the director-general of the USES commented that the most common form of cooperative agreement with the states involved splitting the costs of the offices on an equal basis, although in some states "the municipalities pay one-third, the State pays one-third, and we pay one-third." Densmore felt that such agreements permitted as much control of the state offices "as the Federal Government requires." The exact nature of the control exercised by the USES over cooperating states was a little vague, but it usually involved the supervision of "the manner in which the office is conducted, insistance upon the use of standard forms, and control of the priority given to different requests for labor."[33]

The cooperative agreements also provided for the nomination of a federal director of employment for each state. In those states that supported their own employment offices the individual nominated was usually the director of the state employment system. He was then sworn into the federal service at a nominal salary of one dollar per year to ensure coordination between the USES and the state employment offices. However, the Department of Labor retained the right to veto such nominations if it felt that the appointment would be unduly partisan. The usual arrangement was for the state director to be appointed by the director-general of the USES "with the approval of the Assistant Secretary of Labor and upon the joint recommendation of the State council of defense and organized capital and labor of that State."[34]

The appointment of impartial state directors, particularly in the South and West where there was little prior experience with employment offices, presented a number of problems. In a few states it even proved impossible to secure a nomination that was supported by both management and labor. In those cases, the director-general of the USES usually overrode union objections. In Alabama, for example, George B. Tarrant, a businessman involved in real estate, was appointed over the protests of the Birmingham Trades Council, the Carpenters' District Council, the Brotherhood of Railway Clerks, and the Brotherhood of Electrical Workers. Significantly, Tarrant was the candidate of Alabama's two senators, John H. Bankhead and Oscar W. Underwood. In Montana the state director was the employers' choice and had the "enmity of labor." In Utah and Rhode Island the state federations of labor originally protested the nominations but later withdrew their objections. In New Mexico the appointee was reputed to have a "strong anti-labor bias." In Massachusetts, William A. Gaston, a member of the state council of defense, was appointed over the protest of the Boot and Shoe Workers Union.

The other state directors of the USES were acceptable to labor: at least five were active union members, including two presidents and one secretary-treasurer of state federations of labor. In Arizona, for example, Thomas J. Croaff, the president of the Arizona State Federation of Labor, was appointed with the approval of both the state council of defense and the state governor. Seven state directors had had previous experience in state government administration, often as commissioners of labor. Approximately twelve appointments were Immigration Bureau officials who had been transferred to the Employment Service.[35]

Although special representatives had been sent to the various states in January 1918 to initiate negotiations on closer cooperation, by May only nine states had committed themselves to some formal cooperative agreement.[36] However, by this time, approximately half the states had signified a willingness to cooperate even if no formal agreement was signed. This usually involved the state director agreeing to accept an appointment from the Department of Labor as a dollar-a-year man to ensure some basic cooperation between the USES and the state system. It was not until June that even this minimum level of cooperation had been achieved in all states.[37]

Employment experts watched with dismay the pell-mell expansion of the federal employment service. William M. Leiserson, the moving spirit behind the establishment of the AAPEO and recently appointed as professor of politics and economics at Toledo University, vented his frustration before a meeting of the Ohio Academy of Social Science at the end of March 1918. In a stinging attack on the Department of Labor, he again voiced the rejected advice given earlier by the AAPEO representatives. Already a year had elapsed since America entered the war, but there was still no "comprehensive system of labor market organization to meet the needs of the nation at war." The fundamental reason for this disastrous state of affairs was, he felt, directly attributable to the incompetence of those in charge of the USES.

Leiserson's major criticism of the USES was that, instead of concentrating on the state as the administrative unit and encouraging the development of statewide systems of employment offices that the national service would then coordinate, the Washington office had rushed to establish a nationwide network of local employment offices which unnecessarily duplicated work already being done. Federal offices in New York, Cleveland, Minneapolis, Los Angeles, and many other cities were merely duplicating work already being done more effectively by state and municipal employment offices.[38]

Moreover, Leiserson felt that many of the federal offices were incompetently, or even dishonestly, operated. In Wisconsin, for example, the USES office established in Madison had reported in August 1917 that there were 3,257 positions filled that month; in fact, the officer in charge had merely taken the total business done by the four cooperating state offices and reported that total as the work of the USES office. The reality was that the federal office had not placed anyone. In Los Angeles, Buffalo, and other cities with federal offices, he believed a similar situation prevailed. In those cities with no state or municipal employment office whose figures could be used to boost artificially the USES office placement figures, the results were illuminating. The latest figures available covered only November 1917, but they showed that the USES office at Mobile, Alabama, had only fifteen people apply for work and managed to place one; in Savannah, Georgia, 160 applied for work and nineteen were placed; in Minneapolis, 202 applied for work and one was placed. Other figures were incomprehensible: in Galveston, Texas, fifty-five people applied for work, but 401 were reported as placed.[39]

The record keeping of the USES was, in Leiserson's view, seriously deficient. He commented that the published monthly statistics showing the operation of the various USES employment offices were totally misleading because there was no uniformity in the method of collecting the data. The overall totals for applications for work and successful placements, therefore, did "not make a sum that can have any meaning." It obviously represented a great deal of duplication, and the sources varied from month to month. By contrast, the figures for the British employment system, which were published alongside the American figures each month, presented a complete and accurate statement of the operation of the 383 branch exchanges in that system.[40] The American statistics bore no relationship to reality: there was no agreed, nationally accepted way of reporting statistics. The Department of Labor had "not only neglected to standardize the accounting, record and statistical methods of the state and municipal employment bureaus, but it has not even a good record system for its own offices."[41] At every point, federal officials had ignored the advice offered by the employment professionals. Organizational and political pressures rather than professional and efficiency considerations had dominated the development of the USES.

There were other criticisms leveled by Leiserson. One concerned the use of discredited techniques to attract labor. This criticism was directed at the use of blanket newspaper advertisements that gave misleading impressions of anticipated labor shortages. Because such advertisements were quite indiscriminate, they attracted too many workmen, many of whom lacked the appropriate skills. The USES had also engaged in campaigns to sign up labor far in advance of the actual demand, which again contradicted the best advice offered by the employment experts. A particularly flagrant example of this had been the recent Shipyard Volunteer Campaign.[42] Moreover, the creation of thirteen zone or district offices, each with a separate office and a superintendent, had been unnecessary and again violated the best advice being offered by the employment professionals. The failure to establish an advisory council, composed of representatives of employers, labor, and the states was another serious shortcoming. Leiserson felt that "public criticism" was needed to force those in charge of the USES to adopt policies and practices that were "approved by all experienced public employment officials."[43]

By the end of the winter of 1917–18, the Department of Labor had emerged triumphant. Led by the determined Assistant Secretary of Labor Louis Post, the department had secured sufficient funds to underwrite a rapid expansion of its employment service, had effected an internal reorganization, and had managed to evade attempts to incorporate a special advisory board that might have fettered its control over the expanded organization. The decision to postpone any attempt to secure formal, legislative establishment was the price of this unauthorized expansion. The appointment of the secretary of labor as war labor administrator on January 4, 1918, had further strengthened the position of the Department of Labor in this struggle. Although, among employment experts, there was considerable criticism of both the organization and the operation of the expanded USES, as winter turned to spring it seemed nevertheless that the centralists in the Department of Labor had routed their opponents. However, to confound skeptics in Washington and to silence its critics in the states, the USES had to demonstrate its capacity to supply labor to wherever it was required and to do so efficiently. The enormous wartime expansion of U.S. shipbuilding capacity presented the Department of Labor with the opportunity it needed.

CHAPTER FOUR

The Seattle Labor Market Experiment

For a brief period during the First World War, the United States became the greatest shipbuilding nation on earth. After a faltering start, the Emergency Fleet Corporation (EFC), the construction arm of the U.S. Shipping Board, presided over a staggering expansion of American shipbuilding capacity. In April 1917, the United States had only sixty-one yards, thirty-seven for steel and twenty-four for wooden ships, with a combined total of 211 ways; by November 1918, there were 1,284 ways in American yards, "more than double the ways in the rest of the world." The Emergency Fleet Corporation both expanded existing shipyards and created immense new facilities. Hog Island, built during the war on the Delaware River mud flats south of Philadelphia, had fifty ways and was the largest shipyard in the world in 1918. This phenomenal increase in shipbuilding capacity naturally generated an immense demand for labor. At the time of the armistice, 380,000 workers were employed in American shipyards.[1]

The Department of Labor was extremely anxious to be seen to be of use to the shipbuilding program. Supplying the enormous labor requirements of the shipyards would justify both a rapid expansion of the USES and a request for large congressional appropriations. Edward N. Hurley, the chairman of the U.S. Shipping Board, and his advisers were very concerned about the supply of shipyard labor, and Hurley himself was, almost certainly, instrumental in securing the $825,000 from the President's National Security and Defense Fund for the expansion of the USES in late 1917.[2] In the winter of 1917–18, the USES undertook two separate projects on behalf of the Shipping Board: the Shipyard Volunteer Campaign and the Seattle

U.S. Employment Service poster designed to attract labor to the shipyards. *RG 165 WW, 460-A10, National Archives.*

experiment with a centralized shipyard labor market. Initially, both ventures appeared to be quite successful. In the long run, however, both seriously compromised the reputation of the USES.

Worried about an impending shortage of labor for the new shipyards, Hurley announced in January 1918 a crash program for the registration of 250,000 "shipyard volunteers" who would agree to go to the shipyards when the yards were willing to take them. There had been some talk of such a program in late 1917 and both the State Councils Section of the Council of National Defense and the Department of Labor had been promoting the idea. However, nothing definite had been decided and Hurley's announcement caught everyone off balance. Initially, the state councils of defense were put in charge of the campaign, but the Department of Labor insisted that the Shipping Board had agreed to conduct the campaign through its organization and demanded to have a role. After some confusion, the Department of Labor eventually assumed full responsibility for the campaign although it still relied on the cooperation of the state councils of defense.[3] It was an inauspicious beginning.

The Shipyard Volunteer Campaign, initially scheduled to last for only three weeks, had to be extended for more than three months and caused immense confusion throughout the country. In New Jersey, the state council of defense tried to turn over the registration proposal to the State Department of Labor, which operated the state employment offices, but the commissioner of labor, Lewis T. Bryant, refused to have anything to do with the campaign. His attitude epitomized that of the employment professionals. He pointed out that there were no jobs yet available at the shipyards on the scale projected and that to conduct such a campaign would only cause unrest and dissatisfaction among workmen who, naturally, would expect to be called to the shipyards immediately. He assured the state council of defense that the projected New Jersey quota of 16,000 men could be supplied through the state employment offices at any time the shipyards could actually employ the men.[4] Subsequent events proved his point.

The campaign involved an immense amount of work. In Illinois, for example, fifty-four special enrollment offices were established across the state by February 1. When the Illinois campaign closed one month later, the state council had the names, addresses, and occupations of 29,613 volunteers, the majority from Chicago. This figure was 6,000 above the quota. More than 10,000 personal interviews had been conducted throughout the state and 2,449 letters relating to the campaign were received and answered. The enrollment cards received were then cataloged and indexed.[5] The final outcome was a massive three-volume work. In Ohio, where the Reserve work was conducted solely through the existing state employment offices, a total of 18,198 shipyard volunteers signed the cards.[6] Approximately 10,000 men enrolled in Pennsylvania, where the shipyard volunteer drive lasted until June 15, 1918.[7]

However, in spite of the enormous effort that had gone into the campaign, the vast majority of the men who enrolled as shipyard volunteers were never called upon and the organization was quietly allowed to die. In New York, where the state council had undertaken the campaign, an official report from Buffalo, where 1,000 men had registered, noted that, by April 1918, there was "considerable dissatisfaction because there have been no calls made upon the men enrolled for service."[8] In May, an EFC representative reported from Chicago that about 13,000 men had signed up "a month or two ago" and had since "been running wild in the streets." Many had given up their jobs in expectation of obtaining immediate work in the shipyards. "Others have deserted their families on the pretext that they are needed for government work. As a whole, the situation here is a most wonderful mess."[9] Bryant's criticism of the whole registration had proved to be only too accurate. The campaign had been a fiasco: its only redeeming feature was the attendant publicity given the shipping problem. As a contemporary noted, "It put ships on the front page."[10]

The kind of broadbrush, indiscriminate advertising for workmen that underlay the Shipyard Volunteer Campaign was anathema to the employment professionals. They believed that all statements of demand for labor should be based on specific requests for workers rather than on estimates of likely future needs, which usually proved to be grossly exaggerated. To add to the irritation of the professionals, the publicity for the Shipyard Volunteer Campaign, which was distributed by the Department of Labor and comprised "tons and tons of literature containing instructions, registration blanks, report forms and advertising matter," was quite misleading because of its insinuation that the shipyards would get all their labor through the USES. This misrepresentation was compounded by the failure of the USES to protest the mischievous advertisements of high-paying jobs put out by the shipbuilding companies. In fact, the shipyards were turning men away because they were not yet ready to employ them.

In Leiserson's view, the entire Shipyard Volunteer Campaign demonstrated perfectly "the lack of knowledge of the employment business of those who are supposed to build and operate the national labor market organization."[11] In the eyes of the employment experts throughout the country, the Shipyard Volunteer Campaign demonstrated what they already knew: the USES lacked sufficient expertise to be trusted with the resonsibility for centralized control over the wartime labor market.

The second major campaign involving the USES and the Shipping Board was Seattle's experiment with a centralized labor market. Since U.S. entry into the war, the Department of Labor had been trying to convince the board that the fledgling USES should be used as the sole supplier of ship-yard labor.[12] Toward the end of 1917, responding to growing concern about the available labor supply, the Shipping Board decided to accept the Department of Labor's overtures. It was to be the first major test of the theory that a centralized labor market, under government auspices, could solve the labor problem.

The experiment, which was conducted in Seattle, generated considerable enthusiasm within the wartime administration. Writing to the officials in charge of the new USES office in Seattle, William E. Blackman, director of labor of the Emergency Fleet Corporation, noted that "the whole program throughout the United States depends upon what you are doing. . . . The plan you now are working on is the only feasible one and if we can prove it by actual results it will be a very easy matter to establish like agencies all over the country."[13] The experiment also attracted the attention of academics and those interested in general employment matters.[14] Meyer Bloomfield, a student of labor questions who had been appointed to the the Industrial Service Section of the EFC, declared that it was "a dream of his life come true where employment of labor is conducted as a science and not 'in the anarchy of a wide open labor market.'"[15]

By late 1917, Seattle had four steel yards in operation employing approximately 16,000 workers and another steel yard under construction. There were also twelve wooden shipyards in the area.[16] Because most of the Seattle yards had been constructed since 1914 during a period of great wartime demand, they were able to pay well and to attract adequate labor.[17] The tendency toward higher wages was reinforced by the powerful Seattle metal unions, which had imposed a wage scale that was markedly higher than that found elsewhere on the Pacific Coast. In fact, the strength of the Metal Trades Council of Seattle was reflected in an agreement reached with the four steel shipyards shortly before American entry into the war that had established a virtual "closed shop."[18] In the wooden shipyards, although the unions involved were well organized, no formal agreement was in force.

On December 14, 1917, representatives of the Department of Labor, the Emergency Fleet Corporation of the Shipping Board, the four steel ship-yards in Seattle, and "representatives of the Metal Trades Council, the Boilermakers, Shipbuilders and Helpers, the United Brotherhood of Carpenters, and the Shipwrights, Joiners, and Calkers" signed an agreement concerning a proposed USES office in Seattle.[19] The new office was to supply all the labor required "for War Emergency work in this district."

The Department of Labor was to control the office, which was to be free of charge to workers and employers alike. Acknowledging the existing situation, the agreement specified the right of employees to organize. It also provided for the establishment of an advisory committee composed of representatives of employers, employees, and relevant government departments.

Two clauses in the agreement were extremely important. One specified that existing employment offices maintained by employers or unions in Seattle were to be "combined into a central Government office." This meant, in practice, that the shipyard unions, which operated their own employment services through their business agents, would have the right to nominate some of their own members to the USES office staff. The other clause gave the unions both the authority to rule on the qualifications of all applicants for work in the shipyards and the power to issue work permits to successful candidates.[20]

The achievements of the new system in Seattle were substantial. By centralizing the demand for labor, the USES office was able to meet both shipyard demands and other local needs for labor. By the end of March 1918, Blackman, the director of labor of the Emergency Fleet Corporation, reported to the chairman of the Shipping Board that the Seattle office was meeting "all the needs of the shipyards with the exception of a few wood caulkers in wooden yards."[21] Moreover, a central office was able to make a more accurate estimate of likely shipyard labor requirements: instead of newspaper estimates of a shortage of 20,000 men, for example, the USES office calculated that the increase in workers needed was not more than 6,000, an estimate that still turned out to be higher than the actual need for the first four months of 1918. Production rose as shipyards were able to work two shifts. Yet, in spite of these apparent successes, the Seattle experiment ultimately proved to be a failure.

Open criticism of the Seattle experiment during 1918 focused on whether or not it had deliberately promoted unionism and the closed shop. Technically, the federal government had forbidden discrimination between union and nonunion men working on government contracts. However, the strength of the shipyard unions in Seattle had created what was, in effect, a de facto closed shop, a situation that was not well understood in other parts of the country.[22] The issue surfaced in mid-August 1918 in an article published in the *Business Chronicle of the Pacific Northwest,* a well-known antiunion journal. It purported to be a transcript of an interview between a workman and the director of the USES office in Seattle:

Workman: In order to work, must I join a labor union?

Director: Well, the big plants where men are needed so badly are unionized and so it will be necessary for you to join the union.

Workman: Are they "closed shop"?

Director: Yes.

Workman: But I don't want to join a labor union.

Director: Then we don't want you.

This interview caused a considerable stir in Washington among members of the War Cabinet and other key officials, and it damaged the image of the USES. Given the strength of the union movement in Seattle, it was merely an expression of an unpalatable truth albeit very undiplomatically expressed by a federal government official.[23] However, the overreaction in Washington was a symptom of a related, but much more serious, problem. The trouble in the Seattle office was more complex than simply appearing to favor union men in what was, virtually, a "closed shop" district.

Something did go seriously amiss in the Northwest. Events in Seattle triggered a protracted subterranean struggle within the national wartime administration that never came out into the open because all parties concerned had more to lose than to gain from such publicity. Although it appeared to be a success, the operations of the Seattle office in fact confirmed the worst suspicions of those who felt that the Department of Labor could not be trusted to be neutral in the clash between management and labor. It was not the isolated issue of appearing to favor union labor in the Northwest but the larger question of who controlled the administration of the Seattle office and, by implication, the administration of the USES itself, that was the focus of the struggle.

Within weeks of the establishment of the Seattle office in December 1917, disturbing reports began filtering back to Washington. Criticism centered on the manner in which the office was being administered. The person placed in charge of the Seattle office was Ferdinand A. Silcox, a thirty-five-year-old officer on temporary transfer from the Department of Agriculture whose administrative experience in government service up to that date had been as a district officer in the Forest Service. In late January

1918, the EFC received a confidential report that, either through lack of experience or through deliberate union sympathies, Silcox was allowing union men to control the operation of the office. It was a potentially explosive situation. Gordon Corbaley, the secretary of the Seattle Chamber of Commerce and a trusted confidential adviser of the EFC, tersely wired Blackman that "Silcox is fine man but has head too high above ground to catch little things, as staff beginning to put things over on him." Unless some action was taken immediately, Corbaley feared that the shipyard owners would withdraw from the agreement.[24] Blackman immediately wired Henry M. White, the commissioner of immigration in Seattle, and asked him to make a confidential investigation.[25]

Commissioner White did investigate the Seattle office and his report confirmed Corbaley's estimate of the situation. He saw a pressing need "to put some acceptable outsiders into the middle of the present group" in the office and to remove "some of troublemakers" by sending them out as traveling examiners. Furthermore, he urged that representatives of the employment management departments in the various shipyards should be put into the USES office to keep a check on the activities of the union representatives who had been hired as part of the December agreement. White also suggested that, if Silcox could be sent to San Francisco for a month, he would be able to reorganize the Seattle office.[26]

Silcox, in fact, remained in the Seattle office until August 1918. After a preliminary discussion with Commissioner White, Silcox telegraphed the Washington office of the USES defending the record of the Seattle office in supplying men for the shipyards and stating that "it would help if you would state somewhat more definitely what the disquieting information is."[27] The EFC, however, did not want to arouse the wrath of the Seattle union movement by an open declaration of its suspicions. In early February, the Washington office attempted to move Silcox temporarily to the San Francisco office, but the move was blocked by the Seattle Metal Trades Council. Gordon Corbaley commented to Blackman that Silcox was "stirring up trouble about his transfer to San Francisco."[28] There was not a great deal that Blackman could do without risking a break with the powerful Seattle metal unions. Corbaley tried to impress on Blackman the gravity of the situation, but nothing was done.[29]

At the same time, shipyard management was expressing concern about the operation of the Seattle office.[30] In mid-March, one irate shipyard owner telegraphed Blackman from Seattle reminding him that one of the functions of the centralized employment office was to minimize the "shifting of men from one yard to another." This purpose was being circumvented by shipyard foremen who were making deals with the business agents of the relevant unions to pirate skilled men away from other yards. This was possible through the "close association of business agents with examiners in [the] government office": the latter sent the men where the business agent of the union directed.

> There is no attempt made at fair and equitable play and under present conditions government office occupies position of fifth wheel to coach for in former days we simply did business direct with business agent of union and were furnished with whatever men we required. Our sole idea in doing business with government office was that this office was going [to] supply us with men and that employers would not be permitted [to] do business with union direct.[31]

The Seattle office, instead of acting as a restraint on labor turnover as was intended, was covertly encouraging it through the close relationship between the unions and the staff of the government employment office.

Other employer groups also expressed concern that the USES office in Seattle was not being administered in an impartial manner and was, in fact, being deliberately used to promote unionism. In mid-March the Employers' Association of Washington wrote to Charles Piez, general manager of the EFC, outlining its grievances and attaching five sworn affidavits. The association charged that the former business agent of the Iron Shipbuilders' Union, Dan McKillop, who was now employed in the office as an examiner, was "using his position to unionize the men at the expense of the labor supply in the shipyards." All applications for work in the shipyards seemed to require McKillop's approval. Nonunion men who applied for work permits were either refused outright or given an examination to test their skills that was administered by the union in a blatantly discriminatory manner. Nonunion men who had previously been granted permits to work in the yards were required to take an examination, which many failed, including workers with up to sixteen years of experience behind them. If individuals inquired why they failed the examination "they are told that the union has made it a rule to give out no information."[32] The Employers' Association found this an intolerable situation.

There was a continual drumfire of complaints about the Seattle office throughout the year.[33] As late as October 1918, the Seattle district manager of the Emergency Fleet Corporation made a careful study of the situation and reported that the USES office "does not serve the purpose intended." The cause of this undesirable condition was the degree of union influence over the operation of the office. A majority of employees in the USES office, he felt, "have apparently in their mind that paramount must be the upbuilding and strengthening of their Union and a continuance of conditions whereby the demand for labor shall remain much greater than the supply rather than any spirit of helpfulness to the shipbuilding program." Lawrence Wood, who had succeeded Silcox as office superintendent in August, was unable to do very much because a majority of his associates in the office "were forced on him" by the unions. Wood himself believed that only "about 30%" of the men sent to the shipyards from the Seattle office ever reached their destination because of the deliberate policy of the unions to make it as difficult as possible to obtain a work permit.[34]

The substantial shortfall in the supply of labor available to the shipyards of the Pacific Northwest in the second half of 1918 added urgency to these continued complaints. In October, an EFC representative in Seattle estimated that the four steel yards in Seattle were short 6,600 men and that the total demand for shipyard labor in the Northwest exceeded 11,000 men.[35] Henry McBride, a lawyer and a former governor of Washington, who was an EFC adviser in the Puget Sound district, confirmed the existence of a serious shortage of both common and skilled labor in the Seattle shipyards. Moreover, he believed that the unions were being obstructive: "In the yards there are numbers of helpers who could do the work of a machinist, but the Machinists' Union refuses to grant them permits for doing such work." The shortage of labor had led to increased pirating, or "scamping," of labor, particularly skilled labor, by the various shipyards.[36] Both letters confirmed earlier reports about conditions in Seattle: it appeared that the local unions had captured the administration of the USES office and were using that office to promote union interests rather than the national interest. The Department of Labor seemed unwilling, or unable, to do anything about it.

The continuing criticism of the Seattle office, and the inability of the Emergency Fleet Corporation or the Department of Labor to eliminate the cause of the concern, pointed to the delicate nature of the original agreement establishing that office. In December 1917, the various parties to that agreement had all anticipated some advantage to themselves in the operation of such a centralized, government-funded employment office. The agreement relied on the voluntary cooperation of all interested parties and on the operation of the office in a relatively impartial manner. Yet, once the Seattle office was in operation, the signatories to the agreement found that, for different reasons, they had more to lose by publicly withdrawing their support than by continuing it, despite the flagrantly partisan activities of the staff.

The prime concern of the Emergency Fleet Corporation was maximum ship production with the least possible delay. This could be best brought about by placing existing yards on two or even three shifts. The major threats to such production appeared to be a labor shortage and the related problem of excessive labor turnover. The idea of centralizing the labor market through a national mechanism like the USES seemed to offer the best opportunity to achieve both these objectives.[37] In fact, the Emergency Fleet Corporation quietly contributed one half of the financial support, "not to exceed $10,000 in any one month," for the operation of the Seattle office.[38] Because the Seattle office was reasonably successful in supplying shipyard labor, the EFC was unwilling to risk the disruption that might be associated with any attempt to reform it.

The motives of the shipyard owners were more complicated. The wooden shipyards had never wholeheartedly endorsed the December agreement and were never entirely brought into the orbit of the government employment office.[39] The pool of labor for the wooden yards could be augmented by drawing on house carpenters and woodworkers from allied trades in the region. The situation in the steel yards, however, was markedly different because the available labor supply was quite limited and was entirely controlled by the Metal Trades Council, a fact that was recognized in the "closed shop" agreement.

Although confronted by a powerful and united union movement, shipyard owners in Seattle remained extremely divided. Almost no cooperation existed among the different steel yards and none at all between the steel and wooden yards. In a fiercely competitive situation, the yards were quite fragmented in their response to the highly organized and centralized shipyard unions. In a time of rapid expansion and shortage of labor, the yards were bidding against each other for men, particularly skilled tradesmen, and the unions were able to take advantage of these circumstances to gain wage increases and better conditions.

In the two years prior to U.S. entry into the war, material and labor costs had escalated rapidly. The newer yards, which had the most modern plants and the most recent contracts, were in a better position to pay for the increases than were the older yards with long-term, fixed contracts.

The Skinner and Eddy yard, in particular, had obtained contracts from the EFC in midsummer 1917 for the full capacity of its plant. Anticipating a further escalation in costs, the management had inserted a clause in the contract to permit a 20 percent increase over the wages they were currently paying, which were already well above the $4 per day specified in the latest annual agreement with the Seattle metal unions.[40] This situation was a disaster for other yards in the region.

With one yard in such an advantageous position in a period of great demand for labor, it is not surprising that the employers could not agree among themselves on wage levels and working conditions. As a consequence, there was intense competition between the yards for skilled workmen: the pirating of labor grew worse as the labor market contracted and constituted a serious hindrance to production. For shipyard management, apart from the Skinner and Eddy yard, the establishment of the USES office was, in effect, an opportunity to overcome its lack of unity. Unable to impose uniform wage rates, or to compete with the Skinner and Eddy wage scale, shipyard management saw in a centralized labor market under government control some hope of imposing limits on the escalating labor turnover and related labor costs.[41]

The unions had no such tangible benefits to gain from the establishment of a centralized labor market. Given the traditional suspicion of government-sponsored employment offices that permeated the American Federation of Labor, it is hard to see why the unions agreed to the scheme. Perhaps they saw in the possibility of funneling all shipyard labor through one office an opportunity to promote unionism and the "closed shop" in the wooden shipyards.[42] In the bargain that the unions struck, which gave them virtual administrative control of the employment office, they no doubt felt that they had nothing to lose and possibly something to gain. The fact that the Department of Labor was to be in charge of the USES office may have persuaded the unions to accept the idea. The very favorable experience of British unions with a government-sponsored system of labor exchanges may also have influenced the Seattle unions. A number of British trade unionists visited the United States during 1917 and spoke on that issue.[43] The appointment of Silcox as the first superintendent of the office gave the unions a fortuitous advantage; either because of his inexperience or perhaps through some tacit understanding, Silcox allowed the unions much more influence in the operation of the USES office than they might have expected.[44]

The Department of Labor had an immense stake in the success of the Seattle office. The expansion and successful operation of the USES was a key weapon in the department's struggle to demonstrate that it had the administrative capacity to cope with a major role in the wartime administration.[45] The Seattle experiment was a critical test of its administrative competence. Not surprisingly, senior department officials were reluctant to concede that any problem existed.[46] When they finally admitted that something was amiss in the Seattle office, they took no decisive action for fear that the unions would withdraw their support.[47] In spite of pressure from the EFC and from shipyard management, Silcox, with the support of the Seattle Metal Trades Council, remained in charge of the office until late summer. Complaints about shortages of labor in the Seattle yards and about the deliberate policy of the unions in refusing to grant work permits persisted right up to the armistice.[48] In meeting adverse criticism of the operation of the Seattle office, officials in the Labor Department evaded the issue of administrative partiality and tried to confine the discussion to the less explosive issue of union recognition in a closed shop area.[49]

Nine days before the armistice, John Densmore, director of the USES, made a confidential proposal that he believed would resolve the Seattle imbroglio without antagonizing the Metal Trades Council. He wanted the EFC to issue an order to all shipyards in the Seattle district, including the wooden yards, to employ their labor solely through the USES office. Henry McBride conveyed this proposal to Leon Marshall, director of industrial relations for the Emergency Fleet Corporation. In McBride's view, however, Densmore was putting the cart before the horse: "The remedy it seems to me is more backbone in the employment office."[50] Marshall's reply was succinct: "Densmore's request will be refused."[51] Before being granted a complete monopoly of shipyard labor, the Seattle office first had to demonstrate its independence of undue union influence.

The EFC officials wanted the USES to succeed and were prepared to support Densmore as far as they could; in return, however, the USES had to demonstrate genuine impartiality in its administration before being entrusted with monopoly control of the labor market. This attitude was not confined to EFC officials. Influential members of the national administration remained reluctant throughout the war to grant the USES and the Department of Labor comprehensive powers. The Seattle experiment made them doubt that the department had the capacity to use those powers in an independent and impartial manner.

It was an irony of the domestic mobilization that the Seattle experiment, which was designed to demonstrate the value of centralized control of the wartime labor market, in fact hindered the development of government controls in that area. Both the Shipyard Volunteer Campaign and the Seattle labor market experiment had appeared to be reasonably successful on the surface but both had triggered grave mistrust of the administrative capacity of the USES among wartime government officials and state employment experts. The Shipyard Volunteer Campaign had convinced employment experts that USES officials did not have the requisite level of expertise to operate successfully a centralized wartime labor market. The Seattle experiment had raised doubts as to whether the Department of Labor could be trusted to be impartial in the struggle between capital and labor. In its relations with the shipyards, the USES had failed to demonstrate either employment expertise or administrative competence. It was a bad omen for the ambitions of those in charge of the Department of Labor.

1918
Victory
and
Defeat

CHAPTER FIVE

The Role of the War Labor Policies Board

By the spring of 1918 the Department of Labor's drive to establish a centralized control over the wartime labor market, which had seemed almost within its grasp during the winter, had reached an impasse. Although the USES, with the aid of a $825,000 grant from President Wilson's emergency war fund, had expanded rapidly, the Seattle experiment and other indications of ineptitude had robbed it of any chance of securing the support of either the employment professionals in the states or the major government departments and agencies. Lacking support in Congress, the Department of Labor could only hang on and hope that the wartime drift of events would work in its favor. Evidence of a mounting labor shortage in the spring intensified the pressure on all the parties involved. In the early summer, the newly created War Labor Policies Board finally managed to break the deadlock and secure an agreement that the USES would be given a virtual monopoly over the supply of labor for war industries. The price for that agreement, however, was a fundamental reorganization of the USES and a reorientation of its policy.

During the first twelve months of American involvement in the war, a fierce debate raged between those who believed that wartime demands were creating a labor shortage that was rapidly assuming crisis proportions and those, particularly representatives of organized labor, who feared that reactionary employers were using the issue to try to undermine labor standards.[1] The debate highlighted the complete absence of reliable, up-to-date statistical information on trends in the labor market.[2]

This lack of accurate information on the operation of the labor market meant that government policy in this area, as in many others, was driven by "informed guesswork." However, the wartime crisis forced the state to develop more appropriate statistical data on which to base policy. In this instance, policy preceded rather than followed the creation of appropriate statistical information. The Department of Labor had made little effort to develop adequate statistical flows until the crisis became acute in the spring of 1918; it had heretofore relied on manifestly inadequate data in promoting its role in regulating the national labor market. Policy throughout 1917 and early 1918 had been driven by ideology and guesswork rather than accurate information. The development of a genuine crisis in the labor market forced a reassessment of this policy and highlighted the need for current empirical information on the demand and supply of labor. It was pressure from the various states, rather than from industry or organized labor, that forced the policy reassessment and clarified the need for accurate statistics on the operation of the labor market.[3]

It was not until early March 1918 that the first continuous national register of supply and demand in the labor market was created. In that month the USES instituted a system of daily and weekly reports on general labor conditions from its branch offices in nearly one hundred industrial centers scattered across the country. These reports included estimates of the shortage or surplus of labor, of the availability of housing and accommodation, and of relations between employers and employees in each locality. In addition, about 1,000 large plants, many of them manufacturing munitions, reported each month to the Public Service Reserve on their immediate and future needs for labor.[4]

Although the initial USES reports on labor conditions indicated that no labor shortage existed, by mid-April confidence in the existence of a pool of surplus labor began to evaporate. By the end of June the reports indicated a general shortage of unskilled labor "from Long Island to the mouth of the Chesapeake," across the South, and throughout most of the North Central states.[5] In a speech to a meeting of USES state directors on July 23, Nathan A. Smyth, acting assistant director-general of the USES, declared that the war industries of the country currently lacked "about 500,000 unskilled workers, and the coming requirements of war production necessitate the finding of between 2,000,000 and 3,000,000 more." The demand for skilled workers had also outstripped the supply.[6] The labor situation was becoming desperate.

Throughout the first half of 1918 there was increasing recognition within the wartime administration that some form of more centralized control over the national labor market was required.[7] However, mistrust of the Department of Labor remained a major stumbling block. The Emergency Fleet Corporation (EFC) of the U.S. Shipping Board, for example, which had encouraged greater centralization of the shipyard labor supply through the USES, adamantly refused to give that agency a complete monopoly in spite of constant pressure from the Department of Labor. The Seattle labor market experiment had made EFC officials question the administrative capacity of the USES. In May 1918, Leon Marshall, director of labor at the EFC, commented privately that although he supported a policy of greater centralization in employment matters, he did not believe that the USES was yet capable of doing the job. Moreover, he felt that there was such opposition to the USES among the various government departments and agencies that to attempt to force the issue would create so much friction that it might undermine what he perceived to be "a fairly smooth and continuous drift" toward more centralized control.[8]

Like the Emergency Fleet Corporation, the Department of Agriculture became increasingly frustrated with the actions of the Department of Labor. The announcement, in the spring of 1918, that the third- and fourth-class postmasters and rural mail carriers were to act as agents of the USES in recruiting agricultural labor was interpreted as an attempt to bypass the farm bureaus and county agents sponsored by the Department of Agriculture. Agriculture officials were also alarmed by the Labor Department's announcement that newspapers in various cities were to be asked to become labor agencies. In June, the Department of Agriculture forced a review of its cooperative agreement with the Department of Labor and successfully imposed further limitations on the role of the USES in the recruitment of agricultural labor.[9] Like the professionals associated with the AAPEO, officials in the Department of Agriculture were becoming increasingly skeptical about the degree of employment expertise possessed by the USES.

The USES faced a similar problem in its relationship with the U.S. Railroad Administration (USRA), which had been created at the end of 1917 to control the nation's railroads. The railroads needed vast numbers of seasonal laborers for general track maintenance work, particularly in the sparsely populated area west of the Mississippi valley. In order to facilitate the handling of railroad labor in the area between the Mississippi valley and the Pacific Coast, the USES, in the early summer of 1918, established a regional

Stanley King, special assistant to the secretary of war (1917–18). A graduate of Amherst College and Harvard Law School, King was a director of the W. H. McElwain Company of Boston when the United States entered World War I. He initially volunteered his services as a dollar-a-year man with the Council of National Defense in Washington, D.C., but subsequently moved to the War Department, where he assumed responsibility for industrial relations. *RG 165 WW, 419-P167, National Archives.*

Railroad Division with headquarters in Chicago. In mid-May 1918, after considerable negotiation, the USES and the USRA finally reached a tentative agreement whereby the western railroads agreed to stop using private, fee-charging agencies and to centralize their labor demands through the federal service. However, the USRA directives were ambiguously worded and individual railroads flouted them with impunity.[10] For the USES, particularly in the West, relations with the Railroad Administration paralleled similar frustrating experiences with other federal departments and wartime agencies.

The War Department, which was responsible for an immense wartime construction program, was extremely skeptical of the pretensions of the USES. In May 1918, the director-general of the USES stated before a congressional committee that the War Department was by far the least cooperative government agency. Stanley King, the special assistant to the secretary of war in industrial matters, made no secret of the reason for his skepticism. In response to a request that the War Department force its contractors to funnel all requests for labor through the USES, King simply expressed his belief that the USES "could not do it." Related to this general mistrust of the administrative ability of the USES was the widespread belief in the various departments of the army that the Department of Labor was "not sufficiently free from labor influences to act efficiently."[11] Winning the confidence of the War Department was a slow process, and the USES was never fully successful in its attempt.

In mid-June, Robert Bass, the labor expert attached to the U.S. Shipping Board, voiced the reservation shared by other key government administrators. Although a firm believer in "the principle of centralized control and administration of the employment service," he remained doubtful about the administrative capacity of the Department of Labor "to handle the situation for the whole country. The principle is sound; it is merely a question of whether it will work from a practical point of view."[12] But with the dramatic contraction of the labor market in the early summer of 1918, some way out of this impasse had to be found.

On May 7, 1918, Secretary of Labor and wartime Labor Administrator William B. Wilson announced the creation of a new coordinating agency, the War Labor Policies Board (WLPB), composed of representatives from the various government departments and agencies concerned with war production. This action was a response to the urgent demand for greater centralization of the government's labor policy.[13] The uncoordinated policies of a plethora of separate government wage and adjustment boards was exacerbating industrial unrest and labor turnover. However, the new board had no draconian powers; policy depended on consensus among board members, and implementation relied on the cooperation of each of its constituent government agencies.

Felix Frankfurter, a Harvard law professor with an active interest in social reform, was appointed chairman of the new board and made assistant to the secretary of labor.[14] Frankfurter had originally come to Washington in April 1917 to act as a civilian adviser in the War Department. In the fall, he was appointed secretary and legal counsel to the President's Mediation Commission, which toured vital war industries located west of the Mississippi in an effort to secure industrial peace. Although sympathetic to labor, Frankfurter had been privately quite critical of the role of the Department of Labor in the mobilization. Shortly after America entered the war, he commented that the urgent task of coordinating government labor policy was being hindered by "the lack of organization in the Labor Department, [and] the failure of coordination between the Labor Department activities and the other labor agencies of the government."[15]

Under Frankfurter's prodding, the War Labor Policies Board immediately undertook two major tasks: to develop within the wartime administration a broad consensus in support of a single national policy on wages and conditions of labor, and to secure agreement on a plan for centralized labor recruiting. The first task entailed a slow process of promoting a consensus among all the government agencies, which only started bearing fruit at the time of the armistice. The second task was more urgent. If all labor were to be recruited centrally, it could be distributed in accordance with national priorities. Such action would tend to stifle the uncontrollable competition for labor between employers that was exacerbating the immense turnover of industrial labor and threatening vital war production. To implement such a policy, however, would put an enormous strain on the Department of Labor's embryonic national employment service. Few people, including Frankfurter himself, believed that the USES, as it was then organized, could cope with the pressure.

Frankfurter decided to take immediate steps to force a reorganization of the USES.[16] He selected Fred C. Croxton, the first president of the AAPEO and the moving spirit behind the highly efficient Ohio system of state employment offices, as his expert adviser on employment matters. Croxton was prevailed upon to leave his responsibilities in Ohio as director of the

Felix Frankfurter, chairman of the War Labor Policies Board (1918–19), was instrumental in blocking the attempt by the Department of Labor to create a U.S. Employment Service on nationalist principles. *Courtesy of the Harvard University Law School.*

During World War I, Fred C. (Frederick Cleveland) Croxton was in charge of the employment service in Ohio and was also state food administrator and the chairman of the Ohio
Council of Defense. He was primarily responsible for the victory of a federalist rather than
a nationalist view of the role of the U.S. Employment Service. *Courtesy of Frank C. Croxton,
Columbus, Ohio.*

state employment service, the state Food Administration, and the State Council of Defense in order to be in Washington for a week at the beginning of June. His role was crucial. Frankfurter commented later that without his assistance, "it would have been impossible even to attempt the task. . . . Without him the work would have been impossible."[17] The appearance of Croxton in Washington in June 1918 marked the final phase of the wartime struggle over the organization and control of the USES.

At the first meeting of the War Labor Policies Board, on May 29, 1918, Frankfurter established the Committee on Central Recruiting with representatives from the Labor, Agriculture, War, and Navy departments, the Emergency Fleet Corporation, and the War Industries Board. Croxton and his assistant from Ohio, Charles Mayhugh, were added as expert advisers. The committee endorsed, after considerable discussion, a paper prepared by Croxton that outlined the basic premises on which a nationwide central recruiting program was to be organized: all labor recruiting was to be conducted through the USES; the state divisions were to be the key administrative units; the USES would be guided by the War Industries Board's priority ranking of national labor needs; a rough national survey of total labor resources and requirements was to be conducted immediately, and labor quotas for each state, based on the survey, were to be imposed. For the moment, the central recruiting program would not cover skilled labor, railroad labor, agricultural labor, or employers with less than a hundred employees. To assist in the transfer of workers from nonessential to essential industries within each industrial center, it was suggested that local community boards, composed of equal representatives of labor and management, be established.[18] The document also mentioned the possibility of curtailing nonessential production and the need to take housing and factory conditions into consideration in determing quotas.

On June 7, with one abstention, the War Labor Policies Board voted to accept the recommendations of the Committee on Central Recruiting.[19] This decision was a clear indication of the mounting concern over the labor market among senior government officials. It signaled a dramatic change in government labor policy that would entail a massive increase in the volume of work to be handled by the USES. As the members of the Policies Board were about to vote in favor of the centralized recruiting policy, Leon Marshall quietly voiced the reservation they all felt: "The only question is the ability of the U.S. Employment Service to do the work."[20] As members of the Policies Board understood, the answer to Marshall's question hinged on the reorganization of the USES to be undertaken by Fred Croxton. That reorganization was the price for WLPB support for central recruiting through the USES.

Having secured agreement that the USES would administer the centralized recruiting policy, Frankfurter turned to the task of reorganizing that body to ensure that it would be capable of handling the responsibility. He asked Croxton to prepare a report outlining the problems in the current administration of the USES and recommending appropriate changes. The report recapitulated a number of earlier criticisms. Indeed, Leon Marshall, the former secretary of the Advisory Council to Secretary Wilson in the early months of 1918, who had participated in the discussions leading up to the report, commented that they "sounded just like the [earlier] discussions engaged in by the Advisory Council."[21] The report pointed to the lack of overall policy and direction in the USES and to the general confusion and suspicion that plagued the organization as a consequence:

> The opinion at this time more or less prevails that the Federal Government has no well-defined policy in the matter; that the majority of those appointed have no practical knowledge of employment problems or actual experience in the work; that politics of one variety or another dictates the selection of the personnel; that an effort will be made through this service to unionize industry; and that large amounts of money are being spent for which no adequate service is rendered in return.

The report went on to stress that the mobilization and distribution of labor was the most urgent and "the most difficult task confronting the United States" and that a major reorganization of the U.S. Employment Service had to be undertaken at once.[22]

In Croxton's view, there were three critical issues related to the USES that had to be clarified: (1) the relation of the federal employment offices to state offices; (2) the appropriate basic administrative unit for the national service; and (3) the exact character of the work to be done by the central and the district offices. With regard to the relationship between national and state employment offices, the report recommended that the federal and state governments should jointly manage the U.S. Employment Service offices. Under this arrangement, the federal government would be supreme in matters relating to general policy, and would have supervisory powers and the right to inspect state and local offices. Each state would have a federal director "acceptable to both the State and the Federal Governments" who would have complete charge of all offices within the state. As far as finances were concerned, the report recommended that the "ultimate aim" should be to divide the total cost equally between the federal government on the one hand and the state and municipal governments on the other.

The second critical issue concerned the appropriate administrative unit for the efficient operation of the service. The Department of Labor had created a rather cumbersome layer of regional offices within the USES that acted as a buffer between the states and the head office in Washington. Croxton's report recommended that the state should become the basic administrative unit of the entire system and that all district or zone offices should be abolished for the present. Moreover, each state was to establish a central office, on the Ohio model, which would act as the clearinghouse for all employment offices within that state. Each federal director would be responsible for the efficient operation of all offices within his state. There should be no direct communication between the Washington office and local offices; all communications from the central office should be directed to the federal director for each state. The remaining issue concerned the division of functions as between the Washington office and the state systems. Here the report urged that the principal concern of the Washington office should be to determine the general policies that would guide the operation of the national system and to develop the necessary supervisory machinery. No placement work should be done directly by the Washington office.

The report made a further series of recommendations. The most important concerned the internal administration of the USES, which was suffering from "an over-abundance of red tape . . . from a division of authority, and even in greater degree, from lack of team work." It recommended that both the existing managerial structure and the divisional organization of the USES be overhauled. The report also focused on the lack of experience in employment work that permeated all ranks of the USES and urged the immediate appointment of some individuals with employment work experience as assistants to the director-general. Given the complete lack of experience among the bulk of the personnel who had been transferred from the Immigration Bureau, the report urged that appropriate qualifications for all levels of the service should be decided upon and an internal training program established. Politics, in the selection of personnel or in the operation of the service, had to be "entirely eliminated."[23]

Croxton's group had pulled no punches. In essence, the recommendations contained the substance of the initial proposals of the AAPEO as embodied in the original Robinson-Keating legislation.[24] The opinions of those with professional expertise in employment work were finally receiving serious attention.

On Thursday, June 13, a three-day National War Labor Conference organized by the USES opened in Washington. More than one hundred USES officers were present. It was the first time that the state directors, district superintendents, and head office personnel of the USES and the Public Service Reserve had been brought together as a group. The most important speech was given by Nathan A. Smyth, the acting assistant director-general of the USES, who outlined the central recruiting policy adopted by the War Labor Policies Board the previous week and explained how it was to be implemented by the USES when it went into effect on July 15.[25] Secretary Wilson, Frankfurter, Post, and Densmore all gave speeches at the conference but they were more inspirational than practical. There was no mention of the essential condition accompanying the WLPB decision to give the Department of Labor control of centralized recruiting, namely, the fundamental reorganization of the USES.

In fact, at the time of the conference, it was not clear whether Secretary Wilson, as war labor administrator, was prepared to accept the reorganization of the USES proposed by Croxton and accepted by Frankfurter and the War Labor Policies Board. On June 11, two days before the conference was due to open, Croxton sent Frankfurter a four-page condensation of the recent report of his committee with the suggestion that the secretary of labor might wish to use "the essentials of this summary" in his speech to the forthcoming National War Labor Conference. Croxton believed that if the secretary's speech indicated an acceptance of the key recommendations of the report it would "go far toward winning confidence in the U.S. Employment Service."[26] Secretary Wilson, however, refused to endorse the thrust of the recommendations, and his speeches at the conference remained at the most generalized and noncontentious level.[27] He had decided to delay his decision on whether or not to support an administrative reorganization of the USES.

Immediately after the War Labor Conference, Croxton went back to Ohio. Both Frankfurter and Densmore pleaded with him to return to Washington to assist in the reorganization of the USES, declaring that his presence was "indispensable."[28] Croxton, however, refused to leave his Ohio responsibilities until he had received some assurance that Secretary Wilson was willing to agree to a substantial reorganization of the USES. He was particularly anxious that Densmore should be given a completely free hand, which, in effect, would mean severing Louis Post's connection with the USES. Frankfurter wired Croxton on July 3 that the secretary's temporary absence from Washington "necessarily delays matters" but suggested that at least Leiserson and Maxwell should immediately return to Washington. Frankfurter's plea fell on deaf ears. Replying on behalf of the Ohio group, Croxton commented: "We feel that time spent in Washington pending adjustment would not be profitable for service."[29]

Secretary Wilson still delayed. He understood that he was being asked to reverse the policy that the Department of Labor had pursued since the war began and that appeared to offer the prospect of substantially enhancing its standing in the national administration. Moreover, such a reversal would obviously constitute a direct rejection of his loyal and trusted subordinate, Assistant Secretary Louis F. Post. Yet, if he did nothing and the USES failed to cope with the administrative burden of the central recruiting program, the credibility of the Department of Labor would be ruined. The Secretary had been placed in an unenviable position.[30]

At the beginning of July, Frankfurter wrote to Secretary Wilson outlining the immense administrative burden that the policy of centralized recruiting would thrust upon the employment service. The task would test the service to the utmost, and "the fullest spirit of cooperation" on the part of all concerned was absolutely necessary. This, he felt, was lacking. "Instead of harmony there is discord; instead of driving force, obstruction." Frankfurter declared that Densmore was "working under limitations which are fatal." These included the detailed administrative control over the USES exercised by Post that "begets delays and obstructions" and, even more important, "the fact that an irreconcilable lack of confidence exists between the Director-General and his immediate chief [Post]." Efforts by Frankfurter to resolve this impasse between Densmore and Post through "diplomatic indirection" had failed and the only way to resolve the problem was to remove Post by placing the USES under "the immediate administrative charge of the Secretary of Labor."[31]

Finally, on July 5, Frankfurter was able to wire Croxton a circumspect victory message: "The deck has been cleared." He urged Croxton and his associates to come to Washington without further delay. On the same day, Leon Marshall of the Emergency Fleet Corporation also discreetly wired Croxton that Secretary Wilson had made "a favorable decision on the matter we have discussed so much. This makes it clear that your patriotic duty will be in Washington for some time."[32] Secretary Wilson had finally decided to act: Assistant Secretary Post was to be removed from any connection with the USES and the reorganization was to go ahead. Croxton's conditions, which reflected the views of the AAPEO, had finally been met.

Croxton went to Washington in July and stayed for a month. He brought with him an impressive group of advisers with employment experience in both the public and the private sectors. William M. Leiserson, who, at the time, was teaching political economy at Toledo University in Ohio, returned to assist in the reorganization; Wilbur F. Maxwell and, later, Charles H. Mayhugh of the Ohio Employment Service came to help in the work. Croxton also brought T. J. Duffy, the chairman of the Ohio Industrial Commission, who was known and trusted by trade unionists "throughout the country."[33] The National Carbon Company of Cleveland, Ohio, was persuaded to permit its employment manager, W. H. Winans, to accompany the Ohio group to Washington. In addition, Croxton secured the services of Dudley R. Kennedy, a former Ohio man who was currently engaged as the employment manager of the American International Shipbuilding Corporation at the Hog Island shipyard, Mark M. Jones, the welfare director of Thomas A. Edison Industries, and Ralph G. Wells, employment manager with the Du Pont Corporation.[34] The group of employment experts that Croxton had gathered for the task of reorganizing the USES had the confidence of both organized labor and major employers.

The task of reorganization was daunting and time was short. The date for implementing the centralized recruiting policy was pushed back from July 15 to the beginning of August to give the USES more time to organize. With the USES now directly under the secretary of labor and free of any interference from Assistant Secretary Post, Croxton and his group had a relatively free hand in the reorganization. John Densmore, the director-general of the USES, was very anxious to cooperate. In the sweltering heat of late July and August, amidst ominous rumors of an impending labor shortage of massive proportions, Croxton's group of employment experts, together with ten specially invited representatives from the major state employment services and nine senior USES officials, began work.[35]

The recommendations of the group covered all aspects of the organization and operation of the USES. The role of the state as the basic administrative unit was clearly underlined. All district and regional offices were to be abolished. Within each state, responsibility for the organization and operation of the USES offices was to be centralized in the hands of a federal director. All communication between the Washington office and the offices within each state would go through the federal directors, who would report directly to the Washington office. The director-general was urged to establish a Training Division for USES employees to upgrade their skills. Standard administrative forms were to be developed for the entire system. States and localities were to be encouraged to contribute to the cost of the local offices.[36]

The most radical and far-reaching aspect of the committee's report, however, was the recommendation that both state advisory boards and community labor boards be established immediately. It was an indication of the ascendancy of Croxton's group that only four days later, on July 17, the director-general of the USES signed a special order decreeing the immediate establishment in each state of a temporary state organization committee whose task was to establish a state advisory board and community labor boards.[37] Each state advisory board was to have two representatives of labor and two representatives of employers, and was to be chaired by the state director of the USES. State federations of labor and representative groups of state employer organizations were invited to assist the USES state director to organize these state advisory boards. In addition, community labor boards were to be established immediately in the industrial centers within each state. Each community labor board was to consist of one representative of labor and one representative of employers in the community, together with a chairman who was to represent the USES and "the national interests." The instructions specified that the chairman, who did not have to be a USES officer, was to be "a man of influence and standing in the community, commanding the confidence of both labor and management." Each community labor board chairman was to be sworn in as a special agent of the USES at a nominal salary. All appointments were subject to the approval of the secretary of labor.

The powers of the new boards were considerable. In personnel matters, no major appointments could be made to the state organization of the USES without the approval of the state advisory board. The community labor boards had similar authority over appointments to local employment offices. Both boards had power to recommend the removal of USES personnel, although the final responsibility both for appointment and removal rested with the secretary of labor. These powers were clearly designed to promote confidence in USES appointees and to parry the damaging accusation of partisanship in the selection of USES officers. The state advisory committees also had authority to oversee the plans for apportioning quotas across each state and for determining in which localities recruiting for local war industries would be permitted. Community labor boards were responsible for determining how labor in nonessential industries in the local community was to be transferred to war industries and for the proper distribution of the available labor supply among local war industries.

It was a daring plan. The establishment of this system of advisory boards gave to both employers and employees "a share in the administration of the Government's centralized war labor supplying program and in the responsibility for its success." The USES was to have a genuinely federal administrative structure. The plan gave to the USES the benefit of the knowledge and experience of management and labor in each state and was designed to ensure that no influence, "other than that of efficiency," would affect the choice of personnel in each state. Moreover, the community labor boards would protect the states against the arbitrary use of central power. Densmore himself stated that they would operate to protect local employers "against unfair or unnecessary drafts on labor and to accomplish the greatest good with the least harm." He thought that the community labor boards were "probably the most drastic action that the Government has taken since putting the National Army draft into effect."[38] Felix Frankfurter felt that, next to the operation of the selective service act, "the administration of the war labor supplying program will stand as the supreme monument of what voluntary cooperative effort can accomplish in a democracy."[39]

The USES, under pressure from the representatives of the various state governments, had adopted a policy designed to share power with representatives of both employers and labor in organizing the labor market. It was an example of a wider trend within the wartime administration toward "war corporatism." This move complemented the earlier decision of President Wilson to create the National War Labor Board (NWLB) which also had equal representation of both employers and labor and was the final arbiter in labor disputes in war-related industries.[40] Driven by the wartime pressures, government policy aimed to foster a corporate approach to the resolution of labor problems.[41]

The adoption by the War Labor Policies Board of the centralized recruiting program in early June had included a recognition of the need to allocate quotas to the different states. Such a system of quotas presupposed a knowledge both of the total supply of available labor and the total demand for it. In fact, accurate information on both supply and demand was unavailable and the USES had been obliged to adopt a quite arbitrary approach to labor recruitment in the first half of 1918. This had created considerable resentment, particularly in the Midwest and South. Some states felt that they were being asked to contribute a disproportionate share of labor to out-of-state projects, and pressure mounted for the adoption of some kind of quota system to ensure equity.[42]

By early summer 1918, some states had begun to take drastic action in an attempt to conserve their own labor supply. This reflected the increasing realization on the part of manufacturers in the various states that the only way to prevent indiscriminate "pirating" of labor by private agencies and by the USES itself was to insist on some orderly method of prorating the demand. The assistant director-general of the USES put the matter candidly in mid-June: "One by one the doors are being closed because the individual communities, seeing their own coming needs, are beginning to conserve their labor for their own purposes." Recruiters sent down to Georgia and Florida, for example, "if they don't get locked up in jail they get kicked out in some other way." Even big cities like Chicago and Philadelphia were protesting any attempt to recruit labor within their boundaries. The only solution was to devise some equitable method of distributing the demand so that no particular locality suffered more than any other. Smyth admitted that, up to that point, the quotas allocated to the states by USES had been quite arbitrary.[43]

Any system of quotas required a reasonably accurate estimate both of the available labor and of the anticipated demand in essential industries. To estimate the total available labor supply of the country, the USES launched a special survey in early July. Although an attempt was made to cover rural districts, the main emphasis was on cities having populations of 20,000 or more. Respondents were asked to estimate "the number of males over 18 years of age who have entered military service, or are engaged in essential production or are engaged in work not essential to the winning of the war and therefore potential war workers." Nine different occupational classifications were used.[44]

In addition, a special questionnaire survey of essential industries was undertaken to get some idea of the likely demand for labor. Initially, only unskilled labor was covered. A special form, the "Emp. 15" (Employer's Order for Unskilled Male Laborers), was sent to firms engaged on war contracts requesting estimates of immediate labor needs, of projected additional weekly labor requirements from mid-July to the end of August, and estimates for the first week in both September and October. Estimates of labor needs were to exclude labor turnover. Information was requested about the method of hiring labor, the current number of unskilled male laborers employed, the proportion actually working on war contracts, the weekly turnover of labor, and details on wages and other conditions of employment.[45]

The application of the new quota system highlighted the serious labor shortage facing the country. Requisition order forms for unskilled labor were sent to 35,000 firms working on government contracts for the War and Navy departments and the Emergency Fleet Corporation. The first estimate of labor demand, on which initial quotas for the various states were based, was made at the end of July. The figures indicated that the war industries needed a total of 451,000 additional unskilled laborers. However, because returns from employers were slow to come in, even this figure proved to be far too conservative. By the middle of August, with most of the forms returned by industry, the quotas had be be drastically revised: the shortfall of common labor for essential industries was calculated to be almost double the initial estimate. The lowest quota was now set at 1,140 for New Mexico and the highest was a dramatic 169,140 for New York.[46] It was obvious that a very much larger proportion of men than had been initially anticipated would have to be shifted out of nonessential occupations to supply the needs of the nation's war industries.

The politically explosive task of shifting labor from nonessential to essential industries and the related task of allocating such labor among competing war industries called for a degree of expertise and a level of public support, particularly among employers, that the newly reorganized Employment Service was only just beginning to acquire. Frankfurter was very conscious of the fact that the cooperation of employers was essential to the success of the entire central recruiting program. Indeed, one reason why the implementation of the program had been postponed until August 1 was to give sufficient time to employers to realize the gravity of the entire labor problem in the expectation that they would then be more prepared to cooperate with the USES. Frankfurter actively sought and obtained a good deal of employer support for the USES.[47]

An intensive publicity campaign, designed to show the country the gravity of the labor situation and the necessity for shifting labor from nonessential to essential industries, was also mounted. This campaign, although initially oriented toward central recruiting of unskilled labor, was designed to "have the decks cleared for the handling of the skilled labor employment and wage standardization by October first."[48] A special luncheon was held at Delmonico's at the end of July to enable the secretary of labor to address the nation's major editors and publishers. Forty-seven of the "biggest publicists in the country" attended and all "promised complete support" for the central recruiting policy.[49] The entire publicity campaign generated enormous public support.[50] The success of the central recruiting program now rested primarily on the efficiency of the USES itself.

It was not until August 13 that the Department of Labor officially announced an important reorganization of the USES. A number of discreet administrative changes had preceded the announcement. Early in July, Secretary Wilson, in a decision that was given no publicity, quietly severed Assistant Secretary Louis Post's connection with the USES. At the same time, Hilda Muhlhauser Richards, a protégée of Post who was in charge of the Women's Division of the USES, resigned from the department. Shortly afterwards, in mid-July, Charles T. Clayton, the assistant director of the USES and another Post protégée, was appointed director of the new Civilian Insignia Service of the Department of Labor, which was to take charge of the issuance of war badges to industrial workers engaged in essential production. Finally, on August 6, the Department of Labor announced that the Division of Information, Administration and Clearance, headed by Terence V. Powderly, was to be transferred back to the Bureau of Immigration.[51] This was the division that had been responsible for the operation of the Employment Service in the Department of Labor since before the outbreak of the war.

The editorial in the *USES Bulletin* on August 13 tried to play down the significance of the changes by contending that they did not constitute "a reorganization" but were "simply a realignment or readjustment of the existing administrative machinery and a strengthening of the contact" between the Washington office and the states.[52] In fact, the changes were drastic and embodied the substance of the recommendations made by Croxton's committee of employment experts. The administration of the central office was simplified by grouping all existing divisions and sections into five functional divisions: Control, Field Organization, Clearance, Personnel, and Information. This corresponded exactly with the proposals made by Croxton's group.[53] Relations between the central office and the states were also simplified, as Croxton's group had demanded, by the abolition of the

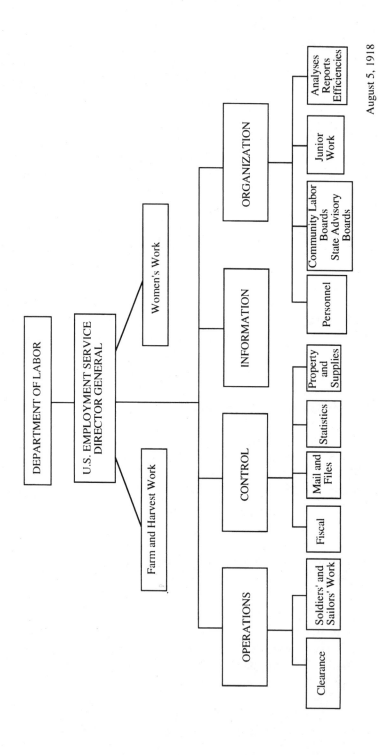

August 5, 1918

U.S. Employment Service, August 1918. Source: *Report of the Director-General, USES* (August 15, 1919), 907.

thirteen regional employment offices, which had only been established at the beginning of April. Henceforth the state was to be the unit of administration, and the federal directors for each state were to report directly to the director-general "and . . . be held responsible by him for results in their respective States."[54]

The question of uniform administrative procedures throughout all USES offices was addressed in General Order B-3, issued by Director-General Densmore at the same time as the announcement of the reorganization. It was a detailed set of instructions on how to operate an employment office and was a big step toward standardizing the definition of "placement" and developing a classification of industries and occupations. The statistics on which the USES relied would now be much more reliable.[55] Croxton's committee of employment experts had triumphed.

There was one contentious issue, however, on which agreement could not be reached. The question of an appropriate strike policy for the USES had been raised by Croxton's committee. It was a sensitive issue. The secretary of labor had long insisted that, if a strike was in progress at a particular plant, the USES would refuse to recognize any requests from employers for men to be employed there. This practice contrasted starkly with British practice, and with the policy of most state employment services, which recognized such calls from employers but advised any applicant that a strike was in progress. It was felt that this approach best preserved the neutrality of the Employment Service. Croxton's committee had, in fact, recommended a compromise: the USES should not send workers to plants where strikes were in progress unless the National War Labor Board decided that the strike was "unjustified." As a sop to employers, the USES was not to offer alternative employment to striking workers unless the employer refused to comply with the rulings of the War Labor Board.[56] Secretary Wilson, however, refused to accept the compromise proposal and insisted on the retention of the original policy: the USES was to refuse to recognize calls for labor from plants where strikes were in progress.

It had been a long and bitter struggle. The USES had achieved its ambition to become the sole representative of the federal government in the labor market but had paid a substantial price for that recognition. The Department of Labor had been forced to abandon its early ambition to create a national employment service that could operate independently of the states, and had been obliged to accept a genuinely federal service in which power was shared with the state employment offices and with state and local advisory boards. Assistant Secretary Post's centralist ambitions had been defeated and his relationship with the USES severed. The states and the AAPEO had shared the victory. Henceforth, policy was to be centralized, but administration of the USES was to be decentralized. The War Labor Policies Board and particularly its chairman, Felix Frankfurter, had been instrumental in strengthening the position of the states in their struggle with the Department of Labor over the administration and structure of the USES. Now the question was: could the reorganized and genuinely federalist USES meet the challenge?

CHAPTER SIX

A Federalist U.S. Employment Service

B y the fall of 1918 the nation was gradually becoming accustomed to the idea of a centralized labor market for war industry under USES auspices. The USES itself had improved its image by accepting the internal reorganization proposed by Croxton's committee, by appointing a number of senior executives from the private sector, and by taking steps to improve the professionalism of the service. The bold decision to create a nationwide system of community labor boards also contributed to a growth in public acceptance of the USES. These boards elicited a surprising degree of public support for the politically sensitive program of moving labor from nonessential to essential industries. Doubts about the administrative capacity of the USES on the part of other government departments and agencies, although not eliminated, began to wane.

The internal changes in the USES started at the top. As part of the administrative reorganization in August, six top administrators—the assistant director-general and the five directors of the new functional divisions—were appointed. Of this group only two were recruited from within the Department of Labor; the other four were effectively dollar-a-year men from the private sector.[1] By early September, the number of dollar-a-year men in this group had risen to five out of the six. This emphasis on recruiting administrative talent from outside the department reflected the influence of the War Labor Policies Board, which was acting, in effect, as a national advisory board to the USES. The steady pressure of the WLPB chairman, Felix Frankfurter, resulted in the selection of administrators who were not only trusted by business and the employment professionals but who had the ability to shape the USES into one of the most important instruments of government policy in the domestic mobilization.

Of the five appointees from the private sector, three had orginally become involved with the Department of Labor through volunteer work with the Reserves. Nathan A. Smyth, a prominent lawyer and a member of the insurance firm of Smyth, Gerard and Sanford of New York City, was one of the founders of the Public Service Reserve and remained an associate national director of that body. He had come to Washington in early 1918 on work for the Reserve and, in May, was appointed acting assistant director of the USES. Felix Frankfurter was impressed with his administrative abilities and, in September, Smyth's temporary position with the USES was made permanent when he was officially promoted to the position of Assistant Director. Another protégée of Frankfurter was Sanford H. E. Freund, a lawyer and the assistant general counsel in the Legal Department of the Great Northern Railroad. In 1917, he had been active in organizing the Public Service Reserve and the Boys' Working Reserve in the midwestern states and, in July 1918, he came to Washington to assist the director-general. His administrative abilities were recognized and he was appointed director of the Clearance Division of the USES in the August administrative reorganization. William E. Hall, a prominent New York businessman and president of the Boys' Clubs of America, had been invited to join the Department of Labor in April 1917 to take charge of the Boys' Working Reserve. In addition to that responsibility he had subsequently been appointed director of the Public Service Reserve. In the August 1918 reorganization, he was put in charge of the Field Organization Division of the USES.

The other two appointees from the private sector were Alexander D. Chiquoine, Jr., and W. H. Winans. Chiquoine, who had been given a leave of absence from his post as secretary of the Philadelphia Bourse to become editor of the *USES Bulletin* in early 1918, was appointed director of the USES Information Division. Winans, an employment manager on loan from the National Carbon Company of Cleveland, Ohio, took charge of the Personnel Division of the USES in September. He had been instrumental in getting the local USES office in Cleveland reorganized and was a member of the team of employment experts that Fred Croxton had brought with him from Ohio in midsummer 1918 to help reorganize the national USES.[2] The appointment of such a well-known employment manager was an important gesture designed not only to strengthen the administration of the service but also to encourage greater business confidence in the USES.

Along with the attempt to strengthen the administrative capacity of the central office, Frankfurter and the WLPB kept up pressure on the USES to improve the quality of the personnel in the state branches. Members of the head office were well aware of the problem.[3] Shortly after the armistice, W. E. Hall listed a number of states with incompetent state directors and commented bluntly: "Our weakest point as a peace-time organization is in our personnel."[4] At the same time, Ernest Hopkins, who had been an extremely influential adviser on labor matters in the War Department, commented to Frankfurter that "the testimony . . . from all the states" was that "an incompetent personnel" continued to compromise the reputation of the Department of Labor.[5] Allegations of incompetence, combined with rumors that the USES employed a disproportionate number of "former union officials," persisted throughout the war and the reconstruction period.[6]

To address this problem, steps were taken in the fall of 1918 to enhance the professionalism of USES staff. At the beginning of November, training courses in up-to-date employment methods were instituted. A special Training Section of the Personnel Division was created in Washington to develop an appropriate program. Fifty-one delegates from nineteen states attended the first Normal Training Conference held in January 1919. A second conference was held in late February for delegates from the southern states.[7] Those attending the conferences were expected to return to their states and organize similar conferences for the personnel in the state USES. In Illinois, for example, a three-day state conference was organized for February 19–21, 1919.[8] The employment experts had long criticized the absence of an adequate staff training program in the USES.

In mid-October 1918 the establishment of a special force of twenty national field organizers also indicated the determination of the Washington office to promote a more professional approach within the state organizations. The field organizers had been selected for their organizing abilities and were on limited-term service.[9] Each of these men was to be assigned to a state as the personal representative of the director-general. After an investigation lasting between two and four weeks, the field organizer was to submit a formal report both to the state federal director and to the director-general. The aim was to make sure that the national policy of the USES was reflected in the state organization and operation. The field organizers, who had been chosen "for their proved ability in private business to visualize a situation quickly and remedy inefficiencies," had received intensive training in Washington in the aims, principles, and practices of the USES.[10]

However, the group had barely been organized before the armistice created a quite different set of conditions.

Related to this effort to develop a more professional approach among staff was the production of an administrative manual to guide individuals in the operation of the service. This was finally ready for circulation at the beginning of 1919. The manual emphasized that the function of an employment officer was not just filling vacant positions but matching "the requirement of the job with the capacity of the worker." Employment office work involved both "a definite professional spirit" and "a distinct code of right practice." It differed from the work of an employment manager in an industrial plant, but "the same professional spirit and standards hold good for both." Indeed, the manual suggested that in some respects the work of the USES officer was broader in scope than that of the employment manager because it was also concerned with "the welfare . . . of the community."[11]

By late 1918, the USES had also begun to address what was a major handicap to its efficient operation, namely the absence of national, agreed-upon definitions of the various skilled trades. The problem was real enough. By mid-June 1918, for example, the shortage of skilled machinists was creating serious industrial bottlenecks, but the Selective Service System felt unable to relax the draft regulations covering machinists because the term was so broad that it covered tradesmen "of all grades of skill." Nothing could be done until someone devised "some means of classifying the different grades of machinist."[12] Similar problems plagued other trades. The USES became involved in two quite different approaches in attempting to resolve the problem.

The first approach relied on the appointment of individual experts. The increasing shortage of skilled workers in the summer and fall of 1918 began to alarm both industry and the War Department, and it was realized that some means of keeping highly skilled workers out of the draft had to be devised. In September, the state advisory boards of the USES were asked to assign to each district exemption board an industrial adviser whose task it was to ensure that, in "necessary" industries, a claim for deferred classification was made for "key" men. The exact skills that identified such individuals were left vague. In discussing the role of the industrial advisers, the *USES Bulletin* commented that they would need subtle powers of discrimination and "the utmost nicety of judgment."[13] The process of selecting these expert advisers took time and the war was over before the new system had a chance to operate.

Paralleling the appointment of industrial advisers, the USES also promoted efforts to develop a national vocabulary defining various skilled occupations. As early as May 1918, the army had produced a book of specifications covering the 565 different trades it required.[14] Shortly afterward, the Department of Labor undertook to produce a standard set of specifications, including "standardized names," for the munitions and shipbuilding trades. This limited initial project expanded in the latter part of 1918 into one designed to classify all occupations as a guide to USES staff. It was not until December 1918 that these trade specifications, in five separate booklets, were published: "In the description of each occupation there are five divisions—the name of the occupation or trade; kindred occupations; description of duties to be performed; qualifications necessary for the occupation, including training and physical requirements; and education required."[15] The USES was contributing to the nationalizing and standardizing of American life and language.

Probably the most important organizational innovation on the part of the USES in the latter part of 1918 was the creation of a nationwide system of community labor boards. Each industrial community in the state was to organize such a board representing local employers, employees, and the public.[16] These community labor boards were designed to give employers and employees some direct involvement both in the administration of the local employment office and "in the responsibility for the success of the plan by which America's industrial man power may be mobilized to the utmost and war industries fully manned."[17]

The community labor boards had one of the most sensitive tasks in the government's entire labor program. Nathan Smyth thought their mission was even "more important than that of the draft boards."[18] More labor for war industries had to be found. Labor was not to be conscripted, yet it had to be moved out of nonessential into essential industries. It was up to these small but representative committees to use community pressure on both local employees and their employers to secure the necessary transfer of labor. The boards had no executive powers and were urged to obtain the necessary labor "so far as possible . . . by securing harmonious and cooperative action on the part of employers and employees."[19]

The potential for opposition to the transfer of labor from nonessential industries was well recognized. Smyth thought that the community labor boards would "undoubtedly meet with some opposition" when their decisions began to affect local industries. However, he felt that employers who were unwilling to cooperate should be made to face "the full force of public opinion" in their communities.[20] To assist the community labor boards in the task of mobilizing public opinion behind the transfer of labor to essential industries, the USES solicited the support of the network of state, county, and community councils of defense that had been created by the State Councils Section of the Council of National Defense. The network of defense councils in each state was an important means by which public opinion could be focused at the local level.[21]

Although Department of Labor and WLPB officials recognized the critical importance of public opinion in supporting the actions of the community labor boards, they were also aware of the need for a more direct and coercive sanction. In early August, the WLPB proposed that, if an employer refused to comply with the ruling of a community labor board, a special WLPB committee should use the priority power of the War Industries Board (WIB) to close down that plant.[22] However, implementation of this recommendation was delayed because of the reluctance of the WIB priority commissioner to delegate the priority power to a committee of the WLPB. The steadily deteriorating labor situation forced a change of attitude, and by the time of the armistice a tentative agreement had been reached whereby the WIB was to delegate its priority powers to the community labor boards "in order to move workers from less essential to more essential industries." The coercive power of the state was to be delegated to volunteer local boards. The cessation of hostilities made the plan unnecessary just as instructions were about to be mailed out.[23]

In the original order creating the community labor boards, women were not mentioned. However, the advisability of including women representatives on the community labor boards, which were so involved in encouraging the substitution of women for men in nonessential industries, soon became obvious. In mid-September, two women, representing labor and management, were added to each community labor board. Initially, the women were to have full voting rights only on matters concerning the utilization of women in industry. This token representation did not last very long. One month later, the order was amended to give the women exactly the same voting rights and responsibilities as the men had. At the same time, two women members with full voting rights were added to the USES state advisory committees. The community labor boards were also given much greater authority to monitor the working conditions of women in industry.[24]

The labor shortage in war industries generated intense pressure to get the community labor boards established as quickly as possible. By the end of the first week in September, there were 737 community labor boards in operation and a further 69 partially organized.[25] By mid-October, almost 1,200 community labor boards were operating, a figure that had risen to approximately 1,650 by the time of the armistice a month later. The number of community labor boards in each state varied considerably: Texas and Maine headed the list with 161 and 152 boards respectively; Pennsylvania had 86; South Carolina and Oklahoma each had 48; Massachusetts and Michigan had 44 each; Connecticut, New York, North Carolina, and Arizona had 14 each; both New Jersey and Vermont had 13 boards.[26]

The community labor boards achieved some spectacular results. In Maryland, by the end of September, they had been instrumental in meeting the entire state quota of 14,340 unskilled laborers by transferring approximately 15,000 men from nonessential industries. In Ohio, the community labor boards in Cincinnati and Toledo, worried about the completion of two huge air nitrates plants before the winter began, transferred 3,000 men in October and another 3,000 in November from nonessential industries in their vicinity. In Connecticut, by November 1918, approximately 1,200 persons per week were being transferred from nonessential to essential industries under the supervision of the community labor boards. Other states reported excellent work done by their boards. In Wisconsin, where thirty community boards had been established, the federal director commented that "all but three or four" were active and extremely helpful.[27]

The advantage of the community labor boards was not confined to their ability to find and to shift desperately needed labor from nonessential to essential industries. They also possessed an important, if less tangible, asset. Major F. W. Tully, the War Department representative on the War Labor Policies Board, reporting to Frankfurter in early August on the progress of the centralized recruiting program, remarked that the community labor board plan had proved "exceedingly popular . . . with manufacturers and trade associations." The creation of the boards had overcome the fear "that the labor recruiting program meant the creation of a partisan and incompetent political machine."[28] At a conference of USES officials held shortly after the armistice, Charles B. Barnes, the assistant federal director of the USES for New York State, declared that the community labor boards "had done more for the Employment Service than had any other single factor." The federal director in Wisconsin thought the community labor boards had given the USES offices in that state "character and standing in the community."[29]

In the latter part of 1918, the USES also made some modest efforts toward dealing with a number of social issues relating to employment, particularly matters affecting unskilled workers. The attempt by the USES, shortly before the armistice, to secure control over all advertising for labor was an attempt to control the disruption to the labor market caused by the fierce competition between private employment agencies. The licensing of such private agencies by the USES would minimize that disruption. However, in addition, it would give the USES some leverage over the more unscrupulous private agencies in preventing them from taking advantage of unskilled labor. In a quite separate move, early in 1918, the USES had established a special Negro Division to look after the needs of that particular group of unskilled workers. Although this action was a pragmatic response to political pressure rather than a real recognition of a special social need, Secretary Wilson subsequently acknowledged the special needs of black workers by establishing a separate Division of Negro Economics within the Department of Labor.[30]

During the fall of 1918, the USES put increasing pressure on government departments and agencies to do something to improve housing and social conditions around major emergency construction sites. Wretched living conditions were a major contributing factor to the enormous labor turnover at such sites. Any improvement in those conditions would assist the war effort by reducing labor turnover and, at the same time, promote the idea that the maintenance of humane industrial conditions was a responsibility of government. For similar reasons the USES lent its support to the drive for wage standardization.[31] In the emergency situation, the USES was making a modest contribution to the promotion of such issues.

A number of administrative changes in late 1918 also reflected this concern with a more humane and socially responsible approach to employment problems. On December 9, 1918, the Junior Section was established as part of the Field Organization Division and charged with the guidance and placement of boys and girls under twenty-one years of age. It was estimated that 14 percent of wage earners in the country fell into this category. Aiming to cooperate closely with the schools and to build on the work done in the latter part of 1918 by a few state and city offices, mainly in New York State, Cleveland, and Chicago, the new section aimed to keep juniors at school for as long as possible and to give them the best advice available about careers.[32]

A U.S. Employment Service poster encouraging women to move into the work force. *RG 165 WW, 460-C7, National Archives.*

Another innovation was the establishment of a special bureau for place-ment of the aged and the handicapped in December 1918. Like the section for juniors, the special bureau for the aged had been foreshadowed in the 1916 annual report of the Department of Labor. Although separate services for the placement of boys and girls had been organized in 1916, they re-mained paper organizations. Lack of funds during the reconstruction pe-riod and the 1920s severely limited the effectiveness of these special sec-tions, and they remained more a promise of future possibilities than effective organizations.

The most important of the administrative changes reflecting a reformist outlook were those relating to the employment of women. A special divi-sion for women and girls had been planned in 1916, but it remained a paper organization until the reorganization of January 1918, when the Women's Division was formally organized and Mrs. Hilda Muhlhauser Richards, a representative of the National League for Woman's Service who had been working in the Department of Labor as a volunteer, was placed in charge of it. The approach adopted by the new division was conservative: it aimed "to maintain normal conditions with respect to women's work, so far as that can be done under the stress of war." Efforts to recruit women workers were made only "when calls have been received for them." Considerable effort was devoted to the establishment of separate employment offices de-voted exclusively to women workers: their number increased from nine to fifty-five in the first half of 1918.[33]

In the summer of 1918 the role of the Women's Division changed dra-matically. Mrs. Richards resigned and was replaced by Mrs. Margaretta Neale, who had previously been in charge of the women's branch of the USES both in New York City and in New Jersey. In the major reorganiza-tion of the USES at midyear, the Women's Division was dissolved as a separate administrative entity and in its place special sections for women were created, where appropriate, in the five functional divisions of the USES; Mrs. Neale was appointed assistant to the director-general for women's work and had supervision over all matters concerning the employment of women.[34] She worked closely with Mary Van Kleeck, the director of the newly orga-nized Women in Industry Division of the Department of Labor, and the USES followed the fairly protective guidelines for women workers pro-moted by that body. Approximately 368,000 women were placed through the women's branches of the USES during 1918.[35] The appointment of women to the state advisory boards and the community labor boards in the fall of

1918 was a further recognition of the important role of women in the industrial labor force.

During the fall of 1918, relations between the USES and other departments and wartime agencies improved slowly but still remained variable. Relations between the departments of Agriculture and Labor, for example, remained cordial but quite distant. They were governed by a memorandum of understanding signed on April 27, 1918, which outlined the methods of cooperation between the departments in supplying farm labor. In very general terms, the Department of Agriculture was to determine agricultural labor needs and, when necessary, to advise the USES of specific needs in particular localities, which the USES would then "use its best endeavors to supply."[36] In June, when the WLPB decided to centralize labor recruiting through the USES, agricultural labor was excluded from the resolution at the insistence of the Department of Agriculture, although it was specified that the cooperative arrangement between the two departments would continue.

In early August, Frankfurter asked Fred Croxton to investigate the question of farm labor and the relationship between the two departments. Croxton reported that he thought the April memorandum of understanding was satisfactory and that the real problem was "to get the spirit of the memorandum carried into effect throughout the country."[37] He felt that more effort was needed to promote "*real* cooperation" between the two departments and, at the state level, he recommended that Department of Agriculture representatives should be physically located in USES offices wherever practicable, with more senior representatives being given some authority by being sworn in as USES officers at a nominal salary.[38] Frankfurter tried to get Department of Agriculture officials to agree to the substance of the Croxton proposals, but they were reluctant to have their state organizations tied too closely to the USES structure. Eventually, in early October 1918, a vaguely worded "memorandum of understanding" was accepted by both departments.[39] The Department of Agriculture had won the struggle to keep its distance from the USES.

Relations with the War Department remained difficult right down to the armistice. In October, in an effort to get more skilled and unskilled labor out of nonessential industries and into essential industries, the War Department proposed extending the "work-or-fight" order to all men placed in the deferred class by local draft boards on the grounds of their having dependents. It was estimated that of the 8 million registrants in the deferred classification because of dependents, approximately 2.5 million were not working in essential industries. This provoked a serious disagreement with USES representatives who were developing less coercive methods that utilized the community labor boards and the priority powers of the War Industries Board to shift men out of nonessential industries and who saw in the War Department proposal a thinly veiled effort to conscript labor.[40] In countering the War Department proposal, USES officials did assert and retain the primacy of civilian control over the domestic labor market.

The earlier War Department suspicion of the administrative capacity of the USES continued throughout the war and into the postwar reconstruction. Immediately after the armistice, Frankfurter was warned that War Department officials doubted the ability of the USES to cope with the demobilization. That lack of confidence was directly related to the belief that those working in the USES lacked sufficient expertise. The War Department's continuing distrust of the administrative capacity of the USES never fully abated. In the immediate postwar period that distrust helped to undermine public support for the continuation of the USES. By contrast, relations between the Navy Department and the USES were quite supportive.[41]

Unlike the Agriculture and War departments, relations with the War Industries Board grew steadily closer during the latter part of 1918. This reflected an increased awareness of the seriousness of the labor shortage on the part of WIB officials. At the end of August, Charles A. Otis, chief of the Resources and Conversion Section of the WIB, commented that, although the newspapers were mentioning a shortage of one million unskilled laborers, "my own opinion is that there is nearer five million shortage throughout the country."[42] By late October, the U.S. Housing Corporation reported that all its projects were only "being manned to the extent of about fifty per cent of their requirements." The situation was so desperate that the Housing Corporation had applied to the chief of staff of the army for 12,500 men to be furloughed from camp to work on its projects.[43]

In early September 1918, the Priorities Division of the WIB established a special Labor Section. One function of this new body was to act with the USES in determining priorities for the recruitment of labor for essential war industries. Throughout September, October, and November, when the WIB was actively promoting the curtailment of nonessential industries in order to release labor for war industries, the closest contact with the USES was maintained.[44] In addition, plans were outlined by the USES for a special two-week campaign, beginning December 1, to register "all skilled workers of certain specific types who are not now engaged in war work." The USES anticipated that it would then be able to force nonessential industries to release these skilled workers "through the arrangements being effected with the War Industries Board."[45]

The increasingly close cooperation between the USES and the WIB in the fall of 1918 resulted in other benefits. In September the Statistics Division of the WIB contacted the USES concerning methods of obtaining reliable labor statistics. As a direct result of this contact, the WIB requested the USES to use the community labor boards to make a monthly survey of all labor employed in eighty-eight specified industries mentioned in the preference list of the board's Priorities Division. The initial results proved so valuable that, one month later, the WIB asked the USES to extend the survey to cover all industries.[46] By late 1918, reliable statistics on the current operation of the labor market were finally becoming available.

The Emergency Fleet Corporation continued to be supportive of the USES, although, like the WIB, it was not prepared to surrender complete monopoly control of the national labor market to the Department of Labor. It was, however, moving in that direction. In the Northwest, the Seattle experiment with quasi-monopoly control, although unsatisfactory, continued to function. In the East, by the fall of 1918, the enormous Hog Island shipbuilding complex near Philadelphia was using the USES exclusively.[47] Moreover, the Emergency Fleet Corporation was prepared to support the USES in its efforts to curb unregulated newspaper advertising for labor. Immediately before the armistice it was preparing to issue regulations approved by the USES governing all shipyard advertising for labor "just to stop competition of one shipyard with another."[48]

In addition to seeking to improve relations with other government departments and agencies, the USES also moved to regulate the activities of the various private employment agents operating in the wartime labor market. Shortly before the armistice, the USES asked the WLPB to approve a set of regulations to go into effect on December 1. These would cover all war-related industries and forbid the use of "labor agents, scouts, private employment agencies, [or] newspaper advertising" in all labor recruiting "except through or under permission of the U.S. Employment Service." The regulations were to cover both unskilled and skilled labor. The proposals were designed to give to the USES virtual control over the activities of the private employment agencies, which were still actively soliciting labor and disrupting the labor market. The proposed regulations did not outlaw private employment agents but severely restricted their freedom. In the future, all such agents supplying war-related industries would be required to be licensed by the USES and would have to operate under its supervision and control. The proposal was discussed at the November 6 meeting of the WLPB, but, with talk of an armistice in the air, no action was taken.[49]

Relations between the USES and nongovernmental bodies also steadily improved during 1918. The U.S. Chamber of Commerce was very supportive. By late June 1918, the Chamber's Industrial Relations Committee was cooperating with the USES in organizing local employment offices and was impressing upon all members the need to support the centralized labor program and the USES. It also urged members to impress on congressmen the need to appropriate sufficient funds for the USES. In July and August, it urged all members of the Chamber to participate in the state advisory boards and community labor boards then being organized by the USES.[50] Similar supportive relations were established between the USES and the National Industrial Conference Board.[51]

The American Federation of Labor was also very encouraging. At the AFL annual convention held in St. Paul, Minnesota, in mid-June 1918, a resolution was passed urging the executive committee to use its best efforts to secure the $2 million requested by the Secretary of Labor for the USES and "to do what is in their power to make the Bureau effective."[52] This was followed up with an editorial in the *American Federationist* in September urging "support and assistance" for the USES. In July 1918 the head of the Clearance Section of the USES had been able to advise all field officers that "practically every [labor] organization is offering its services" in the effort to comb out skilled labor for essential industries.[53] This cooperation continued throughout the rest of 1918.[54] Although the unions cooperated willingly, it was understood that the USES was dealing mainly with unorganized and unskilled workers. Most union men did not use the USES facilities themselves as they preferred to rely on the facilities offered by their own unions.[55]

Under the persistent prodding of Felix Frankfurter, the USES did make a determined effort, in the second half of 1918, to overcome its initial weaknesses in personnel and organization. Over the same period, its relationships with most other departments and government agencies slowly improved, as did its standing with employer and union groups. An increased level of professional competence began to permeate the organization and there was even a modest effort made to address some social issues relating to employment. However, by far the most important initiative was the creation of a network of community labor boards to assist in the sensitive task of shifting workers from nonessential to essential industries and substituting women for men in a broad range of occupations. This successful experiment generated widespread public approval for the USES and its policies. By the time of the armistice, the USES was rapidly gaining strength and status both within the wartime administration and in the nation at large.

The U.S.
Employment
Service
at War

CHAPTER SEVEN

The Industrial Northeast

Connecticut

The geographical distribution of government war contracts during the war reinforced the existing pattern of industrial concentration in the United States. Three-quarters of all government contracts for war purposes, excluding those let by the U.S. Shipping Board, were concentrated in seven states—Massachusetts, Connecticut, New York, New Jersey, Pennsylvania, Ohio, and Illinois. One-quarter of the war contracts went to New York alone, and three states—New York, Pennsylvania, and Ohio—absorbed one half of the total. Contracts let by the Shipping Board for vessels were more dispersed because of the requirement of deep waterways, but the contracts for shipbuilding accessories followed a geographical pattern that was similar to other war contracts.[1] The geographical concentration of war contracts created an insatiable demand for labor in the band of industrial states stretching from Boston to Chicago. It also resulted in a very serious shortage of housing and other social amenities in these industrial areas.

Although geographically diminutive, Connecticut was one of the most industrialized states in the Union when America entered World War I.[2] By the second decade of the century, it was the fourth most densely populated state in the Union, with two-thirds of its population concentrated in urban areas. It was also one of the most industrialized states in the Northeast, with over 50 percent of the work force engaged in manufacturing. The state's industrial base was quite diversified: machine tools, firearms, metals (particularly brass), hats, silks, sewing machines, textiles, insurance, finance, and hardware all contributed to this diversity. Almost all these industries switched to government contracts during the war, so that by 1918, four-fifths of Connecticut's industries were producing goods for the war effort.[3]

Such a heavy concentration of war industries created an immense demand for labor and led to an acute labor shortage within the state by the winter of 1917–18.

Connecticut's response to the change in the labor market was slow. Both employers and organized labor were reluctant to concede that the situation required drastic new initiatives. However, when that recognition did come, Connecticut created one of the most efficient systems of employment offices in the country. The appointment of the director of the Connecticut employment office system as the state director of the USES meshed both state and federal authority in one person and incorporated the state offices into the national system of USES offices. Headed by an able and aggressive administrator, the Connecticut employment offices rapidly gained the confidence of employers and, well in advance of the national USES, began to assert near-total control over the state labor market. However, the mixture of federal and state authority possessed by the director of the employment system in Connecticut highlighted the dilemma confronting a genuinely federal rather than a nationalist USES. In such a system, would national or state interests prevail in the competititon for the limited supply of available manpower?

Because the Connecticut state legislature was not in session during 1917, the task of overseeing the state's early involvement in the war effort fell to the state council of defense. That body had been appointed by the governor, at the request of the federal government, shortly after war was declared. As part of its organization, a Committee on Man Power and Labor was established to assist in adjusting the wartime supply to the demand for labor throughout the state. The original scope of this committee was very broad and included all aspects of working conditions as well as the supply of labor. The committee had no formal powers, although it obviously had the support of the governor. It relied upon "the voluntary cooperation of labor and manufacturing interests."[4]

To chair the new committee, the state council selected Herbert Knox Smith, a former chief of the U.S. Bureau of Corporations and on various occasions acting secretary of the federal Department of Commerce and Labor. A lawyer and vice president of the Hartford Special Machinery Company, Smith was well known among employers. He was also respected by the state labor movement as "an exponent of the square deal."[5] Smith was well aware of the difficulties facing his committee and took pains to get the support of organized labor. Including Smith, there were six members on

the committee: three were employers, two were lawyers who were also involved in the management of corporations, and one, a plumber, was a union
member and the president of the New Haven Trades Council, which was
affiliated with the American Federation of Labor and the Connecticut State
Federation.[6] Although dominated by employer representatives, the committee did include one union member and had a respected and sympathetic chairman acceptable to both management and labor.

By the fall of 1917, the committee had come to focus on two major issues
affecting the labor supply within the state. The first was the problem of high
labor turnover, which the committee believed was "beyond reason, and
indicates unsound economic conditions."[7] The committee also became
convinced that a serious labor shortage was developing within the state.
The huge influx of war orders had led to a rapid expansion of industries
and great labor unrest and shortages. In New Haven alone, the population
engaged in manufacturing increased from 24,993 in 1914 to 46,600 in 1918.
The Winchester Repeating Arms Company, which was the biggest manufacturer in that city, added 14,000 employees in this period.[8] In December
1917, Smith estimated that the labor shortage in the state was "between
25,000 and 30,000" and steadily getting worse.[9] Some means had to be
found to alleviate the situation.

In November, the Council of National Defense pressed the state councils of defense to promote the expansion of existing state employment services and to link them with the USES. The proposal to utilize existing
state-supported labor exchanges created special problems in Connecticut
and prompted an unusual response. The five free state employment bureaus in Connecticut had been in operation in the major industrial cities
for approximately fifteen years and in 1915–16 had filled approximately 37,000
positions.[10] However, they were not highly regarded by either employers or
union men.[11] With both management and unions in Connecticut reluctant
to support the existing state employment offices, the state council of defense finally decided, on December 26, 1917, to establish its own statewide
system of War Production Labor Exchanges to cooperate with the Department of Labor. A grant of $100,000 was secured from the state treasury to
finance the projected system. The new offices were to be closely linked with
the statewide network of local councils that had been organized by the
Connecticut state council of defense. No mention was made of the existing
state system of employment exchanges; the state council had decided to
ignore these offices entirely.[12] The decision to build an entirely separate
system of state-funded employment offices for the war emergency and to

ignore the existing offices was unique to Connecticut. No other state took such an unusual step.

The state council's nominee for director of its system of employment exchanges was Leo A. Korper, treasurer of the Capitol City Lumber Company, one of the two largest lumber companies in the state. The choice of the director was crucial; everybody on the state council recognized that "the success of these exchanges would depend very largely upon the person selected to have charge of them."[13] Korper accepted the appointment as a dollar-a-year man and received no salary for his work. He immediately went to Washington to talk with federal officials in both the Department of Labor and the War Department, which resulted in his appointment as state director of four separate federal employment agencies: the U.S. Employment Service, the Public Service Reserve, the War Service Exchange, and the Civilian Personnel Division of the Ordnance Department. In effect, the Connecticut state council of defense had centralized all employment matters, both federal and state (with the exception of the existing state employment offices), in the one agency and, indeed, in one person, a deliberate policy that it adopted for all other war work in the state.[14] The idea was not lost on Washington, which adapted the idea to other states.

Caution on the part of the Connecticut governor caused some delay in the establishment of the new employment offices. The first office, which was located in Hartford, was not established until the beginning of April 1918. However, by the end of April, four offices were in operation and, in June, a fifth office was established. By the end of September, ten offices were operating, and in October the service attained its maximum expansion with fourteen offices throughout the state. Each office had between two and ten examiners, plus clerks and stenographers to handle the business. The Hartford office acted as a central clearing office for intrastate transfer of labor "where absolutely necessary." The number of applicants actually placed rose from 399 in April to 6,936 in August and 9,658 in October, and the daily average placed rose from 37.7 in April to 231.2 in August and 357.4 in October.[15]

The personnel selected by Korper to operate the new employment system lacked experience in employment office work but were otherwise well qualified. To be associate director, he appointed a Yale graduate, Allen B. Lincoln, who had extensive newspaper experience and had been for twenty years the life insurance manager for Northwestern Mutual. The company gave him a temporary leave of absence to take the position. He took particular responsibility for publicity matters and operated in conjunction with the extremely efficient publicity department of the state council of defense. The superintendents of the employment offices in the six major cities in Connecticut also had impressive qualifications: four had extensive managerial experience, one was a leading union man in the state, and one was a Yale academic. Korper had emphasized representativeness as well as general ability in his choice of superintendents.[16]

Under Korper's guidance the Connecticut system of war employment offices developed into a very sophisticated organization. The head office at Hartford acted as the clearinghouse for the fourteen branch offices throughout the state and had attached to it a number of specialist officers. These included a state field representative in charge of the supervision of local offices and the placing of farm labor, a special representative of the Ordnance Department in charge of recruiting for that department, a farm help specialist from the U.S. Department of Agriculture "who took charge of the coordination of the farm labor work of the Employment Service with the work of the County Farm Bureaus," and a woman with three executive assistants in charge of the Woman's Division, which was "charged with the responsibility of recruiting and placing women, particularly in war industries." Regular conferences of office superintendents were held to coordinate activities and to pool experiences.[17]

Relations between the state branch of the USES and Connecticut employers and organized labor followed a fairly typical pattern. Throughout 1917 and early 1918, manufacturers and unions alike had remained lukewarm toward proposals to expand the number of employment offices in the state. Union members were not convinced that a genuine shortage of labor existed and were therefore unwilling to put aside their traditional distrust of such offices. Manufacturers, on their part, were suspicious of the motives of the Department of Labor and skeptical about the competence of its officials. In 1917, for example, the Department of Labor had established the Public Service Reserve, which had enrolled approximately 300,000 skilled workers all over the country who had agreed, for patriotic reasons, to transfer to government work when called. This had resulted in a considerable transfer of skilled men to the rapidly expanding shipping yards. Connecticut manufacturers, many of whom were involved on government war contracts themselves, viewed such an indiscriminate method of transferring skilled labor with alarm. They felt that they might at any time lose indispensable skilled men who had enrolled in the Reserve.[18]

The Connecticut state council of defense was the first in the region to capitalize on the mounting concern among state employers over the potentially adverse effect of federal labor policies. In January 1918, at a meeting of all members of the Connecticut council of defense organization, Korper stressed the defensive role of the proposed system of employment offices.[19] He wanted to make it clear to employers that the state branch of the USES, under his direction, would be used to protect the Connecticut labor market. As he subsequently remarked, "We didn't get very much cooperation, at first, until they [the Connecticut employers] saw that we could do something for them."[20] Possessing both state and federal authority, Korper was well placed to protect the Connecticut labor market from unreasonable labor demands for out-of-state projects and to promote policies to help relieve the labor shortage within the state. It was a formidable task requiring an aggressive approach, a capacity to use delegated authority to the hilt, and a willingness to assume authority that was clearly not delegated. Korper did not shrink from the task.

The most obvious challenge to Korper's efforts to control the Connecticut labor market came from out-of-state firms that were attempting to recruit labor within the state. Even though some of these firms were working on important government contracts, Korper kept up a constant drumfire of complaints to the Washington headquarters of the USES, demanding that out-of-state recruiters be forbidden in the state unless they were specifically licensed by him. Korper was not afraid to threaten recalcitrants, particularly private employment agents, and his combination of federal and state authority, coupled with his determination to control the state labor market, commanded attention. Even the War Department, which was involved in some massive construction projects in different parts of the country, was not immune to this pressure. In October 1918, Korper wrote to USES headquarters in Washington to ask whether or not the War Department had authority to recruit in Connecticut: "A rumor has reached this state that the War Department were [sic] about ready to launch a campaign to recruit men in this state and preparations have been made to discourage it."[21]

Apart from applying pressure on individual out-of-state firms through both the Washington office of the USES and the War Industries Board, Korper took action to prevent such firms from advertising for labor in Connecticut newspapers. Because the Connecticut USES was so intimately tied into the organization of the state council of defense, it was able to take full advantage of that body's extremely efficient Department of Publicity, which had very close ties with the state newspapers.[22] In April 1918, Korper reported that local newspapers, at his suggestion, were refusing to accept advertisements for labor from the American Brake Shoe and Foundry Company of Erie, Pennsylvania, which was one of the worst offenders. In July, an attempt by the Wright Martin Aircraft Corporation of New Jersey to put a display advertisement in the Hartford *Times* for 2,000 machinists was also blocked by Korper. By mid-August 1918, Korper wrote that he was doing "everything possible" to discourage newspaper advertising for labor in Connecticut, whether such advertisements carried "the signature of a private concern on non-essentials; a concern on direct Government orders; or, in fact, an advertisement by some department of the United States Government itself."[23] In controlling newspaper advertisements for labor, Connecticut was well in advance of the rest of the country. It was not until the beginning of August 1918 that the U.S. Employment Service itself finally received official authority to control newspaper advertising for labor, and even this authority applied only to advertisements for unskilled labor placed by firms with over 100 employees.

Although aggressively protective of the work force of Connecticut industries, Korper did recognize the need to permit some recruiting for essential war industries located in other states. This usually involved cooperation with USES offices in neighboring states and entailed reciprocal obligations. He had been permitted, for instance, in "thirty or forty instances" to recruit for Connecticut industries in New York State and elsewhere: "I do not desire to see any of our needed labor leaving Connecticut, neither do I desire to have the surrounding State Directors refuse to allow us to enter their respective states to recruit." Korper's solution was to permit outside recruiters to operate within the state provided it was for essential war industries and on the condition that such recruiting was done "under the direction and supervision of our own Service within this state."[24]

It was not only out-of-state firms that caused concern. Part of Korper's problem, particularly in the early months, was to convince Connecticut manufacturers that a centralized labor recruiting program, operated through his organization, would be of benefit to all firms within the state and would help to eliminate the endemic pirating of labor between Connecticut firms. By early June 1918, he felt that even the most recalcitrant manufacturers within the state were becoming convinced of the value of cooperating with his office.[25] Korper was always careful to ensure that those firms that did use the USES offices exclusively got good service. Complaints from firms like the Acme Wire Company, which had "been disposed to cooperate with us in every possible manner from the start," were treated with "prompt and careful attention."[26] The Connecticut USES had to be seen to be effective; cooperation had to be matched by demonstrations of utility.

By mid-1918, well before the implementation of the national central recruiting program, which affected only unskilled labor, Korper had begun to secure, through the voluntary cooperation of manufacturers within Connecticut, a general agreement to obtain all labor, both skilled and unskilled, through the state USES offices. By late October, he could report that in the districts covered by nine of the thirteen USES employment offices within Connecticut, "employers are securing [all] labor in no other manner than through the U.S. Employment Service." Agreement for such monopoly control was close in New Haven, Hartford, and New Britain. That would leave only the Bridgeport district and pressure would be exerted "to get the same program in force there."[27] In early November, commenting on employer cooperation in submitting requisitions for help through the USES offices, Korper stated that "the employers are using the Service in Connecticut and are cooperating with it splendidly."[28] By the time of the armistice, the Connecticut USES had much greater control over the state labor market than the Washington office of the USES had over the national labor market. Korper's efforts to secure the voluntary cooperation of management were bearing fruit.

The Connecticut USES, under Korper, was innovative in a number of other areas. Korper's efforts to secure employer cooperation and a monopoly over the supply of labor to Connecticut manufacturers were necessary preliminaries to a campaign to reduce the enormous turnover of labor within the state. This turnover created what was in effect an "artificial" demand for labor and made it virtually impossible to calculate the "real" demand. Korper regarded the reduction in labor turnover as "one of the principal efforts" of the Connecticut USES under his direction. One method he encouraged was for examiners in the various USES offices to talk with the men seeking new employment in an effort to induce them "to return to their former jobs or to another place in the same shop." This method proved fairly successful. Over 6,500 workers were induced to return to their employers instead of changing their jobs after discussion with the USES examiners. Korper estimated that the cost of labor turnover varied between $20 and $200 per man and the total savings to manufacturers in the state to be close to a million dollars.[29]

More aggressive methods were also adopted. Connecticut led the country in the adoption of district cooperative agreements among manufacturers designed to minimize labor turnover and to assist in shifting labor from nonessential to essential industries. In early June, the superintendent of the USES office in Waterbury, Ralph W. Budd, called a meeting of all manufacturers, both essential and nonessential, to discuss the labor situation in that city. Representatives from 120 firms, employing a total of 45,000 workers, attended. The meeting agreed to create a small committee, consisting of two nonessential manufacturers and one essential manufacturer, to work with Superintendent Budd in developing a comprehensive, voluntary plan for transferring workers from nonessential to essential industries, using the USES office exclusively. The "Waterbury Plan," which covered both skilled and unskilled labor, was conceived and put into practice well before the USES was given more limited control over the recruiting of unskilled labor at the beginning of August.[30]

The other aspect of the "Waterbury Plan," the active discouragement of labor turnover, received less publicity. It proved to be highly effective but quite controversial. The June meeting had agreed that each manufacturer in the district would submit to the USES Waterbury office each morning "the name and address of every employee leaving his establishment, either voluntarily or through discharge, together with a statement of the reasons for such leaving." On discharge, each employee received a card stating which company he had been working for and the date of his release. This card was an authorization permitting any other employer in the district to employ him; employers wishing to hire a workman without a card had to receive specific authorization from the USES office. The scheme covered all factories in the district and applied to both skilled and unskilled men. Budd believed that "nine out of every ten men leave the factory without notice. These men will not receive a card from the employers and will find difficulty in getting another job."[31] Employers also agreed to centralize the rather haphazard employment practices operating within the Waterbury factories; the power of foremen to fire employees was to be discontinued and both hiring and discharging functions were to be centralized in factory employment offices.[32]

Budd had made an effort to allay the fears of union representatives that this scheme could develop into an employer blacklist under the aegis of the USES. At the original meeting he had appointed a committee of three members, representing union labor in Waterbury, to work with him in conjunction with the manufacturers' committee.[33] This did not satisfy the Waterbury Central Union. Shortly after the meeting of manufacturers in July that approved the proposed scheme, union representatives met with

Budd and refused to approve the plan, claiming that foremen were using it to intimidate workmen and to force them to give up to a week's notice. Budd denied the charge.[34] One month later, the secretary of the Waterbury Central Union wrote to Korper to complain that workers who wished to change employment were being denied the necessary clearance card and to request a "thorough investigation" of the operation of the scheme. In early September, Korper received a request for an investigation from the director-general of the USES.[35]

Korper's response was circumspect. He did not deny that the clearance card system had the potential for abuse. However, he pointed out that, under the original scheme, if an employee felt that he was being denied a clearance card by his employer, he could complain to Budd, after which a committee composed of equal numbers of employers and workers would decide the case.[36] Korper noted that the Washington office had been kept fully informed of the "Waterbury Plan" from its inception and that the majority of factories in Waterbury had participated "in a proper and helpful manner." He added that the introduction of the community labor boards, "which are now actively at work," would operate to eliminate "whatever objectionable features already exist."[37]

The "Waterbury Plan" had an immediate impact on labor turnover. At the end of July, the USES office in that city reported a brisk business in men who applied for work at local factories but did not have registration cards and hence were sent to the USES office.[38] One Waterbury plant reported that its labor turnover was reduced "from 311% per annum (compiled weekly) to 80% within the space of four weeks."[39] The largest plant in Waterbury, which employed 14,000 people, reported a 50 percent drop in labor turnover in the plan's first week of operation. In late July, Budd even wrote to Washington outlining the scheme and suggesting that it be adopted on a national basis.[40]

Waterbury was in desperate need of some means of augmenting its available labor supply. Given the critical nature of the war production being carried out there, it is perhaps not surprising that the union protests, although acknowledged, were not acted upon. In August 1918, for example, the Connecticut Brass and Manufacturing Company, one of the few producers of thin bronze for aircraft radiators, was working at only half capacity because it could not get a sufficient supply of labor. In mid-August, in response to the critical situation in Waterbury, the War Department decided to furlough men from the army to work in the Waterbury factories to meet the critical shortage of manpower.[41] The Ordnance Department

COULD YOU SAY THIS?

COULD you say that the work you are doing every day right here in Stamford is helping Our Boys over there to win?

Wouldn't you like to be able to say it?

| Stamford has over 10,000 men and women at work NOW in her War Industries.

SHE NEEDS 2,100 MORE | **WAR WORK WHICH YOU MIGHT BE DOING**

If you are a man:
Metal Casting.   Rolling Brass.
Shipping.   Trucking.
General Factory Work

If you are a woman:
Lathe Operating.   Packing.
Inspecting.   Finishing.
Drill Press Operating.
General Light-Factory Work. | Stamford needs
Y O U
today in her war-work if she is to fill the Government's immediate demands for war material. |

MEN are wanted for heavy work, especially that which cannot be done by women.

WOMEN are wanted for hundreds of jobs which men are leaving to take up heavier work.

STAMFORD offers healthful surroundings, good wages, shops, amusements, and everything a progressive, busy community can offer.

BE AN AMERICAN WAR-WORKER

Go to 444 Atlantic Street, ask for Mr. Blodgett, who is here in the Government Service, and let him point out to you some of the things YOU might be doing to help win the war at home.

U. S. EMPLOYMENT SERVICE

444 Atlantic Street   **Stamford, Connecticut**

An example of the adaptation of the U.S. Employment Service wartime message to local circumstances. Source: Edwin S. Blodgett, *How Stamford Is Meeting Her War Labor Problems* (Stamford, Connecticut: USES Employment Office, 1918), 15.

allocated 2,400 enlisted men to the Connecticut brass mills for use as common labor.[42] In Connecticut, the shortage of common labor, rather than skilled labor, was most acute, and this shortage got steadily worse right up until the armistice and, in many plants, "it constituted the limiting factor in the output of war material."[43]

The city of Stamford established a scheme very similar to that of Waterbury at about the same time. The director of the USES office in Stamford took the idea one step further and actively encouraged other, nonemployed groups in the community, particularly women and retired men, to join the work force during the war for patriotic reasons. A committee "representative of all classes in the community, and composed of the leading citizens" was established. Full-page advertisements were placed in the local paper, ministers were asked to preach on the topic, and a corps of four-minute speakers was organized to speak throughout the district. The campaign was successful and a considerable number of people, "stirred by the patriotic appeal," applied to the USES office.

The Stamford office then launched a campaign to pressure men who were not doing heavy work in the factories to volunteer to do "a man's work" and thus allow women or older men to do the light work. A special motion picture, entitled *Mr and Mrs Hines of Stamford Do Their Bit,* which told the story of a Stamford housewife who decided, for patriotic reasons, to join the work force while, at the same time, her husband decided to give up the light work he was doing at the factory and volunteer for heavy work. He took a job in a casting shop and his wife went to work on a lathe in a machine shop. A special educational campaign among employers was also undertaken to overcome the reluctance of management and foremen to employ women.[44] The community labor boards in Connecticut, which were established in the early fall, were able to build on these early initiatives of local USES offices.

The Connecticut branch of the USES was also able to assist state manufacturers in a number of quiet ways. In the case of the Winchester Repeating Arms Company in New Haven, the Washington office of the USES received complaints that the company was trying to replace men with women "on repetition work and the operation of various semi-automatic machinery at wages quite materially lower than paid men for the same occupations."[45] Winchester Bennett, who was in charge of the corporation, was one of the original members of the Connecticut state council of defense. Korper had a long talk with him and, after visiting the New Haven plant, reported that he needed "a little more time before taking any action."[46] In late April, Korper deflected a proposal from the Washington office of the USES suggesting a formal investigation of the situation.[47] Nothing was done. Korper obviously felt that such an investigaton would jeopardize the support of Connecticut manufacturers for the employment service and would be unlikely to lead to any change in the practice. He had, therefore, effectively blocked a federal investigation.

Assisting Connecticut manufacturers could also mean taking aggressive action against some of the international unions. In November 1918, Korper received a memo from Sanford Freund, director of the Clearance Section of the USES, which conveyed a complaint from the general secretary-treasurer of the International Association of Machinists. The union official had protested Korper's refusal to acknowledge the right of a union representative to recruit machinists in Bridgeport for an out-of-state project even when "some of the machinists recruited were men who could not obtain work in Bridgeport." Freund stated that, given the great demand for machinists and toolmakers, if the men could not obtain employment in Bridgeport they should be encouraged to go elsewhere. He also reminded Korper that the USES did not have any formal control over the recruitment of skilled labor and that the USES should remain neutral in any dispute between employers and employees.[48]

In a furious reply, Korper pointed out that he had written a "strong letter" at the request of the chairman of the local community labor board in Bridgeport who was trying to prevent a representative of the Machinists' Union from recruiting machinists and toolmakers currently employed in important Bridgeport war industries for an out-of-state project. Although Korper agreed that the USES did not technically have control over the recruitment of skilled labor, he did believe that "it was proper" for him to assume that authority. He would not allow administrative technicalities to permit either unions or employers to undermine his control of the Connecticut labor market. As a parting shot, Korper added that, if such skilled workers were unemployed in Bridgeport, they could easily find work in any of a dozen other Connecticut cities.[49]

The innuendo in Freund's memorandum that Korper had taken sides with employers in this incident provoked a terse denial. In fact, Korper pointed out, his letter had been written at the request of the chairman of the Bridgeport community labor board who, far from representing employers, was the former president of the Bridgeport Plumbers' Union, a former officer in the Bridgeport Trades Council and the Bridgeport Central Labor Union, and "regarded highly by all the officials of the Connecticut Federation of Labor with whom your Director in this State has acquaintance."[50] Freund tried to calm Korper and stated that he had not intended to criticize his actions, but the Connecticut state director was not easily pacified.[51] Korper was determined to stifle all wartime employment activities within Connecticut carried on by either unions or management and to channel all employment work through his statewide network of USES offices.

The Connecticut branch of the USES was one of the most efficient in the Northeast. In a number of specific ways it was able to use the dual federal-state authority it possessed in quite effective and innovative ways to alleviate the wartime labor shortage within the state. It placed restrictions on recruiting by out-of-state firms, encouraged Connecticut manufacturers to cooperate and to stop stealing each other's labor, approved a number of experimental schemes designed to reduce labor turnover, and introduced imaginative ways of overcoming prejudice against female workers in factories. The Connecticut branch of the USES developed schemes to meet these various needs well in advance of the Washington office. However, in all these activities there was an underlying defensive motivation. Although as patriotic as any wartime administrator in Washington, the Connecticut director of the USES naturally perceived national labor priorities through the prism of state interests.

It was as well that Korper and his counterparts in other states did so. The initial manpower mobilization methods adopted by the Department of Labor were crude and ill-conceived and, as the labor market contracted, these methods became increasingly disruptive. In an unanticipated way, these crude early USES efforts to mobilize labor led both to a heightened employer suspicion of government interference in the labor market and, paradoxically, to the eventual acceptance of the central role of the USES. This acceptance was linked to a growing realization that the state branches of the USES could act as buffers to protect each state's labor pool from indiscriminate federal incursions. The example of Connecticut suggests that wartime manpower policy was not decided solely in Washington. Because of their control over the actual administration of policy and because of the degree of independence they maintained, the branches of the USES in the major industrial states also played an active part in developing a labor policy that tried to balance national and state needs. Given the virtual absence of reliable data on the operation of the labor market, and the lack of administrative expertise in employment matters in the Washington office of the USES until late in the war, it was as well that they did.

CHAPTER EIGHT

The Midwest
and South

During the first half of 1918, as the national labor market slowly contracted, the Midwest and the South both began to recognize the need for a defensive strategy in their relations with Washington. With the exceptions of Illinois and Ohio, both regions were still heavily agricultural and contained significant pools of labor that could be used to meet the national emergency. The heavily industrialized Northeast had attracted the bulk of the war contracts which had created in that region both an insatiable demand for labor and an attractive, high-wage structure. By the summer of 1918, both the Midwest and the South had become very concerned that the wartime migration of their labor to supply eastern industrial plants would have very significant, immediate, and long-term effects on their own economies and were seeking ways to minimize that impact. This created obvious problems for the USES.

The administrative situation facing the USES in the two regions was very different. In the Midwest, unlike the South, the Department of Labor had to negotiate with state governments that were already deeply involved in employment activities. When the United States entered the war, the Midwest was probably the most advanced region in the country in terms of the sophistication of its state-funded employment offices. Wisconsin, Ohio, and Illinois had set the pace in the immediate prewar period. In particular, Ohio, under Fred Croxton's guidance, had created an exemplary public employment system out of the old state offices in 1914–15, and had then dramatically expanded and further improved the system immediately after the American declaration of war. During 1917, the Ohio system was one of the largest and undoubtedly the most sophisticated in the country.[1]

In 1911, the newly created Wisconsin industrial commission had employed William Leiserson, one of the pioneer students of the labor market, to reorganize the state's four employment offices. Over the next three years Leiserson made the Wisconsin offices an example to the rest of the country. With only four offices, however, the Wisconsin state employment system reached only a fraction of the potential labor market and it was not until federal money became available in 1918 that there was any expansion.

In the prewar period, Illinois spent over $40,000 annually on eight state employment offices, which was more than double the outlay of any other state in the Union. Most state employment offices spent only a fraction of that amount.[2] In 1915, the state Department of Labor had reorganized and consolidated the employment offices "along the most approved lines" and had created a General Advisory Board, which included representatives of both employers and organized labor, in an effort to generate greater public acceptance and support.[3] The city of Chicago also operated a municipal employment office unconnected with the state offices. Other midwestern state employment systems, though not as well developed as the ones in Wisconsin, Ohio, and Illinois, were still too strong to be ignored.[4]

Once war was declared, the desirability of some cooperative agreement between the various midwestern state employment systems and the USES was obvious. Although the different state systems cooperated with the USES in various practical ways, formal cooperative agreements were slow to emerge. In Wisconsin, for example, it was February 1918 before an agreement was reached whereby the state Industrial Commission, which operated the four state employment offices, was appointed the USES state director. This arrangement ensured that state authorities retained effective control of employment matters in Wisconsin. Federal funds led to rapid expansion. By the armistice, there were thirty offices in the state. In neighboring Minnesota, an agreement was not reached until May 1918. The agreement specified the appointment of a Minnesota official as state director of the USES. In Ohio, a formal cooperative agreement was not finally signed until the late summer of 1918. Again, effective control of the state offices rested with state officials and Fred Croxton was appointed USES director for the state of Ohio.[5] Because of the importance of the Chicago labor market, the USES had established its own office there before the war and in December 1916 had negotiated a formal cooperative agreement with the Illinois employment offices. However, that agreement was never properly implemented by the federal authorities and remained a source of friction and irritation throughout the war.[6]

The wartime emergency created a genuine alarm in the midwestern states over the availability of sufficient agricultural labor. The need for greater food production in a time of increasing labor scarcity caused by the military draft and the demands of the wartime industrial program brought the problem into sharp focus in the agricultural states. The panicky comments of the midwestern representatives at the National Defense Conference, held in Washington shortly after America became involved in the war, reflected the concern over the issue in that region.[7]

Among the midwestern states, the Ohio employment service led the way in organizing the agricultural labor market. This paralleled the efficient organization of the Ohio industrial labor market, which it also achieved.[8] The first step taken was to make an accurate estimate of the seasonal demand for agricultural labor throughout the state. Shortly after the declaration of war, the Ohio employment service blanketed the state with a questionnaire to farmers, which established, with some degree of accuracy, both the acreage under cultivation and the estimated labor requirements for the season.[9] However, this technique did not give entirely reliable results, and by early 1918 it had been replaced by a more sophisticated procedure. In each local community, the employment service organized meetings at which farmers filled out special forms detailing, one month in advance, their labor needs, the wages to be offered, and other relevant details. With the aid of a large number of volunteer local agents, the Ohio employment service was able to establish a regular, monthly, forward estimate of the demand for agricultural labor based on actual orders placed by farmers.[10]

The Ohio approach to dealing with agricultural labor avoided the pitfalls associated with generalized estimates of seasonal demand. In the midst of increasing national panic about farm labor shortages, the Ohio employment service was able to provide quite accurate and reliable figures on the real demand within the state, which clearly indicated that most agricultural labor needs could be met from within the state's own resources. No publicity campaign seeking farm labor was undertaken until the completion of this careful canvass of "the actual demand for farm help based on orders from the farmers themselves." When the publicity campaign was launched, men were invited to apply at the nearest employment office for information on specific farm jobs that were available, together with the wages and employment conditions being offered. This was in sharp contrast to the clumsy publicity methods then being used by private agencies and by the USES itself, which broadcast indiscriminate advertisements, usually well in advance of the actual need, suggesting a general demand for labor in certain regions.[11]

In Wisconsin, atypically, the demand for farm labor was predominantly nonseasonal; the large dairy farms required steady labor throughout the year. However, as in all farming areas, there was a call for extra labor during the spring, summer, and fall seasons, particularly on those farms in the state that raised special crops such as peas, beans, and cherries. No crops were lost in the state because of a labor shortage, although there was a constant demand for labor that could not be fully met. Part of this shortfall of labor was met by encouraging women and boys and girls of school age to assist on the farms.[12] In the spring of 1917 a special agreement was reached between the state council of defense and the state Highway Commission whereby road workers were released for farm labor during peak periods at the request of the county labor commissioners. This scheme was given national publicity by the Council of National Defense and became known as the "Wisconsin Plan." Other midwestern states took similar action to ensure that an adequate supply of agricultural labor would be available when needed.[13] The methods used by the USES to recruit agricultural labor seemed very clumsy by comparison with the less disruptive and more effectively targeted methods used by the various state employment systems in the Midwest.

By the spring of 1918, in the Midwest fears of a shortage of agricultural labor had been supplanted by a more general concern that the USES was stripping the region of its industrial work force. USES officials even admitted that some of their recruiting methods were quite arbitrary. For example, when the labor supply in a particular area was exhausted, USES policy was "to distribute the demand equably in territory near enough to be considered tributary."[14] Such an informal procedure was no guarantee that the burden of supplying needed war workers would be spread evenly among the various states. Some midwestern states began to feel that the USES was asking them to contribute a disproportionate share of such labor, and pressure mounted for the adoption of some kind of quota system to ensure equity.

The efficient Ohio employment service was the first to protest against the arbitrariness of USES recruiting procedures. In mid-April 1918, in response to a request for 2,500 men for eastern shipyards, it telegraphed the Washington office stating that 2,425 shipyard workers had already been supplied that week and demanded that the USES "indicate total men wanted as well as Ohio's proportion, in order that we can show to employers that

Ohio is contributing only her fair proportion." The Washington office ignored the protest. Two weeks later, responding to another request for labor
for an eastern shipyard, the Ohio state employment director insisted that
the Washington office supply both the total demand for labor at that yard
and Ohio's quota before he would furnish any labor at all. This threat of
noncompliance eventually produced the requested information.[15] The USES
was being forced to devise some method of distributing the demand so that
no particular locality suffered more than any other. However, given the
inadequacy of the available labor market statistics, this proved to be impossible. As late as mid-June, the assistant director general of the USES candidly admitted that, although every state was "clamoring for quotas," the
USES had been unable to obtain, "under present methods, any comprehensive picture of what the demand is," and it was therefore impossible to
allocate meaningful state quotas. He conceded that, up to that time, "such
quotas as we have given have been purely arbitrary."[16] It was not until mid-
July that agreement was finally reached on both the principles on which a
national quota system would operate and on a reliable method for estimat-
ing the total demand for labor.[17] Ohio's action, together with pressure from
other midwestern states, finally forced the USES to reassess the methods it
used to recruit out-of-state labor.

The more industrialized midwestern states also tried to minimize the
outward flow of industrial labor by putting pressure on the federal government to reallocate war contracts. They argued that the massive turnover of
labor in eastern industries was related to poor social conditions, particularly the lack of adequate housing. It was known, for example, that Illinois
had recently shipped to the huge powder plant under construction at Nitro, West Virginia, 6,000 laborers, two-thirds of whom had returned because of "dissatisfaction with employment and housing conditions." At
Nitro, the turnover of labor in the summer of 1918 was 100 percent per
month.[18] Although Nitro was somewhat exceptional, high turnover rates
were endemic in eastern war industries. The midwestern industrial states
argued a plausible case for contract reallocation by linking high labor turnover to inadequate housing and then by demonstrating that they had ample
housing for additional workmen. A survey of one-quarter of the city of
Chicago showed, for example, that accommodation was available for over
36,000 workers in that district alone. Suggestions were made that existing
contracts should be taken away from plants in the East that could not guarantee adequate housing and given to midwestern states where housing and
labor were readily available.[19] A special delegation from Illinois went to

Washington to submit the matter personally to Frankfurter and to Densmore.[20] The delegation received a sympathetic hearing: Frankfurter gave assurances that "definite action" would be taken and the delegation was told that the War and Navy departments had "adopted a definite policy of placing *new* contracts outside" the eastern munitions centers.[21] By the summer of 1918, the practice of shipping labor out of state had become a very sensitive issue throughout the entire Midwest.

In the southern states, as in the Midwest, a similar sensitivity toward the prospect of losing their labor supply developed during 1918. However, given the different circumstances in the two regions, this reaction manifested itself in different ways. In the Midwest, the states with strong employment services cooperated with and, indeed, effectively coopted the USES when it expanded into their territory. They were too powerful to be ignored. By contrast, in the South there were no state-funded employment offices, and state departments of labor, where they existed, were relatively weak. In that region the USES was able to expand without having to worry about cooperation with existing state employment offices. Although it was a different organizational environment and one relatively free of state-imposed administrative restraints, this did not mean, in practice, that the USES had a free hand. Unable to exert pressure on Washington through administrative channels, as the midwestern and northeastern states were able to do because of their powerful position within the USES, the southern states resorted to more aggressive political action to achieve their ends.

A number of southern communities took draconian action in an effort to curb the northward migration of their population. In Macon, Georgia, in an effort to keep out all labor agents, the city council passed an ordinance setting "the license fee for agents at the laughably high figure of $25,000, and compounded the impossible by requiring that agents be recommended by ten local ministers, ten manufacturers, and twenty-five businessmen."[22] Other cities and states passed similarly stringent measures. In May 1918 the director-general of the USES complained that the attitude of the southern states promised to "result in grave curtailing of production and construction" needed for the war effort. He pointed out that Florida had not only arrested numerous private labor agents but "now has in jail at Gainesville two officers of our Service who have been recruiting common labor for the Army projects at Norfolk." A similar situation threatened in Georgia and in Tennessee.[23] Despite Densmore's complaints, there was little that federal authorities could do. At the time of the armistice, for example, local authorities in Wiggins, Mississippi, had arrested the local representatives of the USES for attempting to recruit workers.[24]

By 1918, a situation of near panic over the labor supply gripped large sections of the South. By the time of the armistice, six southern states had imposed taxes of up to $2,000 on the shipment of labor out of state and most southern states had laws making it an offense even to invite someone to quit employment. Florida, Georgia, Mississippi, and Virginia required a license tax of $500 in each county in which an agent operated for the purpose of securing labor to be sent interstate. North Carolina required both an annual state tax and a tax of $100 in each county where such business was transacted. South Carolina was even more severe; its law imposed a tax of $2,000 per year for each county in which the labor agent worked.[25] This spate of restrictive legislation had begun prior to the U.S. entry into the war as a response to the exodus of labor moving to the northern industrial states which were experiencing boom conditions because of European war orders. Since late 1915, private labor recruiters had been active throughout the Southeast. Large numbers of blacks were willing to move and by 1916 the Great Migration was well under way.

In an effort to quiet southern anxieties about a shortage of labor in the region, the Department of Labor took a number of different initiatives. One of the first was to propose the temporary admission of Mexican agricultural labor. Such a proposal inevitably incurred the wrath of organized labor.[26] The Department of Labor tried to accommodate the AFL objections and, in the winter of 1917–18, plans were laid to transport 50,000 islanders from Puerto Rico and the Virgin Islands.[27] However, a shortage of available shipping sabotaged this scheme temporarily and, in April 1918, the Secretary of Labor felt obliged to suspend the clauses in the immigration law relating to the literacy test, the head tax, and the contract-labor prohibition in order to allow the admission of farm labor from Mexico and surrounding countries for periods of not more than six months. In June, the rulings were extended to cover Mexicans hired for railroad track maintenance, all forms of mining, and construction work for the federal government.[28]

The establishment of a separate Negro Division within the USES was another example of the effort made by the Department of Labor to placate the South. The initial pressure to establish some kind of special division to look after black labor had come from Giles B. Jackson, a black lawyer and politician in Richmond, Virginia, who had been agitating for such action for some years. He had a good deal of support from Senator Thomas Martin and from the Richmond Chamber of Commerce and also managed to get Samuel Gompers to support his plans, which clearly involved keeping blacks in the South. Secretary Wilson had himself been moving to establish a special bureau for blacks, and in May 1918 he announced the establishment of the Division of Negro Economics, headed by George Edmond Haynes, a professor of economics and sociology at Fisk University, a co-founder of the National Urban League, an executive of the National League on Urban Conditions among Negroes, and the first black to have received a Ph.D. from Columbia University. At the same time, Secretary Wilson announced the establishment of a Negro Division within the USES to be headed by Giles B. Jackson. Responding to political pressure, the secretary had established two separate but clearly overlapping agencies concerned with black labor within his department.

However, it became clear quite early that Jackson's appointment had more to do with political patronage than with serious labor issues. Jackson had ambitious plans to try to get black labor out of the cities and back onto the farms and wanted to appoint a considerable number of assistants and field agents. The only request that Assistant Secretary of Labor Louis F. Post would approve was Jackson's request for a stenographic secretary. Jackson's proposals for the work of his division were drastically curtailed by Secretary Wilson in early July. In effect, the Negro Division of the USES was not permitted to do anything. The department's Division of Negro Economics, directed by Dr. Haynes, retained complete control over work among the black population. It cooperated closely with the USES field offices and, to all intents and purposes, operated as the Negro Division of the employment service. The Jackson appointment was merely a reponse to southern political pressure.[29]

The director-general of the USES was, himself, willing to go to considerable lengths to appease southern employers. In April 1918, Densmore arranged a conference with a delegation from the Florida lumber industry, the entire congressional delegation from Florida, and representatives of other government agencies to see if anything could be done to assist that state's lumber industry. At the conference, one of the members of the delegation who was himself a sawmill operator stated that a labor agent from Muscle Shoals, Alabama, where the army was constructing a huge nitrates plant, was "offering my niggers . . . $3.80 and $4.00 a day, while I am paying them $2." Densmore commented that one could not blame the laborers for being attracted to the higher wages, but he did offer a solution to the Florida labor situation: the USES would simply not inform black labor of opportunities elsewhere.[30] If the USES was given sole authority to recruit labor for the federal government, monitoring the flow of information about job opportunities would be an effective way to control the movement of black labor and to pacify southern employers.

The USES was also prepared to tolerate some rather questionable initiatives on the part of its officers in the southern states. In August 1918, Cliff Williams, a USES district supervisor in Mississippi, proposed a plan for a "Labor Registration and Card System" designed "for the stimulation of labor power." Williams was a native of Meridian, Mississippi, a large-scale manufacturer of portable sawmills, and was reputedly interested in improving social conditions.[31] His proposal involved holding a General Registration Day during which all able-bodied men and women would sign a blue pledge card agreeing to work six days a week. The general registration would then be followed by a canvass of all workers in the community "forcing all to show Blue card." The pledge card system was designed to be used in conjunction with the passage of city ordinances making idling a punishable offense. The stated aim of the system was to prevent "continual or part-time loafing." The scheme also called for the establishment of an inspection system maintained and paid for by the employers of the locality.[32]

Not all members of the Department of Labor were enthusiastic about the scheme. Assistant Secretary Louis Post was deeply suspicious of the whole pledge card plan and believed that it was just a form of labor conscription for private purposes. This was, he believed, "especially true of the States in which wage earners are for the most part Negroes." Referring specifically to the interracial meetings being held in New Orleans and in Montgomery, Alabama, which were largely the work of Williams, he commented that the work cards "are so framed and so used as to be regarded as operating to coerce the Negro wage earner and his dependents into private service while employers and their dependents are undisturbed."[33]

However, in spite of Post's reservations, the pledge card system was put into operation. Williams eventually addressed approximately 150 mass meetings composed of both blacks and whites where Loyalty Leagues were organized. "These organizations effectively got behind local authorities for the enforcement of antiloafing laws and the prevention of indiscriminate labor recruiting." There was a good deal of local support. In Montgomery, Alabama, 40,000 people were signed up in the first forty-eight hours, and eventually about 80,000 joined the county Loyalty League. A similar success story was reported from Mobile, where, in less than a month after establishing a league, "the city had been cleaned up and loafing abolished."

It was alleged that over 3,000 idlers were put to work in that city: "Some of these, gamblers and touts, confessed that they had not performed an honest day's labor in 25 or 30 years."[34] In the South, the USES conformed to southern racial attitudes and prejudices.

As the labor market steadily contracted during 1918, the USES found itself in an increasingly difficult position in its relations with the Midwest and South. Because these regions had relatively few war industries, they became a primary source of labor for essential industries located in the East. The USES began to be seen in the Midwest and South as a direct threat to the survival of these regions' local economies. Both regions became alarmed at the loss of labor and attempted, in different ways, to cushion the actions of the USES. In the Midwest, where strong state employment systems cooperated with or were incorporated into the USES under conditions that left these states with a good deal of influence, the struggle to curb federal action was an internal, administrative one and was not widely publicized. By contrast, in the South, where there were fewer effective administrative barriers to federal authority, opposition took on a more public and overtly political expression. The political leverage of the southern delegation in Congress no doubt helps to explain why senior USES administrators, in their attempts to placate southern anxieties, were willing to accommodate themselves to the racial prejudices of that region.

Armistice
and
Aftermath

CHAPTER NINE

Reconstruction and Political Misjudgment, 1918–1919

The signing of the armistice on November 11, 1918, had a dramatic effect on the labor market and on the operation of the USES. Cancellation of war contracts began within a few days: $2.5 billion of the $6 billion in outstanding manufacturing contracts were cancelled in four weeks. The effect on specific communities was immediate. In Cleveland, Ohio, contract cancellations in the three weeks after the armistice put 13,000 out of work; in Connecticut, in the three weeks following Christmas 1918, 40,000 war workers were discharged.[1] In November 1918 the USES had received calls from employers for 1,724,943 workers and had been able to find only 744,712; by February 1919, almost 10,000 more workers registered than there were calls from employers. Steps were taken immediately to discontinue the purely war activities of the USES and to shift the organization onto a peacetime basis.[2]

In the months immediately following the armistice, the actions of both the War Department and Congress were a sobering reminder of the weak political position of the USES. However, officials in the Department of Labor chose to ignore these signals and attempted to revive the dream of a nationalist rather than a federalist USES. Again, this action reflected the ambition and determination of senior officials in the Department of Labor rather than pressure from interest groups in the wider society. These officials were trying, singlehandedly, to overturn the basic premise on which the USES had been reorganized in mid-1918. Although their effort was short-lived and Department of Labor officials quickly recognized their mistake, it alienated many potential supporters and delayed the subsequent campaign to muster widespread support for congressional legislation that would formally establish the USES. That delay proved fatal.

Immediately after the armistice, the mistrust of the administrative capacity of the USES within the War Department, which had been muted in the fall of 1918 because of the grave labor problems facing the nation, surfaced again. War Department officials who had been discussing demobilization plans with Department of Labor representatives threatened to establish a special employment service to assist returned servicemen during the demobilization period unless the Labor Department was prepared to "give better assurances through changed personnel in the Employment Service, that it can be safely relied upon to do this work."[3] In early December, at the instigation of officials in the War Department, the Council of National Defense organized a conference between representatives of the USES and "the executive departments, welfare organizations, and other associations" that were interested in alleviating unemployment among returning servicemen and discharged war workers. As a result of this conference, steps were immediately taken to establish cooperative Bureaus for Returning Soldiers, Sailors, Marines, and War Workers in every town and city of importance in the country. The aim was to pool all job opportunities in each community and to make them available to returned men via the bureau. The idea proved popular and a total of 2,594 bureaus was established.[4]

Each local bureau was supervised by a board of management composed of representatives of the community labor board, if one existed in the locality, of the community council of defense, and of the local branch of each organization represented on the Central Committee plus other local organizations. The manager was appointed as a special representative of the Department of Labor at a nominal salary of one dollar per year and, where possible, the local USES office was to provide administrative support. A national board, chaired by Nathan A. Smyth, the assistant director-general of the USES, and composed of representatives of interested government and private bodies, was established to oversee the work.[5] In effect, the War Department had used the Council of National Defense as a vehicle to discreetly shift the responsibility for the demobilization work, at least partially, out of the hands of the Department of Labor.

On March 14, 1919, the War Department again revealed its distrust of the capacity of USES by establishing an Emergency Employment Committee for Soldiers and Sailors. Ostensibly, this was a response to the emergency created by the closure of a number of USES offices as a result of the failure of Congress to pass a deficiency appropriation bill before it adjourned in early March. The Emergency Employment Committee was chaired by Colonel Arthur Woods, former police commissioner of New York City, who was serving as special assistant to the secretary of war. A central employment office was opened in the Council of Defense building, which became known as the Office of the Assistant to the Secretary of War. By May 1919 this office had a staff of forty-six commissioned officers and eighty civilian workers, all maintained by the War Department. Branch offices established in New York City, Indianapolis, and San Francisco were staffed by an additional twenty-eight commissioned officers.[6]

Although, in theory, Colonel Woods's organization was intended to supplement the work of the USES, in practice it operated entirely independently. Indeed, in some parts of the country, a quite bitter division developed between the two organizations.[7] Because of its association with the War Department, the Emergency Employment Committee was able to mobilize a great deal of general support throughout the country. The National Association of Manufacturers, for example, passed a resolution urging Congress to authorize an emergency appropriation to cover Colonel Woods's employment work. In a veiled reference to the USES, the resolution noted that Woods's organization was "efficiently and impartially administered." The National Industrial Conference Board passed a similar motion at its 1919 convention.[8] To witness the successful operation of a separate employment service by the War Department was a galling experience for officials in the Department of Labor.

If relations with the War Department in the reconstruction period were irritating for the Department of Labor, relations with Congress could not have been worse. The great difficulty experienced by the USES in obtaining funds from Congress throughout the wartime emergency should have been a sufficient warning to Department of Labor officials. For the fiscal year 1917–18, the department had originally asked for $750,000. However, neither the Senate nor the House appropriations committees included any funds at all for the USES when they considered the deficiency bill. In the Senate, an amendment proposing a $500,000 appropriation was added to the bill, but this was finally reduced to $250,000 by the conference committee before the Urgent Deficiency Bill for the fiscal year 1917–18 was approved on October 6, 1917. It was only the intervention of the president, who allocated $825,000 on December 5, 1917, from his special National Security and Defense Fund, that enabled the USES to embark on a policy of rapid expansion in the first half of 1918.

For the fiscal year 1918–19, there were similar difficulties. The department had, in late 1917, originally asked for $750,000, but this was followed by a supplemental estimate of $1.25 million at the end of December, making a total request of $2 million for 1918–19. The House Committee on Appropriations approved an appropriation of only $1.8 million. In early June 1918, immediately after getting authorization to handle all unskilled labor recruiting and while the appropriations bill was before the Senate, the department requested additional funds in the light of its new responsibilities. The Senate Appropriations Committee was sympathetic to the needs of the USES and inserted a clause appropriating $7.5 million. This led to a clash with the House committee. Eventually, a compromise was reached on a sum of $5.5 million for 1918–19. The basis of this compromise was "the understanding between the chairmen of the two committees that we should go ahead and do the job we had to do and, if we had to, come back for more money."[9]

On the basis of this understanding the USES went ahead with a rapid expansion and by the end of December 1918, half-way through the fiscal year, had already spent $3.2 million. Recognizing the need for supplementation, the department, in early 1919, asked for a deficiency appropriation of almost $3 million to cover the projected budget deficit for the USES that would be incurred by the end of the fiscal year in June 1919. Because Congress was to adjourn on March 4, 1919, the deficiency appropriation bill had to be passed by that date.

Moreover, it was very desirable that the appropriation for the operation of the USES for fiscal year 1919–20 also be passed by March because the first session of the newly elected Republican-dominated Sixty-sixth Congress might look less favorably on the continuation of the USES than its Democrat-controlled predecessor. The original estimate for the 1919–20 fiscal year, which the Department of Labor had submitted in August 1918, totaled $14.8 million and was based on the assumption that the existing size of the organization would be doubled. After the armistice the need for such a rapid expansion was queried and department officials reluctantly agreed that it would be more appropriate "to go at it rather slowly instead of having a mushroom growth all of a sudden." The budget estimates were pared back to around $10 million, which included provision "for an extension of the service of about 25 per cent beyond its present capacity."[10]

The final session of the Sixty-fifth Congress concluded in early March 1919 without making an appropriation either to cover the shortfall in the USES appropriation for 1918–19 or to cover the operation of the service during the 1919–20 fiscal year. The deficiency bill had passed the House on February 28, 1919, with a slightly decreased appropriation for the USES of $1.8 million, but it was filibustered in the Senate even though it had been favorably reported by the Senate Appropriations Committee. It was an unexpected setback, particularly as the bill had received wide support in the press and from social welfare agencies.[11]

The secretary of labor appealed to President Wilson for assistance in the struggle, declaring that the USES had the support of "the vast majority of employers, as well as working men, throughout the country." He believed that "for many months" the USES had been subjected to "a systematic and underhanded propaganda" carried on by "the remnants of the Manufacturers Association and a few other small organizations of reactionary employers." President Wilson, who was involved in the peacemaking, was unable to offer financial assistance because his National Security and Defense Fund was exhausted.[12] This placed the USES in the unenviable position of having to make a drastic cut in projected expenditures for the last quarter of the financial year up to June 30, 1919.

The failure to pass the deficiency bill had a drastic impact on the USES. In early March, the USES was "at the zenith of its expansion . . . operating 854 offices on a budget exceeding $5,500,000 and . . . employing 4,079 salaried employes in addition to a personnel of 3,075 appointees at a nominal salary of one dollar a year." This situation changed overnight. Most branch offices had to be closed immediately: the USES was able to finance the operation of only fifty-six offices located in major industrial centers. Personnel were reduced to approximately 800.[13] However, the Washington office requested all federal state directors "to urge State and municipal authorities, welfare organizations, chambers of commerce, labor organizations, and other institutions to take over and finance, as far as possible, all offices eliminated by telegraphic order until Congress should have an opportunity to provide an appropriation." The response to this appeal was very generous and enabled 490 USES offices to be kept in operation during this period.[14] The Department of Labor had suffered a major setback, but senior officials still hoped it was only a temporary one.

To compound the injury, Congress failed to make any appropriation for the continuance of the USES during the next financial year. The Sundry Civil Bill, which eventually passed the House, did not include the amended request for $10 million made by the Department of Labor for the operation of the USES in 1919–20. Congress then adjourned before the bill reached the Senate, where Department of Labor officials had been confident that the clause would be reinserted. The omission of the clause from the House bill had not been a decision of a majority of that body but turned on a parliamentary point of order related to the fact that the USES had not specifically been created by Congress and was, technically, only a war emergency body.[15] A new appropriation bill now had to be introduced in the first session of the new Sixty-sixth Congress, which was scheduled to meet on May 19, 1919.

The size of the revised estimate for the peacetime USES had been an indication that the Department of Labor still nursed ambitions to create a centralized rather than a federal employment service. Nathan Smyth later commented that the revised estimate for $10 million, which was submitted to Congress in February 1919, was based on "a straight Federal Service without State help." He added that the revised estimate was requested on the assumption that the USES would be "a solely Federal service, a continuation, not of a cooperative service, on the basis that the service [w]as then operated" but a restructured organization.[16] In spite of the setback experienced in mid-1918, Department of Labor officials had obviously not abandoned their determination to shift the USES away from a federalist and back to a nationalist basis.

In an effort to put pressure on Congress to pass the appropriation bill, the USES had launched a major publicity campaign in the second half of February 1919. State branches of the USES were asked to inundate Congress with "favorable letters, telegrams, resolutions, etc., from your city and state" and to obtain supportive resolutions from "State, city and county legislative bodies and statements from the Governor and mayors; also from soldiers and sailors."[17] As part of the publicity campaign, the Department of Labor publicly released a letter from Secretary Wilson to Representative Edward Keating that outlined the department's policy relating to federal-state cooperation. It was obviously designed to assuage the suspicions of those who supported a federalist USES and who, no doubt, wondered why the department wanted such a large appropriation in peacetime. Secretary Wilson declared that the policy of his department was to work toward a federal, jointly funded system of employment offices, but "in order to avoid hardship and disorder" in the immediate postwar period, he felt that it was necessary for the Department of Labor "to maintain its own system of offices in every state" until such time as the state was ready to assume its responsibility.[18] It was the same rationale that the Department of Labor had used to justify the rapid expansion of the USES on nationalist lines in the first half of 1918. That explanation had failed to convince the employment experts in the states during the wartime emergency; it sounded even less convincing in peacetime.

The action of Congress over appropriations pointed up the vulnerability of the USES. The USES had no independent legislative status and had never been formally recognized by Congress. John B. Andrews, who had earlier lobbied Congress on behalf of the USES, was aware of the vulnerability of the organization and, with others, had tried to get Department of Labor officials to take some action. Such "expert advice" was ignored.[19] However, as the unsuccessful efforts to get legislation through Congress in the winter of 1917–18 had demonstrated, there was no unanimity among the supporters of the USES. No real consensus existed, either during the war or in early 1919, between senior officials in the Department of Labor and employment experts in the states on whether a permanent USES should be organized along federal or national lines, nor was there agreement on a number of specific employment issues.[20] Immediately after the armistice, Felix Frankfurter, chairman of the WLPB, again raised the issue of congressional authorization. At the beginning of January 1919, Nathan Smyth submitted "a first suggestion" for a compromise draft bill, which, on the one hand, avoided any mention of a national advisory board and, on the other, affirmed a strike policy that accorded with that adopted by the states. The proposed bill gave the USES both the right to establish local offices "in such places as may seem desirable to the Director-General" and the authority to enter into cooperative arrangements with state and municipal authorities for jointly operated and funded offices. However, senior Department of Labor officials were opposed to the proposed measure: Louis Post, in particular, was adamantly opposed to the provision relating to strike policy. Secretary Wilson again decided to take no action.[21]

John Densmore, the director-general of the USES, recognized the seriousness of the situation and the impossibility of getting any legislation through Congress without making some concessions to the states to secure their support. He convinced Secretary Wilson to call a conference of state representatives to try to get unified support behind a bill for a permanent USES. In announcing the conference, to be held April 23 to 25, Secretary Wilson stated that its purpose was "to define and establish the most effective form of relationship between National and State employment activities," which would then form the basis for draft legislation for a permanent USES.[22] Approximately fifty representatives of the state governors and eleven representatives of the Department of Labor attended the conference. Calling the conference was a clear admission of defeat for the nationalist policy of the Department of Labor. Secretary Wilson was signaling a radical change of course and a willingness, finally, to compromise. Given the mood of Congress, he now needed the full support of the states.

At the conference, Densmore invited Fred Croxton of Ohio, a longtime opponent of the Department of Labor's centralist aspirations, to lead the discussion. Croxton read out the draft of a bill prepared by a "small committee of employment experts" as a basis for discussion. The bill proposed the creation of an employment service in the Department of Labor, to be in the charge of a director-general appointed by the president. The director-general was charged with establishing a national system of employment offices, "maintained so far as possible in cooperation with States, municipalities, and other political subdivisions," and was empowered to enter into cooperative agreements with individual states to obtain federal funds on a matching dollar-for-dollar basis provided the state employment system abided by the rules and regulations issued by the USES. There was no mention of an advisory council, a strike policy, or the licensing of private employment agencies. Croxton and his federalist supporters were also prepared to compromise.

After considerable debate, the meeting established a special committee with authority to draft a bill that would incorporate the sense of the discussion. The committee was to report the next day. The proposed bill presented by the committee clearly spelled out the role of the USES in the states: it was to establish its own offices only in states that did not maintain employment offices; it was to maintain a role in clearing labor between states; it was to gather and disseminate information on labor conditions throughout the country; and it was to establish uniform policies and administrative procedures. Matching federal funds were to go to states that had established their own employment services, and an appropriation of four million dollars was mentioned as the sum needed to develop the service in the fiscal year 1919–20. The bill also proposed to establish an advisory council to the director-general composed of three representatives of employers, three of labor, and three of the public. The nine representatives were to include three women.

The draft bill was subjected to much criticism and was referred back to a subcommittee for further discussion. When it was reintroduced, discussion centered on the proposed advisory council. The clear provision that an advisory council would be appointed was amended to suggest that such a body "may also be appointed by the President." The amended draft bill, which contained the revised clause on the appointment of the advisory board and which specified that one of the assistant director-generals should be a woman, was then unanimously adopted by the conference.[23] There was no mention of either strike policy or the licensing of private employment agencies in the bill.

Secretary Wilson, however, would still not accept the compromise proposed by the conference. He objected even to the watered-down provision for an advisory council and, at his insistence, all mention of it was taken out of the proposed legislation. The amended bill was then sent to the chairman of the Senate Committee on Education and Labor and to the chairman of the House Committee on Labor. On May 31, 1919, Representative John Nolan, a Republican from California, introduced the bill (HR 4305) in the House and, on June 6, Senator William S. Kenyon of Iowa, another Republican, introduced an almost identical bill (S 1442) in the Senate.[24] On May 23, Democratic senator Joseph Robinson of Arkansas had introduced a similar bill (S 688) in the Senate, which included a vague provision that "an advisory board may also be appointed by the President." There was no mention in any of the bills of strike policy.

In effect, the terms of the final compromise were that the Department of Labor agreed to a genuinely cooperative federal, rather than national, USES in return for agreement that there would be no national advisory council and that the department's strike policy would, in effect, be retained. Unlike the bill originally drafted by Smyth in January, neither the Nolan nor the Kenyon bill mentioned strike policy. Nor did any of the bills mention the licensing or regulation of private agencies; this was obviously now perceived to be too much of a political liability.[25] The three bills were referred to the Joint Committee on Labor and hearings on the proposed legislation began on June 19 and lasted until July 23, 1919.[26] The hearings gave an opportunity for friends and foes to state their cases.

By mid-1919, when the congressional hearings commenced, the major criticisms of the USES had been well rehearsed. Most of the issues had been raised, if in muted form, during the war; after the armistice, critics became more vocal. USES officials were used to the allegations of political partisanship in appointments and of pro-union leanings in policy. Secretary Wilson admitted that there had been some complaints about the political affiliations of a few individuals appointed to the USES, but these, he claimed, were confined to "a very few States." Densmore stated that he was surprised that the USES had been "so free from political urging for appointments." He believed that, far from being a partisan vehicle of the administration, in most states the USES offices contained more Republicans than Democrats.[27]

Secretary Wilson met the criticism of pro-unionism head-on. He defended the action of the USES in recruiting only union men for the Seattle shipyards on the ground that a closed shop agreement already existed in that city between the unions and the yards, which gave the USES no option but to recruit union men. He pointed out that, at the same time, the USES was recruiting hundreds of thousands of workers for the Atlantic and Gulf Coast shipyards, where, because no such closed shop agreements existed, no questions about union affiliation had ever been raised. It was not the function of the government, Secretary Wilson declared, "to promote the theory of trades-unions." To counter the allegation of union bias in appointments within the USES, Smyth produced a list of federal directors in all the states and the District of Columbia together with a statement of their occupations and whether or not they belonged to unions. Only five of the forty-nine were current union members.[28]

The other major allegation of pro-union activity was the Muskegon incident, which had been given a great deal of publicity by the Metal Trades Association and the National Association of Manufacturers in their drive to destroy the USES in the first half of 1919. It concerned some USES examiners who, in the fall of 1918, had been recruiting skilled workers out of nonessential industries in Michigan. One of the examiners, when invited to address a local meeting of the union to which he belonged, gave a brief speech encouraging members in their struggle against the open shop. Informers at the meeting immediately notified the local employers' association and the incident was publicized around the country as an attempt by the USES to force the unionization of open shop manufacturing plants. Densmore countered the allegation by suggesting that the constant harping on this single, unfortunate incident at Muskegon indicated that the critics had been unable to find any substantial evidence to support their charge of a pro-union bias in the USES.[29] The accusation, however, was damaging.

Department of Labor officials knew that the USES was vulnerable to criticism concerning the administration of the service and the efficiency of its personnel. Both the National Association of Manufacturers and the National Industrial Conference Board had recently passed resolutions highly critical of the administration of the USES.[30] However, among organized employers, the USES still had the support of the U.S. Chamber of Commerce and a large number of other employer bodies.

Employment managers were divided in their attitude toward the USES. At the congressional hearings, Mark M. Jones, director of personnel at the Thomas A. Edison Industries in New Jersey and the executive secretary of the National Association of Employment Managers, criticized the proposed bill on the ground that it would perpetuate "the present administration of the employment service." He added that the "great majority" of employment managers were "thoroughly disgusted" with the wartime administration of the USES.[31] On the other hand, Dudley R. Kennedy, formerly director of labor at the Goodrich Rubber Company, who was in charge of wartime labor relations at the giant Hog Island shipyard complex near Philadelphia, felt that the USES had been "a very useful instrument during the war." Kennedy, like Jones, had spent some time in Washington as an adviser to the USES during the reorganization in the summer of 1918 and had an inside knowledge of its operations. He supported the proposed legislation and believed that "progressive manufacturers" were also in favor of it. He thought that many employment managers were "quite unreasonably critical" of the USES.[32]

At the congressional hearings, William E. Hall, director of the Organization Division of the USES, who had been intimately involved in the administration of the USES throughout the war, freely admitted that there had been a number of internal problems. In an oblique reference to the struggle between Densmore and Louis Post, Hall spoke of the lack of a "strong, consistent directing policy" and the "uncertainty as to the location of final responsibility" within the organization that had undermined good administration. He also agreed that there had been "too much shifting in organization and in division of responsibility between Washington and the States."[33] For those who understood the long, internecine administrative struggle over the organization of the USES that had gone on both within the Department of Labor and between that department and the states, Hall's testimony was a model of understatement.

Concerted opposition to the continuation of the USES from private employment agencies was predictable. The fact that the Kenyon-Nolan bill avoided all mention of private employment agencies did not eliminate the private agencies' intense suspicion of federal motivation. A number of USES officials had made no secret of their desire to eliminate private agencies altogether. Secretary Wilson himself felt that, because profits were tied to turnover, there was "a tendency toward dishonesty in connection with the very nature of the business itself." The attitude of the secretary of labor was supported by evidence submitted by Smyth and Hall on the considerable profits garnered from workmen by the approximately 4,000 private employment agencies across the country.[34]

The question of the desirability of a national advisory board or committee was also canvassed at the congressional hearings. Secretary Wilson made his position quite clear. The creation of a national advisory commission was the one recommendation of the April conference that he had been unable to accept because he felt that the advice given by such a body would be impossible to reject even when it directly conflicted with departmental policy.[35] Not all members of the Department of Labor felt so strongly about this issue. Among others, John Densmore, the director-general of the USES, and Royal Meeker, the commissioner of labor statistics, did not oppose the idea of an advisory council. Other witnesses at the hearings, who represented a number of state employment services, enthusiastically endorsed the idea of such a national advisory committee as a way of ensuring complete impartiality on the part of the USES.[36]

Coupled with his refusal to countenance an advisory council, Secretary Wilson had also insisted on his definition of an appropriate strike policy for the USES. He believed that the USES should not supply labor to a plant where a strike had been called.[37] Aware of Secretary Wilson's strong views on the subject, the conference had avoided all reference to strike policy in the draft bill. Within his own department there were many who would have preferred to adopt the approach to strikes taken by most states.[38] Even the secretary of the AFL favored the strike policy adopted by the states. Louis T. Bryant, commissioner of labor in New Jersey, believed that Secretary Wilson's policy had been a mistake and had fostered the erroneous assumption that the USES "was run in the interests of organized labor, that it was controlled by organized labor, and that there was a very decided preference given to organized labor."[39]

In the congressional hearings in June and July of 1919, there was no disagreement among the various parties over the cooperative, federalist structure of the proposed peacetime USES. Officials in the Department of Labor made clear their unqualified support for such a body.[40] Those involved in the state employment systems had fought for this outcome for more than two years. Organized labor supported the proposed bill, although it was clear from the hearings that union members would continue to use union business agents and not the USES in seeking employment. The survival of the USES was seen to be desirable but was not a matter of primary concern to the organized labor movement.[41] Even the representative of the National Association of Manufacturers supported the federal character of the USES contained in the proposed bill, although he was suspicious of the Department of Labor's power to set standards and regulations; he also thought the lack of some kind of advisory board was an additional stumbling block.[42]

Because the previous session of Congress had failed to pass appropriations to cover either the USES operating deficiency for 1918–19 or the projected operating expenses for 1919–20, the new Congress had to address these issues immediately. By mid-June, a deficiency bill appropriating $200,000 to make up the deficit incurred in operating the USES in the 1918–19 fiscal year had successfully passed Congress. However, the appropriations bill for 1919–20 was stalled. The Department of Labor's further amended request for the operation of the USES was $4.6 million, but the House Appropriations Committee had reported out only a sum of $200,000 to maintain the service for the year, with the express provision that no money be spent outside the District of Columbia. USES officials anticipated that this restriction would be removed in the Senate and the appropriation increased to $2 million for a six-month period.[43] Even the $200,000 was struck out of the House bill on a point of order by Representative Thomas L. Blanton, a Democrat from Texas, the third occasion on which he had successfully prevented money being appropriated to the USES on a technicality.[44]

However, after much parliamentary maneuvering, the Sundry Civil Bill for the fiscal year ending June 30, 1920, was finally approved on July 19, 1919. It formally authorized the secretary of labor to operate a nationwide system of employment offices in coordination with the states, but it carried an appropriation of only $400,000 for the operation of the USES for the twelve months. It was stated in the congressional debates that the appropriation was merely an emergency appropriation to enable the Department of Labor to continue the USES until Congress enacted formal legislation in the wake of the hearings being held on the subject. On that basis, the Department of Labor decided to expend the $400,000 allocation on the basis of a five-month period, from July through November 1919, with the expectation that by November the Kenyon-Nolan bill would have been enacted into law together with a sizable appropriation.[45] In fact the latter bill remained stalled in Congress and was never passed.

The failure of Congress to pass the Kenyon-Nolan bill was the final blow. On September 30, 1919, John Densmore was obliged to send telegrams to all federal directors of the USES advising them that, because of the lack of congressional funding, all USES offices in the states were to be closed down by October 10. Activities of the USES would be confined to "maintaining an effective clearance system" between states and "collecting and disseminating information as to general employment conditions." It was anticipated that the existing cooperation of state and municipal employment offices and civic organizations would be maintained and in return the USES would furnish "franking privilege, supplies and forms, equipment and possibly small allotments for clerical assistance and transportation."[46]

It was over. The dream of building a national employment service had been shattered. The related vision of building the Department of Labor into a major federal department based on the Employment Service had also collapsed. In mid-1918, when Congress had finally appropriated more than $5 million for the expansion of the USES, one observer in the department had commented that Densmore, Smyth, Hall, and other senior administrators were "very strong in the statement that within six months the Labor Department will be the strongest in the Administration."[47] The demise of the USES one year later was a bitter end to that aspiration.

Fundamentally, the Department of Labor had never been able to build a sufficiently strong coalition of political groups willing to support the USES. It had never been able to eradicate completely the distrust of its administrative capacity and impartiality, particularly among other government departments and agencies. The long struggle over the stucture of the USES had left the states and the professional employment experts wary of the aspirations of the Department of Labor. Even the AFL, which did support the proposed legislation, made it clear that the USES was of secondary concern; by mid-1919, there were much more serious issues facing the AFL than the survival of an organization that its members would seldom, if ever, use. Employer groups were divided in their support. The failure of the predicted postwar unemployment crisis to materialize during 1919 weakened support for the USES and indirectly assisted the delaying tactics adopted by its opponents.[48]

But it was also a story of missed opportunities. In late 1918 and early 1919, there was a good deal of support for the USES throughout the country; the experience with the community labor councils and the state advisory bodies, in particular, had reassured many skeptics. However, the department itself had dissipated this support by failing to recognize early enough that it would have to give up its ambition to build a centralized national service independent of the states. It was not until late February 1919 that senior officials finally recognized the political reality of the situation and decided to accept a genuinely federal cooperative service rather than continue the attempt to create an independent centralized national service. It also abandoned any direct effort to regulate private employment agencies.

Yet, even at this late stage, Secretary Wilson was unwilling to compromise on two other key issues—the establishment of a national advisory council for the USES and the adoption of a strike policy favored by the state employment services. On these two issues, which had the capacity to defuse the critical issue of administrative partiality, he was intransigent. Secretary Wilson's refusal to countenance either proposal weakened support for the USES among its friends and left it vulnerable to attack from its enemies. As a consequence, a vocal minority was able to delay congressional action until the widespread support, which had emerged by the time of the armistice, changed to neutrality in the second half of 1919 as the labor market returned to normal. Secretary Wilson and his senior officials in the Department of Labor had gambled and lost. It would be another decade, and in response to another national crisis, before the opportunity to secure formal congressional authorization for the USES again presented itself.

CHAPTER TEN

Postwar Reckoning

The wartime USES had been a success, albeit a qualified one. It never became the sole channel for the distribution of labor during the war, although by late 1918 it was beginning to approach that ideal and had certainly become the most significant, single influence on the national labor market. In the period of its greatest influence, between January 1918 and June 1919, inclusive, the USES registered slightly more than 7 million workers, referred 6.5 million to employers, and placed just under 5 million. Total orders from employers numbered just over 12 million.[1]

Most of the placements made by the USES were in war industries, where it was estimated that approximately 7 million men and around 2 million women were employed. The work often involved moving labor across state lines: by the second half of 1918, the USES was moving approximately 3,000 unskilled laborers per week to positions outside their own states. Increasing numbers of women were registering at USES offices. Between July and December 1918, just over 382,000 women obtained positions through the USES and a further 356,985 did so in the first six months of 1919.[2] While interpreting with any precision the statistics of the wartime period is difficult, the record of the USES nevertheless appears impressive.[3]

This achievement was undoubtedly assisted by circumstances. It was not until the summer of 1918 that a serious labor shortage developed and, by that time, the USES had been substantially reorganized and was beginning to function effectively. However, the precise magnitude of the labor shortage in late 1918 remains unclear. One contemporary economist believed that, even during the war, there were never less than a million unemployed although there were many jobs available that went unfilled.[4] The

ACTIVITIES OF THE UNITED STATES EMPLOYMENT SERVICE FROM
JANUARY, 1918, TO JUNE, 1919, INCLUSIVE, BY MONTHS

Month	Registrations	Help wanted	Referred	Reported placed
1918				
January	82,353	89,002	62,642	51,183
February	92,452	92,594	70,369	58,844
March	144,156	177,831	118,079	100,446
April	195,578	320,328	171,306	149,415
May	206,181	328,587	179,821	156,284
June	246,664	394,395	221,946	192,798
July	282,294	484,033	250,152	217,291
August	555,505	1,227,705	500,510	395,530
September	531,226	1,476,282	513,662	362,696
October	594,737	1,588,975	606,672	455,931
November	744,712	1,724,943	748,934	558,569
December	549,593	1,024,330	525,486	392,934
1919				
January	587,200	730,881	514,436	372,186
February	496,299	487,475	406,824	299,118
March	523,736	539,393	440,833	327,660
April	364,061	387,256	309,158	232,135
May	487,929	510,689	424,738	333,587
June	449,155	519,485	404,948	319,813
18 month total	**7,133,831**	**12,104,184**	**6,470,516**	**4,976,320**

Source: *Report of the Director-General, USES* (August 15, 1919), 935.

enormity of the labor turnover, coupled with the paucity of accurate statistics on movements in the labor market, made it impossible to determine
whether or not there was a genuine, national labor shortage by late 1918.
What was absolutely clear was that employers, particularly in the industrial
Northeast, were unable to find and keep sufficient labor to meet their urgent needs.

Any attempt to monitor and to impose some degree of control over the
national labor market in World War I faced almost insuperable odds. For
the Department of Labor, the smallest and least distinguished among federal departments, to attempt to do so almost singlehandedly was to demonstrate an audacity of Napoleonic proportions. Yet, for a time, the
department's dream of organizing the entire wartime labor market, under

the umbrella of a USES organized on nationalist principles, seemed within its grasp. In the spring and summer of 1918 that dream faded. Subsequent attempts to revive it in the immediate postwar period failed.

Any attempt to regulate the labor market had to overcome the barrier posed by the lack of accurate, up-to-date information on how the market operated. Policy was developed on the basis of informed guesswork about the national demand for labor and the available supply. Attempts to develop more accurate information as to the operation of the labor market proceeded haltingly. It was not until the fall of 1918 that the USES developed fairly reliable estimates of supply and demand. In 1919, the economist Don D. Lescohier, commenting on the weekly collection of labor statistics gathered by the USES in the latter part of the war, remarked: "For the first time in its history, the nation was able to obtain reliable information upon the *current* demand and supply of labor in all sections of the country. . . . Labor market data, comparable with stock and commodity market data, were available."[5] The USES made an important initial contribution to the collection of labor market statistics, although, like much else, this initiative was abandoned in the postwar period.

The USES faced other perplexing structural problems. The extremely high labor turnover persisted in spite of various attempts to control it. In the first half of 1918, when the USES was struggling to build its organization, the labor situation steadily deteriorated: "Employers were recklessly bidding against each other for men. Labor scouts infested every large manufacturing center."[6] By the time of the armistice, the USES was developing some innovative methods of combating the labor turnover, but they came too late to have widespread effect. Another problem was the acute shortage of skilled labor throughout the country. Differential wage rates in various sections of the country further hampered the efforts of the USES to move labor to areas of acute national need. These perplexing factors worked to produce a chaotic situation in the wartime labor market and hindered USES efforts.

These structural problems were compounded by the failure of the USES to attract support in the wider community. The two groups with an obvious interest in the operation of the labor market—employers and unions— were both lukewarm in their support. Many employers were suspicious of the Labor Department's motives, fearing that it was "an adjunct of the American Federation of Labor." Others had no faith in the administrative capacity of the USES to provide the labor they requested. Overcoming the reluctance of employers to patronize the service was a major obstacle facing those in charge of the USES throughout the war. Organized labor shared a similar attitude toward the USES: most unions were composed of skilled workers who regarded all employment offices, including the USES, as a service provided primarily for the unskilled. Most unions provided their members with informal assistance in obtaining employment that completely bypassed the USES.[7]

It was not until the fall of 1918, with the creation of state advisory boards and community labor boards, that the USES began to generate more widespread support among employers, unions, and the community at large. The new policy was announced in early July and, by November, 1,644 community labor boards were in operation.[8] Composed of local employers, union representatives, and women, the boards were just beginning to demonstrate their effectiveness and to build support for the USES when the armistice was signed. The boards were a clear signal that the USES was trying to be genuinely neutral as between labor and capital, and their existence "struck at the very roots of that prejudice against employment offices which has been so serious an obstacle to their improvement."[9]

This inability of the USES to generate community support until late in the war was mirrored in its relations with other government departments and wartime agencies in Washington. Senior officials in the War Department remained skeptical of the administrative competence of USES officers both during and after the war. The Department of Agriculture kept the USES at arm's length; although maintaining cordial relations with the Department of Labor, administrators in the Department of Agriculture did their best to minimize the role of the USES in supplying agricultural labor. The Railroad Administration managed to avoid having anything to do with the USES except on its own terms.

However, if the USES had difficulty generating community support, this did not necessarily indicate widespread disagreement over the need for greater centralization and government regulation. By early 1918, there was growing agreement within the administration and among employment experts on the need for greater government involvement in the labor market. The disagreement focused on the proposed unitary administrative structure of the USES and the determination of Department of Labor officials to duplicate the placement role of state employment offices. There was a widespread feeling that officials in the Department of Labor were more concerned with enhancing the position of their department in the national administration than with providing an effective mechanism for meeting the wartime labor crisis or the long-term needs of the labor market. Those who viewed employment office work as primarily a state responsibility, although one requiring guidance and encouragement from the national government, had the support of the recently organized professional group of employment experts, the American Association of Public Employment Offices. This group, which reflected both state interests and professional expertise, ensured that the federalist viewpoint was heard in Washington.

The magnitude of the problems in the national labor market and the lack of support within the wider community were compounded by the actions of the Department of Labor itself. The strike policy adopted by the USES at the insistence of Secretary of Labor Wilson undercut employer support. In spite of opposition from employment experts in the various states, and the example of the British employment service, Secretary Wilson refused to permit any agency of the Department of Labor to supply information concerning employment opportunities at plants where strikes were in progress. In the prewar period, most state employment systems followed the British example by accepting notifications of vacancies from employers but telling workers that a strike was in progress. This seemed a more neutral policy than the one adopted by Secretary Wilson which, in the eyes of employers, seemed to favor organized workers. Shortly after the armistice, in January 1919, the director-general of the USES, at the direction of the secretary of labor, reaffirmed the policy.

Within a year the situation had changed so drastically that Secretary Wilson was obliged to reverse his stand. On January 7, 1920, John Densmore, the director-general of the USES, pointed out that the field activities of the USES were now "confined exclusively to cooperation with states and municipalities" and that fourteen of those states, including the major industrial states of Massachusetts, New York, New Jersey, Ohio, Pennsylvania, and Illinois, had state labor laws under which state employment offices were, if requested, directed to advertise employment opportunities at strike-bound plants while, at the same time, informing applicants that a strike or lockout or other labor disturbance existed. Given this situation and the miniscule federal grants made to the states for employment work by the USES, Densmore felt that it would be foolish to continue to insist that the states accept the department's strike policy. "To insist on this policy, it is believed, would result in the termination of our present cooperative arrangement, and without obtaining the results desired." In spite of his earlier intransigence on the issue, Secretary Wilson finally accepted the logic of the argument and reversed his stand.[10] The USES ceased to have a policy on strikes: each cooperating state employment office could adopt its own policy.

Until very late in the war the Department of Labor also remained impervious to criticisms of its administration. As a consequence, the taint of administrative ineptitude clung to the USES throughout the war. The Seattle imbroglio, the Shipyard Volunteer Campaign, and the uneven quality of USES personnel made most employment experts wary of national initiatives in this field. The very unequal burdens placed on individual states by indiscriminate USES recruiting for war projects in the latter part of 1917 and the first half of 1918 further heightened the suspicion of centralized power and warned of the need to protect state interests. Because of the very uneven distribution of war contracts the greatest demand for labor came from the northeastern industrial states, which developed an insatiable appetite for labor. States outside that region began to demand that the USES provide a rational system of state quotas to ensure that each state provided a proportionate share of the labor needed in the Northeast. Inadequate statistical information made it impossible for the USES to comply with this request. However, the work of the community labor boards in shifting labor from nonessential to essential industries during the final months of the war had begun to address this problem.

The lack of adequate statistical information on the operation of the labor market created enormous friction within the administration of the USES, particularly in relations between Washington headquarters personnel and the various state directors. The state directors had the difficult and, at times, contradictory task of balancing state and national priorities. Like the administrators called from the private sector by the War Industries Board to oversee the industrial mobilization, the USES state directors, like Leo Korper in Connecticut, had to maintain a delicate equilibrium: they wanted to preserve the fundamentals of the status quo whether in business-government relations or in the comparative labor market advantages of individual states and, at the same time, to respond to national needs. They were forced to arbitrate between pressing national needs and the insistent demands of their local constituencies.[11] Recognizing the limits of available labor market information in Washington, they were determined to limit what they felt were excessive national demands for labor placed on their states.

The reluctance of Congress to finance government intervention in the labor market was a further obstacle confronting the USES. As in other parts of the homefront mobilization, the pervasive spirit of voluntarism in the wider community helped overcome congressional parsimony. A very significant portion of the work of the USES, for example, relied on wartime volunteers rather than regular employees. Two important organizations, the Public Service Reserve and the Boys' Working Reserve, relied almost entirely on this pervasive voluntarist spirit. The development of the 1,644 community labor boards, also staffed by volunteers, which were in operation by November 1918, was both a further example of the pervasiveness of voluntarism in the community and an indication of a model of government operation quite different from the hierarchical, centralized, and bureaucratic one embodied in the early USES.

Although Congress had been niggardly with appropriations during the war, the Department of Labor had been able to exercise a great deal of independence; but, once the war ended, Congress reasserted its rights and gave much closer scrutiny to the functions of the USES. USES administrators had anticipated that the transition from war to peace would have a very disruptive effect on the domestic labor market and would thus give the USES an opportunity to demonstrate its value in peacetime. The extraordinarily smooth transition that took place confounded these hopes. The economy proved able to absorb the returning soldiers and switch to normal production without difficulty. Because a number of other agencies, most notably the War Department, stepped in to assist the returning soldiers in finding work, the USES could not even claim much responsibility in that area.

In these circumstances the USES had little defense against congressional efforts to prune it back. The secretary of labor initially requested a budget of $15 million for 1919–20, which assumed a doubling in the size of the USES. However, sensing the extent of opposition, he reduced his request to $10 million in February 1919. Congress eventually adjourned without passing this bill or the deficiency appropriation bill to cover additional expenditures incurred in 1918–19. This, together with the failure of Congress to pass the Kenyon-Nolan bill in 1919, ended the dream of the USES becoming a powerful influence on the peacetime labor market. Wholesale retrenchments had to be made and the USES became a shadow organization dependent entirely on the cooperation of the states.[12]

Two national conferences at the very beginning of the 1920s seemed to offer an unexpected opportunity for resuscitating the USES. In 1920, President Wilson's Second Industrial Conference addressed the issue of unemployment and recommended "a national system of employment exchanges, municipal, state, and federal, which shall in effect create a national employment service."[13] Nothing came of the recommendation. A sharp recession in 1921 caused President Warren Harding to call a Conference on Unemployment in September–October of that year. This was another opportunity to muster support for a rejuvenated USES along federalist lines, and both John Andrews and William Leiserson "energetically worked the committees to obtain an endorsement of substantial action."[14] The conference passed a strong resolution urging the establishment of a permanent federal system of employment offices based on the state as the operating unit and with advisory committees established at the national, state, and local levels. The conference also recommended a special appropriation of $400,000 to make possible the proposed expansion of the USES.[15] The outcome of the conference indicated the continuing strength of those who favored a genuinely federal USES and, for a brief moment late in 1921, it seemed that a rejuvenated USES along federalist lines would be created. Congress, however, pigeonholed the proposal.

The USES remained a skeletal organization throughout the 1920s. It operated no local employment offices, except for seasonal farm labor, and its annual appropriations "hovered around the $225,000 mark."[16] The main work of the USES during the decade was concentrated in the Washington office, which was organized into a general administrative office and four technical divisions. These divisions covered cooperation with states and municipalities; the gathering of industrial employment information; the distribution of farm labor; and junior placement and guidance. In all areas the work done was very limited.

The most important work undertaken in the postwar period concerned relations with the various states and municipalities. The USES attempted to maintain the semblance of a national presence by means of individual cooperative agreements. By the mid-1920s, such agreements had been made with twenty-eight states and twelve municipalities.[17] A cooperative agreement usually specified that the director of the state employment service would be appointed as the federal representative of the USES at a nominal salary and, in return for the franking privilege and a modest federal subsidy, would submit a weekly report covering the activity of the employment offices in his state.[18] The amount of the federal subsidy was related to the amount spent by the state on employment work. In 1924, the USES allocated $79,150 to forty states and municipalities. The grants ranged between a low of $710 to Maryland and a high of $4,320 given to both New Jersey and New York.[19] The overall proportion of federal funds contributed to the state system throughout the decade remained pathetically small. In 1930, for example, federal funds constituted only 3.9 percent of the total annual expenditure of state employment offices.[20] In practice, the USES was reduced to an information gathering role and was totally dependent upon state cooperation.

The work of the industrial employment information division kept alive an important wartime function of the USES. The major work undertaken was a regular survey of "general and specific industrial employment conditions, the distribution of labor, and the fluctuations in employment throughout the country." A monthly bulletin, the *Industrial Employment Information Bulletin,* summarized this information both by industrial groups and by geographical regions. By 1922, this employment survey was based on payroll figures of firms "usually employing 501 or more in 65 of the principal industrial centers of the country, which embrace 1,428 firms employing more than 1,600,000 workers." The same firms were contacted each month. In addition, special agents serving at nominal salaries gathered comments on industrial and employment conditions in 355 industrial centers.[21] The survey offered, in effect, a rough index of employment fluctuation in manufacturing industries throughout the nation.

However, even in this important area the USES seemed unable to respond to criticism. One statistician observed that, given some relatively minor alterations in the methods used to collect the figures, they could furnish "a thoroughly reliable index of employment fluctuation for the country as a whole, and also reliable indexes both for particular industries and for individual cities." No other series of employment statistics offered such detailed information on both particular industries and specific geographical areas.[22] Given the dearth of statistical information on the labor market in the early 1920s, this was an important activity.[23] However, the reliability of the methods used by the USES to gather the statistical information came under increasing criticism, and formal publication of the statistics was finally discontinued in late 1922. Once again, the USES seemed incapable of responding constructively to outside criticism. Although no longer publicly distributed, the USES continued to collect employment statistics throughout the decade.[24]

The function of the Junior Division was to provide information on business developments and employment opportunities to the public schools. The expectation was that such information would assist the schools to estimate the current job market and, where necessary, to introduce curriculum changes to meet changing business demands. The division also established junior placement offices in a few public schools, which involved the appointment of the associate superintendent of the school district as a federal representative on a nominal salary.[25] Each local office was required to send weekly reports on its activities to Washington. The Junior Division offered advice, and representatives made periodic visits to monitor the work being done and to keep the local office informed of new developments. By 1925, the Junior Division had established local offices in twenty-nine cities in fifteen different states.[26] It was a very small-scale operation affecting only a minute proportion of the juvenile population. However, it did keep alive the earlier reformist commitment that had surfaced within the USES late in the war.

The Farm Labor Division was the only federal division established during the war that survived relatively intact through the 1920s. It retained its function of recruiting seasonal harvest labor primarily for the "Big Wheat Belt." This activity usually began in early June in the northern part of Texas and slowly moved northward through Oklahoma, Kansas, Missouri, and Nebraska, ending in the Dakotas around mid-September. Up to 100,000 workers were recruited from outside these states and the obvious interstate character of the work seemed to warrant special USES assistance. A permanent, central office was maintained in Kansas City with another office at Sioux City, Iowa, operated with the aid of that state. During the harvest season approximately forty temporary offices were also opened to assist in guiding the harvesters northward. The success of the USES offices depended on close cooperation between the USES officers and the county farm agents in the various states.

Although the results seemed moderately satisfactory, the approach adopted by the Farm Labor Division was rather crude and represented a reversion to the much criticized, indiscriminate recruiting methods used earlier by the Department of Labor. The USES made widespread use of posters displayed in post offices: in the 1919 campaign, posters were displayed in thirty-nine different states.[27] This information was supplemented with mimeographed material detailing wage rates, numbers required, estimated dates of the harvest, and the location of local employment offices and county farm agents. One investigator noted that during the 1919 harvest season, although the information provided by the USES was not completely accurate or up-to-date, it had probably removed "at least 50 per cent of the uncertainty and misinformation of the harvest situation."[28] However it was a step back from the more exact meshing of labor demand and supply that had been advocated by employment experts.

As farming became more mechanized throughout the decade the need for seasonal harvest hands gradually declined and the attention of the Farm

Labor Division began to shift to other seasonal occupations covering a wider group of states.[29] By 1931, for example, it was claimed that the division had been responsible for "recruiting and directing 400,000 cotton pickers . . . 20,000 cotton choppers, 10,000 mesquite and cactus grubbers, 100,000 small grain harvesters, 50,000 berry pickers, 25,000 fruit pickers, 25,000 vegetable workers, and 40,000 miscellaneous seasonal farm laborers."[30] This claim doubtless exaggerated the direct role of the USES, but it did indicate the increasing diversity of the seasonal farm labor serviced by the Department of Labor in conjunction with the state employment offices.

If the federalists won the wartime struggle over the first USES, neither they nor the nationalists could claim victory in the postwar reconstruction. The emaciated organization that survived into the 1920s represented a stalemate rather than a victory for either side. The federal structure of government in the United States shaped the manpower mobilization both during and after the Great War. The long struggle between federalists and nationalists over the nature of government intervention in the labor market helps explain the ambivalent response to the first USES. It was not until 1933 that Congress, in the Wagner-Peyser Act, finally resolved the issue by creating a USES that clearly embodied federalist principles.

The history of the first USES is not easily accommodated by existing theories. Neither interest group theory nor neo-Marxist theory fits easily over the events. However, one conclusion that seems clear is the ability of senior government bureaucrats, in certain circumstances, to impose their views regardless of the degree of support these views enjoy in the wider community. It was the determination of Assistant Secretary of Labor Louis F. Post, in particular, to build a centralized employment system, independent of the states, that precipitated the long, wartime administrative struggle over the USES. Post very nearly won. It was only a combination of chance events that gave another wartime administrator, Felix Frankfurter, the chairman of the War Labor Policies Board, the opportunity to raise the issue again in mid-1918 and—eventually, with the assistance of key employment experts— to reverse Post's policy. Secretary Wilson's refusal to accept a national advisory board undercut support for the USES, as did his insistence on a particular strike policy that was opposed by most groups associated with employment work and that had only muted support even from organized labor. The failure of Department of Labor officials, in the immediate aftermath of the war, to recogize the political hazards involved in resurrecting the specter of a centralized USES doomed whatever chance the service had of maintaining a major role in the national labor market. If political ineptitude and ideological intransigency doomed the efforts of the Department of Labor, what is remarkable is the degree of autonomy, both in promoting their own program and blocking alternatives, that those senior administrators demonstrated. Although their plans were eventually frustrated, the war had offered a tantalizing window of opportunity.

Epilogue

Keeping the Federalist
Faith, 1920–1933

The postwar depression at the beginning of the 1920s briefly focused public attention on unemployment and on the role of public employment offices, but this interest soon waned. The USES and its parent body, the Department of Labor, faded into obscurity under successive Republican administrations during the decade. Those outside the national administration who had been advocating a federalist style of national employment service tried to keep the issue alive, but without much success. Congress remained skeptical about the value of such an organization in spite of lobbying efforts. It was not until the economic collapse of the Great Depression that interest in the problem of unemployment and in the role of a national public employment system revived. Even then, it was not until 1933, with the return of the Democrats to power in Washington, that the USES was finally given formal legal status by Congress and the long struggle between the nationalists and the federalists over the structure of that body was finally resolved.

If the Department of Labor had lost all ability to influence events during the postwar decade, the employment experts located in the states did not give up hope of securing congressional support for a revived USES structured along federalist lines. Shortly after the armistice, the Russell Sage Foundation announced that it would conduct a detailed survey of public employment offices in order to learn from their wartime experiences what kind of employment system was best suited to American conditions. In early 1919 a small group of advisers, consisting of William M. Leiserson, Charles B. Barnes, Louise C. Odencrantz, Bryce M. Stewart, and Mary

Van Kleeck, was appointed to assist in the planning of the project. Leiserson and Barnes were well known for their federalist views. In the second half of 1919 a group of specially appointed researchers, all of whom had some experience in either public or private employment work, visited seventy cities in thirty-one states and Canada. Special attention was paid to the work done in Ohio, Wisconsin, New York, and Massachusetts. By late 1920, a preliminary draft of the manuscript had been written, although the final version was not published until November 1924.[1]

The Russell Sage study concluded, after an exhaustive examination of the various types of employment offices and the great variety of existing practices, that there was a clear need for a nationwide employment system based on federal-state-local administration. Although acknowledging that a case could be made for a purely centralized, national system, the report concluded that "existing conditions" and "practical considerations" made a federated system of federal-state-local administration a more appropriate and attainable goal. To ensure the nonpartisan character of the service, the report recommended the establishment of a national advisory board appointed by, and directly responsible to, the President. The report also referred to the need for a strike policy that would guarantee the neutrality of the service—a clear criticism of the wartime policy of the Department of Labor.[2] The report, in fact, constituted further support for the position advocated by the employment experts located in the state employment offices and in the AAPEO. Croxton, who was quoted a good deal throughout the report, must have been pleased with the final recommendations.

Also in 1924, William M. Leiserson published *Adjusting Immigrant and Industry,* one of a series of eleven books on aspects of Americanization funded by the Carnegie Corporation. The first three chapters made a sustained plea for a revitalized USES organized on federalist lines. Leiserson felt that such a publicly funded employment agency would be of immense benefit to immigrants. In the early chapters, Leiserson described the problems facing immigrants trying to find work in American industry and argued for a government-funded placement service for immigrants that would be part of a national employment service available to all workers. Drawing specifically on the USES experience in World War I, he argued in favor of a federal rather than a unitary, nationalist type of organization. During the war, he recounted, the USES was not originally built on federalist assumptions, but the pressure of "public opinion . . . and the force of the circumstances of placement" eventually forced the Department of Labor to reverse its policy. Congress, he argued, should pass a law creating, "after the

manner of the highway and vocational education laws, a federal administrative body, with authority to supervise and aid states which adopt the law
and operate local employment offices in accordance with placement policies devised or approved by the national authority."[3]

Throughout the 1920s individual congressmen continued to introduce legislation designed to establish the USES on a formal basis. Bills to provide
for a federal-state system of employment agencies financed by federal grants-
in-aid, with matching state appropriations, were introduced in every Congress. In 1921, for example, Senator William Kenyon of Iowa, and in 1925,
Representative Mae Ella Nolan, widow of the former Republican representative from California, reintroduced bills to establish a national employment service, but both were shunted aside. However, by the late 1920s rising levels of unemployment once more began to spur congressional interest
in public employment offices.

In early 1928, the Democratic senator from New York, Robert F. Wagner,
introduced a bill (S 4157) that practically repeated the original Kenyon-
Nolan proposals of 1919. Like those bills, Wagner's bill had been drawn up
in consultation with John B. Andrews of the American Association of Labor Legislation. The bill was buried in committee, but two years later, in
January 1930, in the immediate aftermath of the stock market crash, Wagner
reintroduced the bill (S 3060). Sentiment in Congress by then was changing and the bill received a favorable hearing in committee and passed the
Senate comfortably. However, it was kept from a vote in the House.

As pressure mounted for some federal action to alleviate the rising unemployment, President Herbert Hoover, alarmed by the federal grant-in-
aid feature of the proposed bill, attempted to sidetrack the issue with a
counterproposal in the form of a bill prepared by William N. Doak, his
new secretary of labor. Doak's bill, in essence, proposed to expand the existing USES along nationalist lines, but it was roundly defeated in the House.
Going one step further, the House then passed the Wagner bill on a voice
vote and sent it to the Senate, which also passed it. By this time it was late
February and Congress adjourned on March 4, 1931. Three days later, with
unemployment figures reaching unprecedented levels, President Hoover
vetoed the bill.[4]

Hoover, however, had decided that positive action was required. In a
move that echoed the Department of Labor's earlier, centralist response to
the wartime crisis, he moved to reorganize and vastly expand the existing
USES without obtaining formal legislative sanction for the organization.

In March 1931, John R. Alpine, a former vice president of the AFL who had become a business executive, was appointed a special assistant to the secretary of labor. Then, on April 18, Secretary of Labor Doak announced a complete reorganization of the USES. In addition to reorganizing the Washington office, forty state directors were to be appointed and at least one employment office was to be opened in each state, with suboffices established "from time to time as circumstances justify." A special appropriation of $500,000 was rushed through Congress. It was with a sense of *déjà vu* that state employment officials watched the USES appoint state directors and establish local employment offices throughout the country in direct competition with existing state employment offices.[5] The specter of a resurgent USES, organized on nationalist lines, had suddenly reappeared, this time under a Republican rather than a Democratic national administration.

The "Doak reorganization" prompted a resurgence of all the wartime fears of state employment experts concerning the motives of the federal administration. Rumors coming out of Washington indicated that no consideration was being given to whether or not the individuals appointed as state directors "had any experience in labor placement."[6] In fact, the entire exercise looked like an effort to buy the support of organized labor by giving well-paid jobs "to fifty or more A.F. of L. officials in the U.S. Employment Service." The administration seemed to be trying to force William Green, the president of the AFL, to reverse his attitude and to secure the support of organized labor for the "Doak reorganization."[7]

The rapid expansion of the reorganized USES into the states provoked as much irritation on the part of state officials as the wartime expansion of the USES had done. In mid-1932, R. G. Knudsen, one of the industrial commissioners in Wisconsin, wrote to Senator Robert La Follette complaining of the actions of the USES both in Wisconsin and elsewhere. In Minneapolis, the USES had opened an employment office "a block and a half from the state office"; in Des Moines, the USES had "opened an office directly across the street from the state office." A similar situation had developed in New York State. He could only conclude that this meant "nothing less than direct competition on the part of the federal department with the employment services rendered by the states."[8]

By June 1932, the USES had established a total of 151 independent employment offices. These included the offices of the forty-nine state directors, thirty veterans' offices (a special Veteran's Division of the USES had been established in 1930 in response to pressure from the American Legion), twenty farm labor offices, and fifty-two branch offices. Excluding the farm labor and the veterans' offices, the USES established independent employment offices in ninety-six cities, in fifty-three of which the states were already operating at least one employment office. Of the thirty veterans' offices, twenty-one were placed in cities that also had a newly established USES office. Moreover, there was no cooperation at all between the veterans' offices and the USES offices. Special demonstration centers, "which served as laboratories in which procedure, technique, and general operation can be tried and tested," had been established by state employment services in five major cities throughout the country. In four of them, additional and separate USES offices were opened.[9] The entire expansion of the USES reeked of politics and expediency.

The Social Science Research Committee of the University of Chicago decided to finance an investigation of the reorganized USES in 1932. It was undertaken by Ruth M. Kellogg, who, beginning in mid-August 1932, spent twelve weeks in the field visiting employment offices and conferring with interested parties in sixteen states. Her book, which came out strongly for the Wagner bill, was published in early 1933. Kellogg commented that, in her research, she had tried to ascertain the principles on which cities had been chosen by the USES and had been repeatedly told "by those well qualified to know, that it was politics."[10] The entire "Doak reorganization" only made sense in political terms. This view had also been expressed by the professional employment experts. In September 1931, the annual meeting of the International Association of Public Employment Services (formerly the AAPEO) had passed a formal resolution condemning the entire reorganization.[11]

At the elections in November 1932, the Democrats were swept into power. At the beginning of the new Congress in 1933, Wagner once again introduced his bill. With the economy in a deep depression, the bill, known as the Wagner-Peyser Act, had a swift passage through both houses and was signed into law on June 6, 1933, by the new president, Franklin D. Roosevelt. At long last, Congress and the executive branch had formally conferred independent, legal existence on the USES. The bill represented the final victory of those who had fought for a genuinely federal USES over the previous two decades. The issues that had divided USES supporters throughout this period had finally been resolved.

The newly created USES was "to assist in establishing and maintaining systems of public employment offices in the several States" and was to coordinate these state agencies "by developing and prescribing minimum standards of efficiency" and by "promoting uniformity in their administrative and statistical procedure." In addition, it was to maintain "a system for clearing labor between the several States." In order to encourage the states to cooperate, a system of matching grants was introduced: $1.5 million was appropriated for the first year and $4 million per year for the succeeding four years. The franking privilege was also extended to participating state offices.

The contentious issues of advisory boards and strike policy were also finally resolved. The new USES was to have a federal advisory council "composed of men and women representing employers and employees in equal numbers and the public" that would formulate general policy and oversee the operations of the organization. Similar advisory councils were to be established in each state. The legislation also spelled out the strike policy that would guide the new organization: the director of the USES was "authorized and directed to provide for the giving of notice of strikes or lockouts to applicants before they are referred to employment." The strike policy adopted by the states, which had been very reluctantly accepted by Secretary Wilson in 1920, had now been enshrined in federal legislation.[12] It was an appropriate symbol of the final victory of the federalists over the nationalists in the protracted struggle over control of the national labor market.

It had been a long, exhausting struggle. Fred Croxton, whose work in Ohio and in Washington during the war had done so much to strengthen the hand of the federalists, had kept the faith. Only three years before, at the 1930 conference of the International Association of Public Employment Services in Toronto, he had reiterated his long-held, federalist beliefs concerning public employment offices.[13] Others had also kept the faith. William Leiserson, for example, who had assisted Croxton both in the prewar reorganization of the Ohio employment offices and in the wartime reorganization of the USES, had continued to promote the cause throughout the 1920s.[14] The passage of the Wagner-Peyser bill reflected the final triumph of that federalist vision of the appropriate relationship between federal and state authority in the labor market.

Notes

Introduction

1. The statistics are drawn from the *Second Annual Report of the U.S. Employment Service (August 15, 1919)*, 66th Cong., 2d sess., H. Doc. 7734, 63:898–99.
2. See, for example, David M. Kennedy, *Over Here: The First World War and American Society* (New York: Oxford Univ. Press, 1980), 258–70; Valerie Jean Conner, *The National War Labor Board: Stability, Social Justice, and the Voluntary State in World War I* (Chapel Hill: Univ. of North Carolina Press, 1983). If the war resulted in greater government intervention in the economy and accelerated trends toward centralization and consolidation, it was also true that the outcome often proved more ambiguous in practice than such a straightforward model of change suggests. For a detailed example of the ambiguity that could surround greater centralization and government intervention in World War I, see Robert D. Cuff, *The War Industries Board: Business-Government Relations during World War I* (Baltimore: Johns Hopkins Univ. Press, 1973).
3. For a study of the effect of crisis on government growth, see Robert Higgs, *Crisis and Leviathan: Critical Episodes in the Growth of American Government* (New York: Oxford Univ. Press, 1987); see also Julie Z. Strickland, "War Making and State Building: The Dynamics of American Institutional Development, 1917–1935" (Ph.D. diss., Stanford University, 1988).
4. Stephen Skowronek, *Building a New American State: The Expansion of National Administrative Capacities, 1877–1920* (New York: Cambridge Univ. Press, 1982), 8.
5. Ellis W. Hawley, "Social Policy and the Liberal State in Twentieth-Century America," in Donald T. Critchlow and Ellis W. Hawley, eds., *Federal Social Policy: The Historical Dimension* (University Park: Pennsylvania State Univ. Press, 1988), 120.
6. Hawley, "Social Policy and the Liberal State," esp. 119–25. See also Ellis W. Hawley, "The Discovery and Study of a 'Corporate Liberalism,'" *Business History Review* 52 (Autumn 1978): 309–20; Louis Galambos, "Technology, Political Economy, and Professionalization: Central Themes of the Organizational Synthesis," *Business History Review* 57 (Winter 1983): esp. 478–85; Donald T. Critchlow, *The Brookings Institution, 1916–1952: Expertise and the Public Interest in a Democratic Society* (DeKalb: Northern Illinois Univ. Press,

1985), 3–16; Stephen D. Krasner, "Approaches to the State: Alternative Conceptions and Historical Dynamics," *Comparative Politics* 16 (Jan. 1984): 223–46.

7. For a recent discussion of the different models of state building and the emergence of this more state-centered view, see Melvyn Dubofsky, *The State and Labor in Modern America* (Chapel Hill: Univ. of North Carolina Press, 1994), intro. See also Theda Skocpol, "Political Response to Capitalist Crisis: Neo-Marxist Theories of the State and the Case of the New Deal," *Politics and Society* 10 (1980): 155–201; Fred Block, "The Ruling Class Does Not Rule," in idem, *Revising State Theory: Essays in Politics and Postindustrialism* (Philadelphia: Temple Univ. Press, 1987),51–68; Louis Galambos, "Technology, Political Economy, and Professionalization," esp. 478–85; Jonathan Zeitlin, "Shop Floor Bargaining and the State: A Contradictory Relationship," in Steven Tolliday and Jonathan Zeitlin, eds., *Shop Floor Bargaining and the State: Historical and Comparative Perspectives* (Cambridge: Cambridge Univ. Press, 1985), 1–45, esp. 16–31; Gerald Berk, "Corporate Liberalism Reconsidered: A Review Essay," *Journal of Policy History* 3, no. 1 (1991): 70–84.

8. Dubofsky, *The State and Labor*, xv.

9. Hawley, "Social Policy and the Liberal State," 125.

10. Although the term "manpower policy" was not used during World War I, it is used throughout this study to describe government policy specifically related to the labor market as distinct from the more inclusive term "labor policy," which, in addition to labor market concerns, also incorporates broader industrial relations issues.

11. "Historically, the Labor Department and its associated agencies lacked the administrative capacity, as defined by budgets, bureaucratic scale and skill, and a history of triumphs, to turn their policies into unchallenged writ." Dubofsky, *The State and Labor*, 234. On "administrative capacity," see also Skocpol, "Political Response to Capitalist Crisis," esp. 173–75.

12. Galambos added, "For the most part they [historians] have been no more interested in the intricacies of administrative history than have the American people. Only in recent years have they begun to describe and analyze some aspects of the elaborate bureaucratic structures that have come to characterize our federal government in this century." See Louis Galambos, "By Way of Introduction" in idem, ed., *The New American State: Bureaucracies and Policies since World War II* (Baltimore: Johns Hopkins Univ. Press, 1987), 5.

13. For the best introduction to this literature, see Mary O. Furner and Barry Supple, eds., *The State and Economic Knowledge: The American and British Experiences* (New York: Woodrow Wilson Center Press and Cambridge Univ. Press, 1990); and Michael J. Lacey and Mary O. Furner, eds., *The State and Social Investigation in Britain and the United States* (New York: Woodrow Wilson Center Press and Cambridge Univ. Press, 1993).

14. For more detail on this incident and on the sources for this study, including a detailed discussion of the secondary literature on the USES, see the "Essay on Sources" at the end of this volume.

1. State Initiatives and National Ambitions
Origins of the U.S. Employment Service

1. For recent work on unemployment, see Alexander Keyssar, *Out of Work: The First Century of Unemployment in Massachusetts* (Cambridge: Cambridge Univ. Press, 1986); Paul

T. Ringenbach, *Tramps and Reformers, 1873–1916: The Discovery of Unemployment in New York* (Westport, Conn.: Greenwood Press, 1973); John A. Garraty, *Unemployment in History: Economic Thought and Public Policy* (New York: Harper and Row, 1978). See also Walter Licht, *Getting Work: Philadelphia, 1840–1950* (Cambridge, Mass.: Harvard Univ. Press, 1992).

2. *American Labor Legislation Review* 5 (June 1915): 173. Although in this period there were a number of surveys and reports attempting to measure with some precision the extent of unemployment, the results must be treated with some caution because of the inadequacy of the information-gathering process. By the eve of World War I, "no means to achieve satisfactory results had yet been worked out." See Udo Sautter, *Three Cheers for the Unemployed: Government and Unemployment Before the New Deal* (Cambridge: Cambridge Univ. Press, 1991), 42–51.

3. Quoted in Sautter, *Three Cheers for the Unemployed*, 30 (see also 26–31).

4. Ibid., ch. 2.

5. Ellen Fitzpatrick, *Endless Crusade: Women Social Scientists and Progressive Reform* (New York: Oxford Univ. Press, 1990), 130–37, 157–59.

6. The British system was organized on a grand scale. In the first two years of operation, 430 exchanges were opened together with 1,066 subagencies. See B. Lasker, *The British System of Labor Exchanges*, U.S. Bureau of Labor Statistics (hereafter BLS) Bulletin No. 206 (Washington, D.C., October 1916), 8.

7. J. Michael Eisner, *William Morris Leiserson: A Biography* (Madison: Univ. of Wisconsin Press, 1967), 30–35.

8. Sautter, *Three Cheers for the Unemployed*, 41–42, 68.

9. Don D. Lescohier, *The Labor Market* (New York: Macmillan, 1919), ch. 4, esp. 113.

10. Sumner H. Slichter, *The Turnover of Factory Labor* (New York: D. Appleton, 1919), ch. 2, esp. 20–22.

11. Lescohier, *Labor Market*, 117.

12. U.S. Commission on Industrial Relations, *Final Report and Testimony Submitted to Congress by the Commission on Industrial Relations Created by Act of August 23, 1912*, 64th Cong., 1st sess., 1916, S. Doc. 415. (11 vols.), vol. 1:109–11.

13. See William M. Leiserson, "The Movement for Public Labor Exchanges," *Journal of Political Economy* 23 (July 1915): 707.

14. *Final Report and Testimony of Commission on Industrial Relations* 1:113.

15. Lescohier, *Labor Market*, chs. 6–7. See also Sautter, *Three Cheers for the Unemployed*, 52–94.

16. Leiserson, "Movement for Public Labor Exchanges," 708–9. On Ohio, see William J. Breen, "The Labor Market, the Reform Impetus, and the Great War: The Reorganization of the State-City Employment Exchanges in Ohio, 1914–1918," *Labor History* 29 (Fall 1988): 475–97.

17. The relationship between the new Department of Labor and the American Federation of Labor was close. A recent study argues that "the Department of Labor aggressively advocated trade unionism's case inside the administration. . . . As he [Secretary Wilson] wrote to Gompers after eight years of service as secretary, the most important of his department's duties was 'to have someone as its directing head who can carry the viewpoint of labor into the councils of the President.' Whenever possible he [Secretary Wilson] chose appointees sympathetic to the labor movement or drawn directly from

the trade unions. . . . In a real sense, then, the Labor Department acted as organized labor's advocate in Washington." Melvyn Dubofsky, *The State and Labor in Modern America* (Chapel Hill: Univ. of North Carolina Press, 1994), 54. However, Secretary Wilson saw the role of the Department of Labor as more than a mouthpiece of the AFL. Although a keen advocate of trade unionism and sympathetic to AFL initiatives, he and his trusted lieutenant, Assistant Secretary Louis Post, wanted the new department to be an independent institution representing all workers, not merely an adjunct of the union movement. See John Lombardi, *Labor's Voice in the Cabinet: A History of the Department of Labor from its Origins to 1921* (New York: Columbia Univ. Press, 1942), 92–95.

18. Lombardi, *Labor's Voice in the Cabinet,* esp. ch. 15.

19. See U.S. Department of Labor, *Report of the Secretary of Labor, 1913,* quoted in Lombardi, *Labor's Voice in the Cabinet,* 150. See also ibid., 144–51.

20. Lombardi, *Labor's Voice in the Cabinet,* 91.

21. Ibid., 357.

22. U.S. Department of Labor, Bureau of Immigration, *Report of the Commissioner General of Immigration, July 1, 1914,* Appendix II, "[T. V. Powderly], Report of the Chief of the Division of Information, August 1, 1914," 63d Cong., 3d sess., H. Doc. 1555, 300.

23. U.S. Department of Labor, *Fourth Annual Report of the Secretary of Labor, June 30, 1916,* 64th Cong., 2d sess., H. Doc. 7205, 56. The report includes a complete list of the employment offices, which makes the overlap with the Immigration Bureau obvious. Existing immigration stations, staffed by immigration officers, were used as the branch employment offices in each of the eighteen zones initially established throughout the United States. See also Lombardi, *Labor's Voice in the Cabinet,* 152.

24. *Final Report and Testimony of Commission on Industrial Relations* 2:1309 (testimony of Terence V. Powderly, May 20, 1914). Leiserson, who cross-examined Powderly before the commission, was highly critical of this rather amateur approach to employment work.

25. Lombardi, *Labor's Voice in the Cabinet,* 152–53.

26. For copies of the correspondence (and the constitution that was adopted), see *Proceedings of the American Association of Public Employment Offices, Annual Meetings: First— Chicago, Dec. 19 and 20, 1913; Second—Indianapolis, Sept. 24 and 25, 1914; Third—Detroit, July 1 and 2, 1915,* BLS Bulletin No. 192 (May 1916), 8–10.

27. Leiserson, "Movement for Public Labor Exchanges," 712. For Leiserson's reminiscences concerning the formation of the association, see "What Constitutes a Good Employment Service," *Proceedings of the Sixteenth Annual Meeting of the International Association of Public Employment Services, held at Cleveland, Ohio, September 18-21, 1928,* BLS Bulletin No. 501 (Oct. 1929), 21–29.

28. See "Report of the Committee on Standardization [presented and adopted at the fifth annual meeting of the association (AAPEO) held at Milwaukee, Wis., Sept. 20 and 21, 1917]," BLS *Monthly Review* 5 (Nov. 1917): 116 [950].

29. For a comment on the success of the policy in Wisconsin see *Final Report and Testimony of Commission on Industrial Relations* 1:355 (testimony of William M. Leiserson, Dec. 30, 1913).

30. Ibid., 348.

31. For a convenient summary of existing legislation concerning private employment agencies, see Mabelle Moses, "The Regulation of Private Employment Agencies in the United

States," in Susan M. Kingsbury, ed., *Labor Laws and Their Enforcement with Special Reference to Massachusetts* (1911; reprint, New York: Arno and the New York Times, 1971), ch. 6.

32. The resolution adopted at the Indianapolis meeting, on September 25, 1914, read: "That this association go on record as favoring the elimination, as soon as possible, of all private employment agencies operating for a profit within the United States." See *Proceedings of the American Association of Public Employment Offices: Annual Meetings, . . . 1913 . . . 1914 . . . 1915,* 141. Not all members of the association favored this approach. See "Relation of Public to Private Employment Offices—Discussion" (Dec. 1913); M. B. Hammond, "Regulation and Control of Private Employment Agencies" (Sept. 1914), 38–39, 79–80. For a discussion of the 1914 annual conference including a brief report on the session on private agencies, see Charles B. Barnes, "Unemployment and Public Responsibility," *Survey* 33 (Oct. 10, 1914): 48–50.

33. Barnes, "Unemployment and Public Responsibility," 49; *Proceedings of the American Association of Public Employment Offices, Annual Meetings, . . . 1913 . . . 1914 . . . 1915,* Appendix A, 141.

34. W. M. Leiserson to R. H. Seager, Mar. 12, 1915, William Morris Leiserson Papers, Professional Correspondence, box 36, file: "Seager, R. H., 1910–1924," State Historical Society of Wisconsin, Madison. Leiserson had served as the very successful director of the Wisconsin public employment offices in 1911–13.

35. For a detailed report on the conference including the verbatim address by Secretary Wilson, see BLS *Monthly Review* 1 (Oct. 1915): 5–13. The 1915 conference produced few tangible results; it did, however, elect an advisory board to survey members on how best to achieve cooperation between federal and state employment offices. Copies of the survey replies (32 pp.) from thirteen respondents, including Leiserson, are contained in RG 183, Bureau of Employment Security, U.S. Employment Service (USES), box 1515, Junior Division, Personnel, file: "Early USES material, 1907–Nov. 1918" [marked in pencil on side of folder], National Archives, Washington, D.C. (NA). See also Sautter, *Three Cheers for the Unemployed,* 87–88.

36. *National Employment Bureau, Hearings* (1916), 13–14 (testimony of Secretary of Labor, Hon. William B. Wilson, Feb. 3, 1916). A recent historian has claimed that "the main push for federal intervention in the employment exchange field appears to have come from the Department of Labor's bureaucratic desire to enlarge its area of responsibility." See Udo Sautter, "Unemployment and Government: American Labour Exchanges before the New Deal," *Histoire Sociale—Social History* 18 (Nov. 1985): 340.

37. *National Employment Bureau, Hearings* (1916), 36, 42 (testimony of Royal Meeker, commissioner of Labor Statistics, Feb. 10, 1916).

38. In 1916 the Department of Labor began to experiment with individually tailored cooperative agreements with various state employment offices. Only a few of these proposed agreements were actually put into practice, and they failed to promote either harmonious cooperation or increased efficiency. See William M. Leiserson, "The Labor Shortage and the Organization of the Labor Market," *Survey* 40 (Apr. 20, 1918): 68. See also chs. 3 and 10 below.

39. See, for example, W. M. Leiserson to G. R. Taylor, Jan. 25, 1915. Leiserson Papers, Professional Correspondence, box 39, file: "Survey Associates, Inc., 1911–1932." Even Royal Meeker, who favored a centralized system in the abstract, recognized that it was not

172 NOTES TO PAGES 16-22

attainable at that time. See his testimony in *National Employment Bureau, Hearings* (1916), 36 (testimony of Royal Meeker, Feb. 10, 1916).

40. William M. Leiserson, "A Federal Labor Reserve Board," *Proceedings of the Fourth Annual Meeting of the American Association of Public Employment Offices, Buffalo, N.Y., July 20 and 21, 1916,* BLS Bulletin No. 220 (1917), 33–45. Leiserson also published two similar versions of this paper: "A Federal Labor Reserve Board: Outlines of a Plan for Administering the Remedies for Unemployment," *National Conference of Charities and Correction: Proceedings, 1916,* 43d Annual Session, Indianapolis, May 10–17, 1916, 161–76; and "A Federal Reserve Board for the Unemployed," *Annals of the American Academy of Political and Social Science* 69 (Jan. 1917): 103–17.

41. See Sautter, "Unemployment and Government," 340–42; John B. Andrews, "A National System of Labor Exchanges," *New Republic* 1 (Dec. 26, 1914): 7–8.

42. *Fourth Annual Report of the Secretary of Labor, June 30, 1916,* 73. For more detail on the early efforts to pass legislation establishing a national employment service, see Sautter, *Three Cheers for the Unemployed,* esp. 81–88.

43. *Fourth Annual Report of the Secretary of Labor, June 30, 1916,* 73; *Fifth Annual Report of the Secretary of Labor, November 10, 1917,* 65th Cong., 2d sess., H. Doc. 7405, 93–94.

44. Leiserson, "Movement for Public Labor Exchanges," 714–15.

45. On traditional union suspicions of public employment offices, see Andrews, "A National System of Labor Exchanges," 6; "Government Labor Exchanges" (editorial), *American Federationist* 17 (Nov. 1910): 995. By 1916 the attitude of the American Federation of Labor had begun to soften a little as a result of satisfactory dealings with the better state employment bureaus. See also the survey on union and employer attitudes reported at the first annual meeting of the AAPEO in September 1914: Charles B. Barnes, "A Report on the Condition and Management of Public Employment Offices in the United States, Together with Some Account of the Private Employment Agencies of the Country," *Proceedings of the American Association of Public Employment Offices: Annual Meetings, . . . 1913 . . . 1914 . . . 1915,* 69–70.

2. Federalist Aspirations in the States

1. See Breen, "The Labor Market, the Reform Impetus, and the Great War," 475–97.

2. The Ohio Industrial Commission supervised the state's employment offices and one of Croxton's first responsibilities when he was appointed in 1913 was to overhaul their operation. In doing this he gained a reputation as one of the foremost employment office experts in the country. He was elected as the first president of the newly formed professional association, the American Association of Public Employment Offices, at its first meeting in December 1913. See ibid., 476–77.

3. Ohio Branch, Council of National Defense, *How Ohio Mobilized Her Resources for the War: A History of the Activities of the Ohio Branch, Council of National Defense, 1917–1919* (Columbus, 1919), 66–69. The number of main offices was later increased to twenty-two and suboffices were subsequently created to tap the labor resources of the small towns; by the end of the war there were forty-one state employment offices in Ohio. See also Fred C. Croxton, "War Employment Work in Ohio," BLS *Monthly Review* 4 (June 1917): 995–1002.

4. See Breen, "The Labor Market, the Reform Impetus, and the Great War," esp. 479–92.

5. *How Ohio Mobilized*, 72. Croxton had requested the assistance of C. H. Mayhugh, assistant statistician in the Ohio Industrial Commission, to operate the employment offices; he was Croxton's right hand man. For a description of the operation of the central office, see William M. Leiserson, "The Labor Shortage and the Organization of the Labor Market," *Survey* 40 (Apr. 20, 1918): 67. For further detail, see "First Annual Report, Ohio Branch, Council of National Defense, March 22, 1918" (36-page mimeo), ser. 1135, Ohio Branch—Council of National Defense Papers (hereafter Ohio Branch—CND Papers), box 4, file 5, Ohio Historical Society (hereafter OHS), Columbus.

6. Leiserson, "The Labor Shortage and the Organization of the Labor Market," 65. The Ohio employment service also dramatically reorganized the state agricultural labor market. See ibid., ch. 8.

7. "First Annual Report, Ohio Branch, Council of National Defense, March 22, 1918," 13.

8. See, for example, Croxton, "War Employment Work in Ohio"; W. M. Leiserson, "Mobilizing and Distributing Farm Labor in Ohio," BLS *Monthly Labor Review* 6 (Apr. 1918): 781–91; idem, "The Shortage of Labor and the Waste of Labor," *Survey* 39 (Mar. 30, 1918): 701–3; idem, "The Labor Shortage and the Organization of the Labor Market," *Survey* 40 (Apr. 20, 1918): 65–68.

9. Charles B. Barnes (chairman AAPEO), Hilda Muhlhauser (vice president AAPEO), and H. J. Beckerle (secretary AAPEO) to National Council of Defense, Mar. 31, 1917, RG 62, Council of National Defense (CND) Records, Committee on Labor, Chairman's Office, Correspondence, 10A-A1, box 317, file: "Coordination of Employment Agencies (Sub-Cmttee)."

10. For the complete text of the resolution, see "Proceedings of the Fifth Annual Meeting of the American Association of Public Employment Offices: Report of the Committee on Standardization," BLS *Monthly Review* 5 (Nov. 1917): 121–22 [955–56]. The members of the committee were Royal Meeker, chairman, U.S. Commission of Labor Statistics; Charles F. Gettemy, director, Massachusetts Bureau of Statistics; C. H. Mayhugh, Ohio Industrial Commission; and Luke D. McCoy, secretary, Illinois Bureau of Labor Statistics.

11. The full report of the Committee on Standardization was presented and adopted at the fifth annual meeting of the AAPEO in Milwaukee, Wisconsin, on September 20–21, 1917. That meeting also unanimously adopted a proposed draft bill for a national employment service on federalist principles drawn up by a special committee of the AAPEO for introduction into Congress. For the text of the proposed bill, see "Proceedings of the Fifth Annual Meeting," 127–30 [961–64].

12. F. Croxton to Mildred Chadsey, July 27, 1917, ser. 1135, Ohio Branch—CND Papers, box 36, folder 8. See also Chadsey to Croxton, Aug. 2, 1917, ibid., box 36, folder 8; Leiserson to Croxton, June 16, 1917, ibid., box 38, folder 2; Croxton to Leiserson, June 14, 1917, Leiserson Papers, Professional Correspondence, box 10, file: "Croxton, Fred C., 1917–1931"; W. McClellan to J. W. Sullivan, June 13, 1917, RG 62, CND Records, Committee on Labor, Chairman's Office, Miscellaneous Papers, 10C-C2, box 359, file: "Employment Agencies."

13. See "Weekly Reports of Gompers, Chairman, Committee on Labor, to W. S. Gifford, Director, Council of National Defense," June 9, 16, 23, 1917, RG 62, CND Records,

Committee on Labor, Chairman's Office, 10A-A4, box 334, file: "Gifford, W. S.—Memos and Reports."

14. Typescript headed "W. S. Gifford Report" (pp. 6–7), RG 62, CND Records, Director's Office, 2-C1, Weekly and Monthly Reports to Director, box 112. This is probably part of a monthly report from the Committee on Labor to W. S. Gifford, the director of the CND. Note that the typescript has a complete list of all who attended both meetings. See also James W. Sullivan, Jeremiah W. Jenks, and William McClellan to W. C. Redfield, July 5, 1917 (with attached list of those who attended the July 5 conference), in RG 174, Department of Labor Records, W. B. Wilson Papers, box 209, file 20/76. Those present at the July 5 conference included representatives of the following agencies: the Bureau of Commerce, the U.S. Civil Service, the Bureau of Foreign and Domestic Commerce, the Committee on Manufacture, the War Department, the Intercollegiate Intelligence Bureau, the Department of Labor, the Department of Agriculture. Representatives from the following divisions of the Council of National Defense were present: the General Munitions Board, the Committee on Women in Industry, the Section on Cooperation with States, and the Committee on Labor of the Advisory Commission. W. S. Gifford, CND director, was also present.

15. J. W. Sullivan to W. Lippmann, July 11, 1917, RG 62, CND Records, Committee on Labor, Chairman's Office, 10A-C2, box 359, file: "Employment Agencies."

16. W. B. Wilson to Messrs. James W. Sullivan, Jeremiah W. Jenks, and William McClellan, July 9, 1917, RG 62, CND: Committee on Labor, Chairman's Office, 10A-C2, box 359, file: "Employment Agencies." See also Secretary Wilson's instructions to the two representatives he sent to the conference. Secretary Wilson to C. T. Clayton and to T. V. Powderly, memoranda, July 9, 1917, RG 174, Department of Labor Records, Wilson Papers, 1913–21, box 209, file 20/76. A carbon of W. B. Wilson to Sullivan, Jenks, and McClellan is also in this file.

17. C. T. Clayton and T. V. Powderly to Secretary Wilson, memorandum, July 10, 1917, RG 174, Department of Labor Records, Wilson Papers, box 209, file 20/76. This memo contains a list of those present, which included representatives from the Agriculture, Navy, Interior, and Labor Departments; the Civil Service Commission; the General Munitions Board, CND; the Committee on Women in Industry, CND; the Committee on Labor, CND; the Intercollegiate Intelligence Bureau; and five representatives of the AFL. See also the one-page typescript report of the meeting (with list of those present) headed "A meeting was held by the Committee on Labor, Room 1042, Munsey Building, Tuesday, July 10th at 10 o'clock" (n.d.), RG 62, CND Records, Committee on Labor, Chairman's Office, Misc. Papers, 10A-C2, box 359, file: "Employment Agencies."

18. See J. W. Jenks to W. B. Wilson, Aug. 13, 1917, RG 174, Department of Labor Records, Wilson Papers, box 209, file 20/76.

19. [J. W. Jenks], "War Service Board: Needs and Work" (n.d.; 4-page transcript), attached to J. W. Jenks to W. B. Wilson, Aug. 13, 1917, RG 174, Department of Labor Records, Wilson Papers, box 209, file 20/76.

20. W. B. Hale to J. W. Sullivan, Sept. 14, 1917, RG 62, CND Records, Committee on Labor, Chairman's Office, Outgoing Letters of J. W. Sullivan, July–Dec. 1917, 10A-A6, box 336, file: "Employment Agency Letters."

21. J. W. Sullivan to Herbert Hoover, "Memorandum as to the Supply of Labor (August 15, 1917)," pp. 6–7, RG 174, Department of Labor Records, Wilson Papers, box 208, file 21/31: "Scarcity of Labor, 1917."

22. Louis Post to Secretary Wilson, memorandum re: "U.S. Employment Service," Aug. 29, 1917, William B. Wilson Papers, box "1917," file: "Employment Service, 1917," Historical Society of Pennsylvania, Philadelphia.

23. Senate Special Committee Investigating the Munitions Industry, *Council of National Defense: Minutes of the Advisory Commission,* 74th Cong., 2d sess., 1936, Committee Print No. 8 (meeting of Sept. 6, 1917), 87–88. See also *Digest of the Proceedings of the Council of National Defense During the World War,* 73d Cong., 2d sess., S. Doc. 193, 258–59; J. W. Jenks to D. Willard, Aug. 27, 1917, carbon, RG 174, Department of Labor Records, Wilson Papers, box 209, file 20/27. The proposed board was criticized by William Browne Hale, assistant chief of the State Councils Section, CND, because it lacked any representation of agricultural labor or women in industry and because "the Intercollegiate Bureau and the Engineering Council are given equal prominence with the American Federation of Labor." See W. B. Hale to W. S. Gifford, Sept. 10, 1917, copy, RG 62, CND Records, Committee on Labor, Chairman's Office, Outgoing Letters of J. W. Sullivan, July–Dec. 1917, 10A-A6, box 336, file: "Employment Agency Letters."

24. See *Council of National Defense: Minutes,* Print No. 7 (Sept. 26, 1917), 181–82. The minutes only say that the council deferred any decision. The information about the narrow vote is from Leon C. Marshall, "The War Labor Program and Its Administration," *Journal of Political Economy* 26 (May 1918): 431–32. Note that Marshall incorrectly refers to the meeting as taking place in late August instead of late September. The article contains a verbatim copy of the proposal as it was made to the Council of National Defense (p. 431). Secretary Wilson was still absent from Washington on the President's Mediation Commission trip to the West and Southwest.

25. Marshall, "The War Labor Program," 431–32; Lombardi, *Labor's Voice in the Cabinet,* 234.

26. For the text of the proposed bill see BLS *Monthly Review* 5 (Nov. 1917): 127–30 [961–64].

27. *Report of the Committee on Industry and Employment, December 21st, 1917* (New York: Mayor's Committee on National Defense, 1918), 6.

28. C. B. Barnes to J. B. Andrews, Nov. 22, 1917, American Association for Labor Legislation (AALL) Records, 1905–43, John B. Andrews Papers, ser. 1, Correspondence 1905–43, Labor-Management Documentation Center, M. P. Catherwood Library, Cornell University, Ithaca, New York.

29. *Report of the Committee on Industry and Employment, December 21st, 1917,* 6.

30. The first session of the 65th Congress lasted from April 2 to October 6, 1917. The bill was introduced in the second session, which began on December 3, 1917.

31. C. B. Barnes to J. B. Andrews, Nov. 22, 1917, AALL Records, Andrews Papers.

32. Keating had been recommended both by Grant Hamilton of the AFL and by Charles Clayton of the Department of Labor. See J. B. Andrews to C. B. Barnes, Dec. 6, 1917, AALL Records, Andrews Papers.

33. J. B. Andrews to Sen. J. Robinson, Dec. 6, 1917, AALL Records, Andrews Papers. In addition to obtaining the support of the individuals named, Charles B. Barnes sent a copy of the proposed legislation to Secretary Wilson, who was out of Washington at the time. The postscript in the accompanying letter mentioned that all reference to federal licensing of private employment agencies had been eliminated as a matter of tactics in order to avoid unnecessary opposition to the bill. See C. B. Barnes to Secretary Wilson, Dec. 4, 1917, copy attached to C. B. Barnes to F. Frankfurter, Dec. 4, 1917, RG 1, War Labor Policies Board (WLPB) Papers, Correspondence of Chairman and Exec. Secr., file: "Employment Service: May–June–July: C-l-f."

34. J. B. Andrews to C. B. Barnes (quote), and to L. C. Marshall, Dec. 6, 1917, AALL Records, Andrews Papers. See also John B. Andrews, secretary AALL, "Report of Work, 1917," *American Labor Legislation Review* 8 (Mar. 1918): 116–17. *The New Republic,* which supported the bill, referred to "both the Labor Adjustment Committee of the Shipping Board and the high officials in the Labor Department . . . insisting on the need of passing the proposed legislation." See "National Labor Exchanges," *The New Republic,* Dec. 15, 1917, 166–67. Henry R. Seager, speaking before the joint session of the AALL and the American Economic Association in December 1917, was cautiously optimistic and felt that, in spite of the disagreement over "minor features" in the bill, an acceptable compromise could be worked out and that "legislation will speedily follow." He felt that support was divided between two groups: those favoring a strong USES controlled by representatives from the departments and boards directly involved in war production and those anxious to protect the prerogatives of the Department of Labor. See H. R. Seager, "Coordination of Federal, State and City Systems of Employment Offices," *American Labor Legislation Review* 8 (Mar. 1918): 24.

35. See Gompers to Andrews, telegram, Dec. 10, and Marshall to Andrews and Andrews to Marshall, telegrams, Dec. 14, 1917, AALL Records, Andrews Papers. Andrews subsequently congratulated Marshall on his ability, during the final meetings of the committee, to "smooth out" the different viewpoints represented. See Andrews to Marshall, Jan. 17, 1918, AALL Records, Andrews Papers.

36. L. F. Post, "Report of the Assistant Secretary on Administration during the Secretary's Absence beginning September 17, 1917 (December 31, 1917)," pp. 16–17, RG 174, Department of Labor Records, Chief Clerk's File, box 132, file 129/14. Post also stated in his report that Andrews had asked him for assistance in drafting the bill. Post had referred Andrews to Charles Clayton, "who helped him in the revision by way of advice but not for Departmental purposes, and suggested Senator Robinson and Representative Keating as appropriate persons to introduce the bill" (p. 16). Barnes and Andrews had spent "half a day" with Clayton studying the projected bill, and Seager later saw Clayton and discussed with him and secured his approval of the changes the group had made. It is not surprising that this was interpreted as support from the Department of Labor. See C. T. Clayton to L. F. Post, Dec. 3, 1917 (weekly report), RG 174, Department of Labor Records, Chief Clerk's File, box 132, file 129/14. For the text of Secretary Wilson's bill, see *Fifth Annual Report of the Secretary of Labor, 1917,* 93–94.

37. Post, "Report of the Assistant Secretary on Administration during the Secretary's Absence," p. 17, RG 174, Department of Labor Records, Chief Clerk's File, box 132, file 129/14. In early January 1918, Gompers described the proposal as one establishing a "labor dictator or director, with great powers" together with an appointed board. He believed that this created an impossible situation: "In other words the Secretary of the Department of Labor might be placed in the position that a board over which he had no control and to which he was not responsible might dictate the conditions under which that great function should be performed." See "Statement made by Mr. Samuel Gompers, President of the American Federation of Labor, to Secretary Wilson in the Latter's Office on January 10, 1918," (4-page typescript), RG 174, Department of Labor Records, Wilson Papers, box 209, file 20/76.

38. Post, "Report of the Assistant Secretary on Administration during the Secretary's Absence," p. 17, RG 174, Department of Labor Records, Chief Clerk's File, box 132, file 129/14.

39. Ibid.

40. See "Statement made by Mr. Samuel Gompers," RG 174, Department of Labor Records, Wilson Papers, box 209, file 20/76.

41. Robert D. Cuff, "The Politics of Labor Administration during World War I," *Labor History* 21 (Fall 1980): 559. See also Leon C. Marshall, "The War Labor Program," 439–41.

42. The Advisory Council was comprised of former Governor John Lind of Minnesota, chairman, representing of the public; Waddill Catchings and A. A. Landon, representing employers; John B. Lennon and John J. Casey, representing labor; and Agnes Nestor, representing women.

43. For a brief outline of the work of the Advisory Council, see Gordon S. Watkins, *Labor Problems and Labor Administration in the United States during the World War*, University of Illinois Studies in the Social Sciences, vol. 8, nos. 3 and 4 (Sept.–Dec. 1919), 158–62.

44. The Advisory Council conferred with senior USES officials and also invited a group of employment experts, mainly drawn from the AAPEO, to advise it. The latter group submitted a statement of general principles that was, in effect, a restatement of the federalist principles espoused by the AAPEO and embodied in the Robinson-Keating bill. The employment experts who attended the conference were Charles B. Barnes, president of the AAPEO and director of the New York state employment service; Fred C. Croxton, ex-president of the AAPEO, food administrator of Ohio, and in charge of the Ohio state employment service; Don D. Lescohier, chief statistician of the Minnesota Department of Labor and Industries and wartime superintendent of the Minneapolis state employment office; Professor Matthew B. Hammond of Ohio State University, an economist and a former commissioner of the Ohio Industrial Commission; and C. H. Mayhugh, a statistician with the Ohio Industrial Commission, who was in charge of the central clearing office of the Ohio system of state employment offices. Both Hammond and Mayhugh had been involved in the reorganization of the Ohio state employment offices. J. W. Sullivan, representing the American Federation of Labor and Gompers' Committee on Labor of the CND-AC, also attended the meeting. See Advisory Council, "Minutes (Mtgs of January 24, 25, 26, 28, 30, February 1)," bound typescript minutes under title "The Advisory Council to the Secretary of Labor, Department of Labor, Washington, D.C., January, 1918," found in Leon C. Marshall Papers, Archive of Contemporary History, University of Wyoming, Laramie. (Another set, in the John Lind Papers, Minnesota Historical Society, St. Paul, is not as complete.) For the statement of general principles submitted by the group of experts, see "Some Outstanding Propositions" (n.d.), 2-page typescript attached to Advisory Council, "Minutes (Mtg of February 2, 1918)," Marshall Papers. Because the minutes make no reference to dissenting voices, it seems that J. W. Sullivan assented to the document. It is unclear whether Gompers was aware of Sullivan's action.

45. Memorandum from the Advisory Council to the Secretary of Labor headed "Organization of the United States Employment Service (February 6, 1918)" and typescript headed "A Bill to promote the more effective utilization of the labor resources of the nation" attached to Advisory Council, "Minutes (Mtg of Feb 6, 1918)," Marshall Papers. The memorandum recommended that the attached bill, which was a slightly amended draft of the Robinson-Keating bill, be placed before Congress. Copies of the memorandum and the text of the amended Robinson-Keating bill are reproduced in U.S. Congress,

Joint Committees on Labor, *National Employment System, Hearings,* 66th Cong., 1st sess., 1919, 475–80.

46. See, for example, John Lind to Fred Wheaton, Feb. 12, 1918, Lind Papers, P933, box 3; J. B. Andrews to Sen. Joseph Robinson and to Rep. Edward Keating (identical letters), Feb. 13, 1918, AALL Records, Andrews Papers.

47. Memorandum from the secretary of labor to the Advisory Council, Feb. 21, 1918, attached to Advisory Council, "Minutes (Mtg of Feb 23, 1918)," Marshall Papers. The Advisory Council had suggested that the USES be organized into five, rather than eight, divisions: Administration, Clearance, Supervision and Personnel, Agricultural, and Women. Secretary Wilson did simplify the USES administrative structure but retained the essentials of the existing organization. The reorganized USES contained five divisions: the Division of Information, Administration, and Clearance (the existing Division of Information inherited from the Bureau of Immigration, which was given expanded jurisdiction); a temporary Division of Training of Personnel; and the three existing divisions of Farm Service, Women, and Reserves, which remained unchanged.

48. Secretary Wilson to assistant secretary, memorandum, Feb. 22, 1918, copy in RG 174, Department of Labor Records, Chief Clerk's File, box 132, file 129/14.

3. Nationalist Initiatives in the Department of Labor

1. "Department of Labor: Plan for Extending the System of Employment Exchanges, in Cooperation with the Department of Agriculture and the Council of National Defense (Revision of July 7, 1917)," RG 62, CND Records, Committee on Labor, Chairman's Office, Miscellaneous Papers, 10A-C2, box 359, file: "Employment Agencies."

2. Compare, for example, the proposed powers of the national supervisory committee outlined in the draft versions of June 12, July 7, and August 16. See "Department of Labor: Plan for Extending Labor Exchange System, Especially to Meet the Farm Labor emergency and for Cooperation with the Department of Agriculture (Tentative Plan for Basis of Discussion)," n.d., attached to G. F. Porter, CND, to B. T. Galloway, Department of Agriculture, June 12, 1917, RG 16, Department of Agriculture: Office of the Secretary, B. T. Galloway File on National Defense, file: "Geo. F. Porter" [18.E.4., row 2, comp. 11]. Also, "Department of Labor: Plan for Extending the System of Employment Exchanges, in Cooperation with the Department of Agriculture and the Council of National Defense" and "Department of Labor: Plan for Establishing Additional Employment Exchanges within the States and Coordinating All Agencies in a National Clearing House System (Washington, D.C., August 16, 1917)," Henry Mauris Robinson Papers, container 8, file: "Council of National Defense: Labor," Hoover Institution Archives, Stanford University.

3. W. M. Leiserson, "Report of Secretary-Treasurer," Second Annual Meeting of the AAPEO, Indianapolis, Sept. 24–25, 1914, *Proceedings of the American Association of Public Employment Offices. Annual Meetings [1913–1915],* BLS Bulletin No. 192 (May 1916), 103.

4. "Memorandum of Understanding Concerning Cooperation Between the United States Department of Labor and the United States Department of Agriculture in Securing Labor for Farm Work during the Crisis arising from the Entrance of the United States in

the European War (April 27, 1917)" (copy signed by W. B. Wilson and D. F. Houston), RG 16, Office of the Secretary of Agriculture, Incoming Correspondence, "1917: Labor," acc. 234, dr. 411.

5. R. A. Pearson to F. P. Harrison, memorandum, June 21, 1917, RG 16, Office of the Secretary of Agriculture, Incoming Correspondence, "1917: Labor," acc. 234, dr. 411; see also related correspondence in "1917: National Defense (5), Labor (June–Aug.)," acc. 234, dr. 454.

6. W. E. Hall, National Director, Boys' Working Reserve (BWR), "National Director Explains Reserve," *Report of National Conference of Directors of United States Boys' Working Reserve, Department of Labor, Washington, D.C., Friday and Saturday, June 29 and 30, 1917*, pamphlet, p. 7, copy in State Council of Defense Records: Boys' Working Reserve, file: "National Conference," Illinois State Archives, Springfield.

7. Hall had an undergraduate degree from Yale, a law degree from Harvard, and was admitted to the New York bar in 1904. In 1917 he was the president of the Trojan Powder Company, the Trojan Chemical Company, and the Stackpole Carbon Company and vice president of three other companies and involved on the board of directors of a number of others. He had a lifelong concern for the welfare of underprivileged boys and was the nonsalaried president of the Boys' Clubs of America from 1916 to 1954, when he became the honorary president. He also served for thirty-two years as a trustee and vice president of the Children's Aid Society of New York. See *Who Was Who in America*, 9 vols. (Chicago: Marquis–Who's Who, 1943–89), 4:396; *New York Times*, Jan. 24, 1961, 29 (obit.); U.S. Congress, Joint Committees on Labor, *National Employment System: Hearings*, 66th Cong., 1st sess., 1919, pt. 2:298–302 (statement of William E. Hall).

8. "United States Boys' Working Reserve," undated memo attached to W. B. Wilson to "My dear Sir" (form letter), May 7, 1917, Councils of Defense Papers: State Councils of Defense, World War I, General Correspondence, 1917–19, ser. 76/1/2, box 35, file S.147: "Labor Dept.—Sec'y W. B. Wilson, U.S.," Historical Society of Wisconsin, Madison.

9. Ibid.

10. Hall, "National Director Explains Reserve," 7.

11. *Report of National Conference of Directors of United States Boys' Working Reserve*, 10.

12. Ibid., 10–11. For further detail on the work of the Boys' Working Reserve, see William J. Breen, *Uncle Sam at Home: Civilian Mobilization, Wartime Federalism, and the Council of National Defense, 1917–1919* (Westport, Conn.: Greenwood Press, 1984), 26, 105–6.

13. National Director, U.S. Boys' Working Reserve, "Memorandum for the Secretary through the Assistant Secretary," Sept. 13, 1917, RG 174, Department of Labor Records, Chief Clerk's File, box 132, file 129/14 (1). In this memo Hall noted that these assistants had recently been withdrawn and that private contributors were querying why the federal government would not provide funds for the Reserve now that it had demonstrated its usefulness.

14. W. B. Wilson to President Woodrow Wilson, Jan. 7, 1918, Woodrow Wilson Papers, ser. 4: Executive Office File, 1913–21, case file: 19-E, Manuscript Division (microfilm ed., reel 172), Library of Congress, Washington, D.C.

15. *Sixth Annual Report of the Secretary of Labor (October 31, 1918)*, 212. See also *U.S. Employment Service Bulletin* (hereafter cited as *USES Bulletin*) No. 16 (May 14, 1918), 3.

16. The connection between the USES and the Public Service Reserve (PSR) grew progressively stronger during 1918. By August 1918, the Reserve had been completely absorbed

into the USES. See chapter 6 below. See also William J. Breen, "The Mobilization of Skilled Labor in World War I: 'Voluntarism,' the U.S. Public Service Reserve, and the Department of Labor, 1917–1918," *Labor History* 32 (Spring 1991): 253–72.

17. See Post's outline of the congressional struggle over the appropriation in L. F. Post, "Report of the Assistant Secretary on Administration during the Secretary's Absence," 11–13. Some members of the department felt that Commissioner of Immigration Anthony Caminetti had deliberately thwarted the secretary's wishes and had actively lobbied congressmen to prevent the transfer of the Division of Information from his bureau. See C.T. Clayton, "Memorandum for the Assistant Secretary (September 26, 1917)," p. 5, William B. Wilson Papers, box "1917," file: "Employment Service, 1917."

18. For Post's justification of his action, see L. F. Post, "Special Report of the Assistant Secretary to the Secretary of Labor with reference to Estimates for Congressional Appropriations in support of the United States Employment Service (December 31, 1917)," p. 2, William B. Wilson Papers, box "1917," file: "Employment Service, 1917."

19. Ibid., 2. Post felt sure that Edward N. Hurley, chairman of the U.S. Shipping Board, was responsible for bringing the issue to the attention of President Wilson. The request from the president must have come as a relief to Post, because there were rumors that the Shipping Board was considering the establishment of a national network of employment offices under its own jurisdiction solely for the recruitment of shipyard workers. See C. B. Barnes to J. B. Andrews, Nov. 22, 1917, John B. Andrews Papers, Catherwood Library, Cornell University, Ithaca, New York.

20. L. F. Post to President Wilson, Nov. 27, 1917, reproduced in Post, "Special Report . . . with reference to Estimates for Congressional Appropriations . . . (December 31, 1917)," 2–4.

21. In his estimates, Post projected the establishment of one hundred federal employment offices, twenty district offices, and a force of one hundred traveling examiners.

22. Post, "Special Report . . . with reference to Estimates for Congressional Appropriations . . . (December 31, 1917)," 4–6.

23. See text of Post's departmental order dated December 13, 1917, reproduced in full as "Exhibit B" attached to Post, "Report of the Assistant Secretary on Administration during the Secretary's Absence."

24. Gordon S. Watkins, *Labor Problems and Labor Administration in the United States During the World War,* University of Illinois Studies in the Social Sciences, vol. 8, nos. 3 and 4 (Urbana, 1919), 185–86; Darrell H. Smith, *The United States Employment Service: Its History, Activities and Organization* (Baltimore: Johns Hopkins Univ. Press, 1923), 34. The Division of Information (now called Information, Administration, and Clearance) was eventually restored to the Bureau of Information on July 1, 1918. The various division chiefs appointed in January 1918 were Terence V. Powderly, Division of Information; Hilda Muhlhauser Richards, Woman's Division; William E. Hall, Division of Reserves; A. L. Barkman, Farm Service Division; Alexander D. Chiquoine, Jr., Division of Investigation; Charles T. Clayton, Division of Service Offices; Royal Meeker, Statistical Division (under Bureau of Labor Statistics). See *USES Bulletin* 1, no. 1 (Jan. 28, 1918), 4.

25. See Post, "Report of the Assistant Secretary on Administration during the Secretary's Absence," 15. Post had orginally suggested that the Public Service Reserve and the Boys' Working Reserve be treated as separate divisions making a total of eight. He also urged that Charles T. Clayton, his private secretary whom he had placed in charge of the service, be made permanent director, and that Hilda Muhlhauser Richards be made

assistant director. Secretary Wilson appointed John B. Densmore, solicitor of the department, as director, with Charles T. Clayton as assistant director in charge of field work and quasi-official bodies, and Robert Watson, formerly chief clerk of the department, as assistant director for administrative work. Hilda Muhlhauser Richards was appointed to head the Woman's Division.

26. U.S. Congress, House Appropriations Committee, *Sundry Civil Bill, 1919: Hearings Before a Subcommittee of the Committee on Appropriations, House of Representatives, on Sundry Civil Appropriation Bill, 1919,* 65th Cong., 2d sess., 1918, 1587 ("Memoranda submitted by Department of Labor," n.d.).

27. Watkins, *Labor Problems and Labor Administration,* 187.

28. Lombardi, *Labor's Voice,* 194.

29. These figures are drawn from the lists published regularly in the *USES Bulletin.* They include offices that were cooperating with the USES but were, effectively, state financed and state controlled. The exact number of wholly federally financed offices at any one time is difficult to establish with certainty partly because of the range of different agreements with different states and partly because of the persistent effort of Department of Labor to count all offices that were even remotely cooperating as USES offices.

30. *Sundry Civil Bill, 1919: Hearings,* 1573 (Densmore testimony, May 1, 1918).

31. Ibid., 1596 ("Memoranda submitted by Dept. of Labor").

32. Ibid., 1589, 1593; *USES Bulletin* 1, no. 16 (May 14, 1918), 6.

33. *Sundry Civil Bill, 1919: Hearings,* 1573–74 (Densmore testimony, May 1, 1918).

34. *USES Bulletin* 1, no. 4 (Feb. 18, 1918), 3.

35. H. Reid to L. F. Post, memorandum "Concerning the affiliations of the State Directors of the U.S. Employment Service," n.d. [Aug.–Sept. 1918], RG 174, Department of Labor Records, Chief Clerk's File, box 133, file 129/14F. Because the amount of information on the forty-two state directors listed in the memorandum varies considerably, the statistics quoted are approximate only.

36. These states were Arizona, Colorado, Georgia, Oklahoma, Minnesota, Wisconsin, Illinois, New Jersey, and Massachusetts. The nature of the cooperation varied. See *Sundry Civil Bill, 1919: Hearings,* 1588 ("Memoranda submitted by the Department of Labor," n.d.).

37. For the list of the state directors appointed, see *USES Bulletin* 1, no. 23 (July 2, 1918), 4. A formal, cooperative agreement, however, did not necessarily guarantee a harmonious relationship between state authorities and the Department of Labor. Pennsylvania, for example, cooperated with the USES and signed a detailed agreement in May 1918 that appeared to establish a unified federal-state employment service. However, the Department of Labor continued to maintain a separate USES office in Philadelphia, which created enormous friction and confusion. Wanting cooperative agreements with state employment services while at the same time maintaining independent USES offices inevitably created resentment on the part of the states and generated suspicion of the motives of the Department of Labor. See E. C. Felton, "Final Report of the Department of Civilian Service and Labor of the Pennsylvania Council of National Defense, January 31, 1919," esp. pp. 1–12, Pamphlets, Newspapers, Clippings, folder marked: "Committee of Public Safety (G. W. Pepper, Chairman) Memo," Papers of the Committee of Public Safety of the Commonwealth of Pennsylvania, 1917–21, Historical Society of Pennsylvania, Philadelphia.

38. William M. Leiserson, "Organizing the Labor Market for the War and after the War (March 29, 1918)" (unpublished ms.), p. 10, Leiserson Papers, box 48, file: "Speeches and Articles, 1918–1921."

39. William M. Leiserson, "The Labor Shortage and the Organization of the Labor Market," *Survey* 39 (Apr. 20, 1918): 68.

40. Leiserson, "Organizing the Labor Market for the War," 5.

41. Ibid., 11.

42. Ibid., esp. 4–5. See also chapter 4 below.

43. Leiserson, "Organizing the Labor Market for the War," 6, 8–9.

4. The Seattle Labor Market Experiment

1. Robert H. Ferrell, *Woodrow Wilson and World War I, 1917–1921* (New York: Harper and Row, 1985), 99–102. See also David M. Kennedy, *Over Here: The First World War and American Society* (New York: Oxford Univ. Press, 1980), 304–5, 325–26, 329. Had the war lasted into 1919 or 1920, ship production would have been very impressive. In fact, by the time of the armistice only 178 ships had been finished.

2. See chapter 3 above.

3. Frederick L. Allen, "The Council of Defense System: A History submitted to the Director of the Council of National Defense (May 5, 1919)," 135–36, RG 62, Council of National Defense Records, Files and Records Division (Post-War), 17-B.1., Administrative File, box 1053.

4. On the attitude of Bryant, see Claude H. Anderson, secretary, New Jersey State Council of Defense, to Frederic E. Foster, assistant secretary, New York State Council of Defense, Jan. 28, 1918, New York State Defense Council Records: U.S. Public Service Reserve, box 17, file: "Miscellaneous Correspondence of State Director: N," New York State Archives, Albany.

5. Charles A. Munroe, chairman, Public Service Reserve Committee, Illinois State Council of Defense, "Public Service Reserve Committee [Final Report], (December 3, 1918)," in *Final Report of the State Council of Defense of Illinois, 1917–1918–1919* (Springfield, 1919), Appendix 20, 246.

6. *How Ohio Mobilized Her Resources for the War* (Columbus, 1919), 76.

7. Felton, "Final Report of the Department of Civilian Service and Labor of the Pennsylvania Council of National Defense (January 31, 1919)," 20–21.

8. See Frederic E. Foster to Henry D. Sayer, New York State Industrial Commission, Apr. 5, 1918, New York State Defense Council Records, State Department, Commissions, etc., box 4, File: "Industrial Commission," New York State Archives.

9. Extract from letter from unnamed Chicago District Production Officer [Charles A. Munroe?] included in William Blackman, "Report of Division of Labor for week ending May 4, 1918 (May 4, 1918)," RG 32, U.S. Shipping Board (USSB) Records, Construction Organization, Industrial Relations Division, General Correspondence of Labor Section [tray 7].

10. Allen, "The Council of Defense System," 135–36.

11. W. M. Leiserson, "Organizing the Labor Market for the War and after the War (March 29, 1918)," 4–5.

12. A cooperative agreement between the Department of Labor and the Shipping Board was actually approved by the two agencies on April 25, 1917. However, it bound the Shipping Board to inform the Department of Labor only of where contracts had been let and of the current wages and conditions in the various yards. The right of shipyard management to use existing employment methods, including private employment agents, was preserved. The text of that agreement is reproduced in C. T. Clayton to Rear Adm. W. L. Capps, U.S.N., general manager, Emergency Fleet Corporation, July 27, 1917, RG 32, USSB Records, Construction Organization, Industrial Relations Division, Industrial Service Section, box 9, file: "Employment Offices—Establishment of." See also Clayton to Samuel L. Fuller, assistant to general manager, EFC, ca. July 19, 1917, reproduced in Clayton to Capps, July 27, 1917.

13. W. E. Blackman to J. L. Hughes and F. A. Silcox, telegram, Dec. 11, 1917, RG 32, USSB Records, Construction Organization, Industrial Relations Division, General Records, box 70, file 53814/1: "Labor—Location and Distribution of Supply."

14. For example, in December 1917 the joint session on "Employment and the War" of the American Economic Association and the AALL drew attention to the experiment. See Henry R. Seager, "Coordination of Federal, State and Municipal Employment Bureaus," Papers and Proceedings of the Thirtieth Annual Meeting of the American Economic Association, Philadelphia, Pa., December, 1917, *American Economic Review* 8 (Mar. 1918): 141–46. The essay is reprinted with a slightly amended title in Henry R. Seager, *Labor and Other Economic Essays,* edited by Charles A. Gulick, Jr. (1931; reprint, Freeport, N.Y.: Books for Libraries, 1968), 293–302.

15. *Seattle Union Record,* Apr. 6, 1918, 1. Shortly after his return from Seattle, Bloomfield addressed the annual meeting of the U.S. Chamber of Commerce in Chicago and enthusiastically reported on the success of the Seattle office. See U.S. Chamber of Commerce, Minutes of Sixth Annual Meeting, Apr. 10–12, 1918, Chicago (meeting of Apr. 11, 1918); bound copies of transcript of meeting found in U.S. Chamber of Commerce Building, LaFayette Square, Washington, D.C. See also Bloomfield, "Labor and Ships on the Pacific Coast," *American Federationist* 25 (June 1918): 483. Bloomfield had not been directly involved in public employment office work in the prewar years but had been particularly influential in the vocational guidance movement that was closely tied to the early personnel management movement. See Sanford M. Jacoby, *Employing Bureaucracy: Managers, Unions, and the Transformation of Work in American Industry, 1900–1945* (New York: Columbia Univ. Press, 1985), esp. ch. 3.

16. Shipbuilding in Seattle was of comparatively recent origin. Prior to the outbreak of the European war in 1914, there was only one shipbuilding corporation in the city. Between 1914 and U.S. entry into the war in 1917, two additional steel yards were built and several wooden shipyards were opened. See Willard E. Hotchkiss and Henry R. Seager, *History of the Shipbuilding Labor Adjustment Board, 1917 to 1919,* BLS Bulletin No. 283 (1921), 15–16. During 1918 the Seattle yards produced sixty-one steel freighters and thirty-five wooden vessels. Seattle yards built approximately 26 percent of all ships constructed by the EFC during the war. Robert L. Friedheim, *The Seattle General Strike* (Seattle: Univ. of Washington Press, 1964), 57–58, 195n.12.

17. Alexander M. Bing, *War-Time Strikes and Their Adjustment* (New York: E. P. Dutton, 1921), 20–21.

18. The text of that agreement is reproduced in J. L. Hughes to C. Piez, June 26, 1918, RG 174, Department of Labor Records, Wilson Papers, box 205, file 13/117: "Seattle Shipyards."

19. *Second Annual Report of the United States Employment Service covering the fiscal year ended June 30, 1919,* 66th Cong., 2d sess., H. Doc. 7734, 896.

20. "Plan for Handling Needed Labor on War Emergency Work (December 14, 1917)," appendix to eighty-six-page, verbatim, typescript report of conference of Piez and Schwab with Seattle labor leaders, July 18, 1918, RG 32, USSB Records, Construction Organization, General Records, Records of Charles Piez, 1917–19, file 128/3: "Labor Conference— Seattle—7/18/18—Mr. Piez and Mr. Schwab with Labor Leaders—Duplicate Copy." A copy of the agreement was published in *Seattle Union Record,* Dec. 22, 1917, 3.

21. W. Blackman to E. Hurley, "Report of the Division of Labor, William Blackman, Director (March 26, 1918)," pp. 2–3, RG 32, USSB Records, Construction Organization, Industrial Relations Division, box 58, file 53710/4: "Labor Supply Section: Reports Weekly."

22. Friedheim, *Seattle General Strike,* 59.

23. See F. Frankfurter, chairman of War Labor Policies Board, to J. B. Densmore, director-general of USES, Aug. 29, 1918, RG 1, War Labor Policies Board (WLPB) Papers, Correspondence of Chairman and Exec. Secr., file: "Fuel Administration." See also related correspondence with H. A. Garfield, fuel administrator, in same file. This was not the first complaint about the Seattle office. See J. B. Densmore to J. S. Cravens, Apr. 27, 1918, copy attached to J. H. Winterbotham to D. R. Cotton, May 6, 1918, Donald Reed Cotton Papers, box 2, P617, Minnesota Historical Society, St. Paul.

24. G. C. Corbaley to W. Blackman, telegram, Jan. 24, 1918, quoted in Blackman to Densmore, memorandum, Jan. 24, 1918, RG 32, USSB Records, Construction Organization, Industrial Relations Division, box 64, file 53793/1: "United States Employment Service—General."

25. W. Blackman to H. White, telegram, Jan. 24, 1918, RG 32, USSB Records, Construction Organization, Industrial Relations Division, box 64, file 53793/1: "United States Employment Service—General."

26. G. C. Corbaley to W. Blackman, telegram, Jan. 28, 1918, ibid. Corbaley had been in contact with White shortly before telegraphing Blackman. Under the December 1917 agreement, officials from seven different shipyard unions were appointed to assist the Seattle USES office. These seven men resigned their positions as union officials in order to go into government employment as USES "examiners." Four were chosen from the metal trades, one from the building trades, and two from the lumber and woodworking trades. See editorial, *Seattle Union Record,* Dec. 22, 1917.

27. Copy of Silcox telegram in C. T. Clayton to W. Blackman, Jan. 25, 1918, RG 32, USSB Records, Construction Organization, Industrial Relations Division, General Records, box 87, file 53832/1, pt. 1: "Seattle District—Labor—General."

28. G. C. Corbaley to W. Blackman, telegram, Feb. 13, 1918, ibid., box 64, file 53793/1: "United States Employment Service—General."

29. See G. C. Corbaley to W. Blackman, telegram, Feb. 14, 1918, and W. Blackman to G. C. Corbaley, telegrams, Feb. 14 and 17[?], 1918, ibid.

30. J. F. Duthie to G. C. Corbaley, telegram, Jan. 24, 1918 ("Approved Blackman" inked in), ibid., box 87, file 53832/1, pt. 1: "Seattle District—Labor—General."

31. C. W. Wiley to W. Blackman, telegram, Mar. 17, 1918, ibid.

32. George F. Russell, secretary-manager of Employers' Association of Washington, to C. M. Piez, EFC, Mar. 18, 1918, ibid.

33. See, for example, L. C. Marshall to J. B. Densmore, June 29, 1918, ibid., box 64, file 53793/1: "United States Employment Service—General."

34. J. F. Blain to C. Piez, memorandum re: "Labor Situation Seattle (Personal and Confidential)," Oct. 5, 1918, RG 32, USSB Records, Construction Organization, General Records, Records of Charles Piez, 1917–19, file 120/1: "Labor—General."

35. Ibid.

36. H. McBride to L. C. Marshall, Oct. 12, 1918, RG 32, USSB Records, Construction Organization, Industrial Relations Division, General Records, box 87, file 53832, pt. 1: "Seattle District—Labor—General."

37. The EFC also attempted to organize a centralized shipyard employment office on the Great Lakes, but this initiative was rebuffed by employers. See M. E. Farr to C. Piez, Apr. 15, 1918, ibid., box 70, file 53814/1: "Labor—Location and Distribution of Supply."

38. J. B. Densmore to L. C. Marshall, July 3, 1918, ibid., box 64, file 53793/1: "United States Employment Service—General."

39. F. A. Silcox to H. M. White, Feb. 7, 1918, ibid.

40. Hotchkiss and Seager, *History of the Shipbuilding Labor Adjustment Board*, 16. Seager and Hotchkiss do not name the company involved; it was, however, the Skinner and Eddy shipyard.

41. Shortly before the armistice, Henry McBride, who was in Seattle, commented: "Employment office here dominated in the past by Metal Trades Council and made use of in some instances to boost wages and to discriminate in favor of concerns paying highest wages stop." See H. McBride to L. C. Marshall, telegram, Oct. 31, 1918, RG 32, USSB Records, Construction Organization, Industrial Relations Division, General Records, box 87, file 53832/1, pt. 2: "Seattle District—Labor—General."

42. Some of the shipyard owners felt they had good evidence for this view. The J. F. Duthie Shipyard, for example, had a sympathetic workman in the local union who made regular reports between April 1917 and February 1918. In January he reported that the union had established a man at the USES office "presumably to give such information as applicants wish to know regarding the Union, but actually to hinder in every way possible any applicant whom this man thinks will not put the Union interests foremost in accepting a position regardless of his ability as a workman." Carbon copies of these reports by Theodore M. Finch are in RG 174, Chief Clerk's File, box 205, file 13/117: "Seattle Shipyards." Finch was arrested in March 1918 on charges of bootlegging and possession of indecent photographs. See *Seattle Union Record*, Mar. 30, 1918, 1.

43. *British Labor's War Message to American Labor: Addresses and Discussions at a Meeting of the Committee on Labor of the Council of National Defense held in Washington D.C. on May 15, 1917*, 65th Cong., 1st sess., S. Doc. 84. See especially the discussion by James H. Thomas, M.P., former general secretary of the British National Union of Railway Men, ibid., 91–92.

44. Silcox was almost certainly pro-union and it was rumored that his political philosophy was radical. Speaking to the Seattle Central Labor Council in March 1918, Silcox stated that "he believed if there is anything in industrial democracy it should be practiced instead of being merely preached, and he looked upon the employment service as a first step along that line." See editorial, *Seattle Union Record*, Mar. 2, 1918. A confidential

report on Silcox made in September 1918 commented that "it is understood that Mr. Silcox is a close friend and associate of one, Anna Louise Strong, . . . a rank Socialist and an I.W.W. agitator. She has the confidence of the most radical, torch and dynamite members of the I.W.W. organization. This is merely called to your attention to indicate the influences entrenched in the Seattle Government Employment Bureau." See confidential report, Sept. 23, 1918, enclosed in D. Whitcomb, Fuel Administration, to G. Bell, War Labor Policies Board, Oct. 11, 1918, RG 1, WLPB Records, Correspondence of Chairman and Exec. Secr., file: "Fuel Administration." For details on Anna Strong, see Friedheim, *Seattle General Strike,* esp. 30, 52–53, 110–11, 149–50.

45. See especially Robert Cuff, "The Politics of Labor Administration during World War I," *Labor History* 21 (Fall 1980): 546–69.

46. See, for example, G. C. Corbaley to W. Blackman, telegram, Feb. 14, 1918, RG 32, USSB Records, Construction Organization, Industrial Relations Division, General Records, box 64, file 53793/1: "United States Employment Service—General."

47. See especially H. McBride to L. C. Marshall, telegram, Oct. 31, 1918, ibid., box 87, file 53832/1, pt. 2: "Seattle District—Labor—General."

48. See, for example, H. McBride to L. C. Marshall, Oct. 12, and C. Piez [vice president and general manager of the EFC] to L. C. Marshall, Oct. 14, 1918, ibid.

49. See, for example, J. B. Densmore, director-general of USES, to J. S. Cravens, State Councils Section, Council of National Defense, Apr. 27, 1918, copy attached to J. Winterbotham to D. R. Cotton, May 8, 1918, Donald Reed Cotton Papers, box 2, P617.

50. H. McBride to L. C. Marshall, telegram, Nov. 2, 1918, RG 32, USSB Records, Construction Organization, Industrial Relations Division, General Records, box 87, file 53832/1, pt. 3: "Seattle District—Labor—General." In related file, see also H. McBride to L. C. Marshall, telegram, Oct. 31, 1918, file 53832/1, pt. 2: "Seattle District—Labor—General."

51. L. C. Marshall to H. McBride, telegram, Nov. 5, 1918, ibid., box 87, file 53832/1, pt. 3: "Seattle District—Labor—General." For a comment on the important role of Marshall in developing EFC labor policy, see Bernard Mergen, "The Government as Manager: Emergency Fleet Shipbuilding, 1917–1919," in Harold Issadore Sharlin, ed., *Business and Its Environment: Essays for Thomas C. Cochran* (Westport, Conn.: Greenwood Press, 1983), esp. 64–66. Mergen suggests that Marshall "may have been labor's strongest advocate in the Wilson administration."

5. The Role of the War Labor Policies Board

1. See S. Gompers, "No Scarcity of Workers" (editorial), *American Federationist* 24 (June 1917): 463–64. Organized labor refused to accept that a labor shortage existed. See J. W. Sullivan to H. Hoover, "Memorandum as to the Supply of Labor, August 15, 1917," RG 174, Department of Labor Records, Wilson Papers, box 208, file 20/31: "Scarcity of Labor, 1917." In January 1918 Sullivan, who was the assistant to Gompers on the Advisory Commission of the Council of National Defense, circulated a copy of the optimistic labor market report that had been printed in the January 1918 issue of the *American Federationist.* See J. W. Sullivan to D. F. Houston, secretary of agriculture, Jan. 4, 1918, RG 16, Department of Agriculture Records, Office of the Secretary, Incoming Correspondence, "1918: Irrigation-Labor (Jan.)," acc. 234, dr. 152. For a more pessi-

mistic view of the labor market, see "Report of U.S. Public Service Reserve on labor demand as obtained in Washington and on labor supply from trade union sources," in Post and Hale, "Report to Interdepartmental Advisory Committee Pursuant to Resolution adopted . . . October 5, 1917 (October 19, 1917)," 88–95 (Appendix G); see also ch. 6, "Is There a Shortage of Labor?" in ibid., 17–23. This report, while urging caution in interpreting the statistics, concluded that there was a shortage of 400,000 workers on direct government contracts. For a discussion of the response of the Selective Service System to the increasing clamor over the alleged shortage of labor, see John Whiteclay Chambers II, *To Raise an Army: The Draft Comes to Modern America* (New York: Free Press, 1987), ch.7.

2. The Bureau of Labor Statistics, the forerunner of the Department of Labor, had been established in 1884 to provide data on issues related to labor. Although limited by inadequate funding, it had done much good work. However it had completely failed to develop any system that could provide *current* statistics on wages and employment. See Mary O. Furner, "Knowing Capitalism: Public Investigation and the Labor Question in the Long Progressive Era," in Mary O. Furner and Barry Supple, eds., *The State and Economic Knowledge: The American and British Experiences* (Cambridge: Cambridge Univ. Press, 1990), 241–86, esp. 246–68.

3. This aspect of the work of the Department of Labor relates to the recent discussion among historians "on the connections between the state and development of a knowledge base for social policy." See especially the essays in Furner and Supply, eds., *The State and Economic Knowledge* and *The State and Social Investigation in Britain and the United States* (Cambridge: Cambridge Univ. Press, 1993), 173. For more detail on the effort to collect usable statistics on the operation of the labor market in the World War I era, see William J. Breen, "Labor Market Statistics and the State: The United States in the Era of the Great War, 1914–1930," *Journal of Policy History* 8, no. 3 (1996).

4. *USES Bulletin* 1, no. 6 (Mar. 4, 1918), 4. A set of USES weekly reports on labor conditions in the United States, March 16–August 10, 1918, is located in Woodrow Wilson Papers, ser. 4, case files no. 19, file: "Department of Labor" (reel 171). For an example of the monthly Public Service Reserve labor reports, see *USES Bulletin* 1, no. 10 (Apr. 2, 1918), 1–2. In fact, the information on the demand for labor obtained from the one thousand plants reporting every month was never used. The schedules were not mailed out until May, the USES did not have a statistical office capable of handling the data when it came in, and there were serious reservations about the accuracy of the information provided. The project was discontinued in July when a new system of reporting was instituted. H. W. Tyler, "Memorandum for the Chairman, Committee on Centralization of Industrial Statistics [WLPB], June 10, 1918" and "Minutes of the Meeting of the Committee on Statistics [WLPB] held at Room 709 Labor Department Building, June 10th, [1918], at 11.30 A.M.," RG 1, War Labor Policies Board Records, Correspondence of Chairman and Exec. Secr., file: "Standardization Committee."

5. *USES Bulletin* 1, no. 24 (July 9, 1918), 3. Summaries of the weekly labor survey were printed in the *USES Bulletin.*

6. Ibid., no. 26 (July 23, 1918), 3.

7. Even Bernard Baruch, chairman of the War Industries Board, conferred with Shipping Board officials about the labor problem and the possibility of establishing some kind of

central committee. See War Industries Board, "Minutes (Mtg of May 9, 1918)," p. 598, RG 61, WIB Records, Chairman's Office, 1-C1, Minutes of WIB Meetings, box 73.

8. L. C. Marshall to F. Frankfurter, May 29, 1918, RG 32, USSB Records, Construction Organization, Industrial Relations Division, General Records, box 64, file 53793-1: "United States Employment Service—General."

9. E. K. Eyerly to Secretary Houston, memorandum, June 4, 1918, RG 16, Department of Agriculture, Office of the Secretary, Incoming Correspondence, "1918: Labor (June)," acc. 234, dr. 156. On the review of the cooperative agreement, see in same file E. K. Eyerly to Secretary Houston, memorandum, June 6, 1918.

10. See *USES Bulletin* 1, no. 16 (May 14, 1918), 1, 5. In fact, the major railroads continued to use private, fee-charging agencies. See, for examples, P. L. Prentis to R. H. Aishton, July 1, 1918, and H. V. Koch to P. L. Prentis, July 17, 1918, War Records Commission: USES, 1918–19, State Headquarters Files, box 7, file 9-3, Minnesota Historical Society.

11. For King's comment, see *Sundry Civil Bill, 1919: Hearings*, 1577 (testimony of John B. Densmore, May 1, 1918). On alleged labor influence, see War Department, "War Emergency Construction Work. Report by Board of Review of Construction. (Francis Blossom, Chairman; submitted September 8, 1919)" (Washington, D.C., 1919), 414–15 (hereafter cited as "Blossom Report"), copy found in RG 77, Office of the Chief of Engineers, Construction Division, ser. 401, National Archives, Washington, D.C.

12. R. P. Bass to E. Hurley, memorandum, June 14, 1918, RG 32, USSB Records, Subject Classified General Files, 1917–20, box 93, file 4439, pt. 2.

13. The composition of the WLPB consisted of representatives from the Departments of War, Navy, and Agriculture and from the War Industries Board, Fuel Administration, Shipping Board, Emergency Fleet Corporation, Food Administration, Railroad Administration, and Committee on Public Information. In addition there was an industrial adviser (H. F. Perkins, an executive with International Harvester, Chicago), a labor adviser (John R. Alpine, AFL vice president), and an economic adviser (Prof. L. C. Marshall, University of Chicago). The executive officer was George L. Bell, a graduate of the University of California and Harvard Law School. Bell had been working as the executive officer of the California State Commission on Immigration and Housing.

14. Frankfurter was not Secretary Wilson's first choice. He had previously offered the position to Leon C. Marshall. See W. B. Wilson to S. Gompers, May 13, 1917, William B. Wilson Papers, Official Correspondence 1913–21, box 197-A-8 (in pencil), file: 13/101 (ser. 13, folder 101). On Frankfurter's early career, see Michael E. Parrish, *Felix Frankfurter and His Times: The Reform Years* (New York: Free Press, 1982), esp. chs. 5–6.

15. F. Frankfurter to H. Croly, May 9, 1917, Felix Frankfurter Papers, General Correspondence, box 50, folder 000921 ("Croly, Herbert"), Manuscript Division, Library of Congress.

16. F. Frankfurter to R. E. Miles, June 8, 1918, RG 1, WLPB Records, Correspondence of Chairman and Exec. Secr., file: "Employment Service: Croxton."

17. F. Frankfurter to R. E. Miles, Aug. 20, 1918, ibid. Frankfurter was very impressed with Croxton. In this letter he added that "he [Croxton] has done it all with surpassing disinterestedness. The world outside knows little of his share in what is being done and in what will be achieved. His self-effacement was one of his greatest contributions, for it was necessary to do the task as disregardful of self as possible. I need not tell you how

finely Mr. Croxton rose to the occasion." Frankfurter wanted Croxton to stay in Washington for the duration of the war, but Ohio's governor, James M. Cox, refused to release him. Croxton did, however, spend part of June, a good part of July, and virtually all of August in the capital assisting in the reorganization of the USES.

18. N. A. Smyth, chairman of the Committee on Central Recruiting, "Recommendations of Committee on Central Recruiting," June 5, 1918, and attached "Proposed Resolution by the War Labor Policies Board," RG 1, WLPB Records, Correspondence of Chairman and Exec. Secr., file: "Committee on Central Recruiting: 3, Report to WLPB."

19. See WLPB, "Minutes (Mtg. of June 7, 1918)," RG 1, WLPB Records, Minutes, box 1; a copy of the "Proposed Resolution by the War Labor Policies Board" (n.d., n.s.) is included with these minutes. The resolution is also printed in the *Report of Proceedings of the National War Labor Conference, Washington, June 13–15, 1918* (Washington, D.C.: Government Printing Office, 1918), 90–91, and in *First Annual Report of the U.S. Employment Service (August 1, 1918)*, 65th Cong., 3d Sess., 1919, H. Doc. 1449, 700–704.

20. WLPB, "Minutes (Mtg. of June 7, 1918)."

21. LCM [Marshall], "Memorandum concerning United States Employment Service, June 10, 1918," RG 32, USSB Records, Construction Organization, Industrial Relations Division, General Records, box 64, file 53793-1: "United States Employment Service—General."

22. "Report and Recommendations," (n.d., n.s.), attached to Croxton to Frankfurter, June 10, 1918, RG 1, WLPB Records, Correspondence of Chairman and Exec. Secr., file: "Employment Service: May–June–July: C-1-f."

23. Ibid., 2–5, 6–7, 12–13.

24. W. M. Leiserson to H. P. Seager, July 13, 1918, William M. Leiserson Papers, Professional Correspondence, box 36, file: "Seager, H. R., 1910–24," Historical Society of Wisconsin.

25. *Report of Proceedings of National War Labor Conference, Washington, June 13–15, 1918*, 21–36. The starting date of the campaign was later pushed back from July 15 to August 1.

26. F. C. Croxton to F. Frankfurter, June 11, 1918, RG 1, WLPB Records, Correspondence of Chairman and Exec. Secr., file: "Employment Service: Croxton." The summary statement, headed "Aims and Purposes of the United States Employment Service" (n.d., n.s.), is found in ibid., file: "Employment Service: May–June–July: C-1-f."

27. See Secretary Wilson's speeches in *Report of Proceedings of the National War Labor Conference: Washington, June 13–15, 1917*, 5–7; 68–71.

28. See exchange of telegrams between F. Frankfurter and Gov. James M. Cox on June 20 (copy; date missing), 21, and July 8, and note also the letter from Frankfurter to Cox, July 10, 1918, RG 1, WLPB Records, Correspondence of Chairman and Exec. Secr., file: "Employment Service: Croxton." See also *How Ohio Mobilized Her Resources*, 85. Secretary of War Newton D. Baker, who was himself from Ohio, also urged Croxton to return to Washington.

29. Frankfurter to Croxton, telegram, July 3, 1918, and Croxton to Frankfurter, telegram, July 5, 1918, RG 1, WLPB Records, Correspondence of Chairman and Exec. Secr., file: "Employment Service: Croxton."

30. Secretary Wilson must have found it hard to reject Post's USES policy; the secretary relied very heavily on his assistant secretary in managing the Department of Labor, having worked with him since its creation in 1913. Moreover, Post had offered his resignation

over the January reorganization of the USES when Secretary Wilson had appointed Densmore to head the USES. See Lombardi, *Labor's Voice,* 194. It is possible that Secretary Wilson was not as committed to the centralist concept of the USES as Post was and was prepared to take a wider view. Numerous contemporaries attest to his fairmindedness and breadth of vision. See, for example, Leon C. Marshall, "The War Labor Program and Its Administration," *Journal of Political Economy* 26 (May 1918): 457n.2, 458n.1.

31. F. Frankfurter to Secretary Wilson, memorandum, July 1, 1918, RG 1, WLPB Records, Correspondence of Chairman and Exec. Secr., File: "Sec'y Wilson: to August. C-1-a."

32. Frankfurter to Croxton, telegram, July 5, 1918, ibid., file: "Employment Service: Croxton"; L. C. Marshall to F. C. Croxton, telegram, July 5, 1918, ibid., box 32, file: "Emergency Fleet Corporation: May to October: C-11-f."

33. See F. C. Croxton to F. Frankfurter, telegram, July 22, 1918, F. Frankfurter to T. J. Duffy and T. J. Duffy to F. Frankfurter, telegrams, July 23, 1918, ibid., box 19, file: "Employment Service: Croxton."

34. See *How Ohio Mobilized Her Resources,* 85; *First Annual Report of the U.S. Employment Service (August 1, 1918),* 705. The Ohio report does not mention R. G. Wells.

35. There was talk of an existing shortage of half a million unskilled laborers and the possibility of a shortage of up to three million by the end of the year together with a growing demand for skilled workers that could not be met. On the shortage of unskilled labor, see the speech by N. A. Smyth delivered on July 19, reported in *USES Bulletin* 1, no. 26 (July 23, 1918), 3. On the increasing shortage of skilled labor, see *Address by Darragh de Lancey, Chairman Second District Board, State of Connecticut, Before Conference of Chiefs of Ordnance District Offices, New York City, June 27, 1918,* pamphlet, p. 2, copy in Donald Reed Cotton Papers, box 3, P617. De Lancey was attached to the Office of the Assistant Secretary of War, Edward R. Stettinius.

36. "Minutes of Committee Called by Mr. Croxton (Mtgs. of Saturday, July 13, 1918, at 2.00 P.M. and 8.30 P.M.; mtg. of Sunday, July 14, 1918, at 9.30 A.M.)," RG 1, WLPB Records, Correspondence of Chairman and Exec. Secr., file: "Employment Service: Croxton." There were also a number of other quite specific recommendations concerning newspaper advertising, recruiting, and related issues. Transportation costs were one source of friction. In March, 1918, Congress had appropriated $250,000 for a revolving transport fund to enable the USES to advance transportation costs to workmen who were moving long distances. Other government agencies had similar funds. Conditions both for receiving and repaying transport funds varied considerably, and the committee recommended greater uniformity. The committee also urged that immediate action be taken to establish a standard rate for the wages of unskilled labor with no differential between different regions in an effort to curb the high labor turnover. It also recommended a national classification of job occupations.

37. USES Special Order B-1, "Instruction Concerning State Advisory Boards, Community Labor Boards, and Organization Committees (July 17, 1918)." The text of the Special Order is reproduced in *USES Bulletin* 1, no. 26 (July 23, 1918), 2–3.

38. John B. Densmore, "How Employers and Workers Will Share in Administration of War Labor Supplying Plan Explained," *USES Bulletin* 1, no. 26 (July 23, 1918), 1, 2. For the reference to the military draft, see J. B. Densmore to A. H. Fleming, July 10, 1918, mimeo copy attached to State Councils Section, CND, Bulletin No. 101, "Labor Mobilization (July 12, 1918)," Henry Suzzallo Papers, box 2, folder 2-30, University of Wash-

ington Archives, Seattle. The draft was sent to all state councils of defense urging both cooperation with the plan and the appointment of special committees at the state, county, and local levels "to render all assistance possible."

39. See report of Frankfurter's speech at the special conference for those involved in the state organization committees held in Washington on July 19, 1918, in *USES Bulletin* 1, no. 26 (July 23, 1918), 4. For a detailed report on the conference, including a list of those present, see ibid., 3–5. For details on the cooperation of the Chamber of Commerce with the program, which was discussed by Earl D. Howard at the conference, see the printed newsletter of the Committee on Industrial Relations, Chamber of Commerce of the United States, *Organization of Local Labor Administrations* (July 22, 1918), RG 1, WLPB Records, Information File, box 45, file: "Chamber of Commerce."

40. See Dubofsky, *The State and Labor in Modern America*, 71–74; Valerie Jean Conner, *The National War Labor Board*.

41. An earlier generation of historians, writing about the first half of the twentieth century, portrayed a largely successful struggle in which the forces of liberalism were able to use the state to regulate business and the economy in the public interest. Since the 1960s this interpretation has been seriously questioned. Far from the clear dichotomy between public and private interest and between regulator and regulated that the older historians saw, more recent critics have pointed to the role that organized interests, particularly large corporations, played in the process of expanding the role of the state over the economy. They suggest that this development was a response not to a desire to further the public interest but rather to the need to provide order and legitimation for the new industrial order. The critics have also questioned the clear division in the old interpretation between the state and private interests and have argued, instead, that the public-private distinction was increasingly blurred as the state moved to "achieve coordination through enlightened concerts of recognized interests." In this particular instance it is clear that it is the state itself, rather than business or labor, that is promoting the corporatist approach. The most useful overview of this new interpretation is Ellis W. Hawley's "The Discovery and Study of a 'Corporate Liberalism,'" *Business History Review* 52 (Autumn 1978): 309–20, 311. See also Hawley, "Society and Corporate Statism," in Mary K. Cayton, Elliott J. Gorn, and Peter W. Williams, eds., *Encyclopedia of American Social History*, vol. 1 (New York: Scribner's, 1993), 621–36.

42. See the successful protest by Ohio against this arbitrary method in *How Ohio Mobilized Her Resources*, 83–84. See also chapter 8 below.

43. N. A. Smyth, "The New Labor Recruiting Program," *Report of Proceedings of the National War Labor Conference, Washington, June 13–15, 1918* (Washington, D.C.: GPO, 1918), 23.

44. *USES Bulletin* 1, no. 23 (July 2, 1918), 1.

45. A copy of "Emp. 15" ("Employer's Order for Unskilled Male Laborers") is attached to "L. C. Marshall to All Firms Engaged in Work for the Emergency Fleet Corporation," memorandum re: "Central Recruiting of Unskilled Labor," July 10, 1918, RG 32, USSB Records, Construction Organization, General Records, Records of Charles M. Schwab, Apr.–Dec. 1918, file 35: "Industrial Service Department: Publications."

46. See *USES Bulletin* 1, no. 28 (Aug. 6, 1918), 1; ibid., no. 30 (Aug. 20, 1918), 1.

47. See, for example, F. Frankfurter to F. Croxton, telegram, June 18, 1918, F. Croxton to F. Frankfurter and F. Frankfurter to F. Croxton, telegrams, June 19, 1918, RG 1, WLPB

Records, Correspondence of Chairman and Exec. Secr., file: "Employment Service: Croxton." The National Industrial Conference Board supported the central recruiting program. See Frankfurter's report to the War Labor Policies Board in WLPB, "Minutes (Mtg of June 21)." The U.S. Chamber of Commerce also supported the plan and even the National Association of Manufacturers cooperated. See U.S. Chamber of Commerce, War Bulletin No. 37, *Distribution of Unskilled Labor* (June 24, 1918), p. 1, copy in, RG 1, WLPB Records, Correspondence of Chairman and Exec. Secr., file: "Chamber of Commerce." See also report of speeches by Earl Dean Howard, chairman of the Committee on Industrial Relations, U.S. Chamber of Commerce, and Nathan B. Williams, attorney for the National Association of Manufacturers, at the meeting of state organization committee representatives from the twenty-eight states east of the Mississippi, in *USES Bulletin* 1, no. 26 (July 23, 1918), 4.

48. D. M. Reynolds to H. M. Robinson, July 18, 1918, Henry M. Robinson Papers, box 4, Correspondence, file: "Reynolds, D. M.(1)," Hoover Institution, Palo Alto, California. See also N. A. Smyth to H. M. Robinson, June 7, 1918, and D. M. Reynolds to H. M. Robinson, July 3, 6, 1918, ibid. Reynolds, who directed the publicity campaign, came from California, where he worked as a publicity man for the Pacific Electric Railway Company of Los Angeles, the Edison Company, and the Los Angeles Telephone Company. He spent two months in Washington working on the central recruiting campaign. Reynolds had directed the Shipyard Volunteer Campaign in early 1918. In fact, skilled labor never was controlled. The armistice came too soon. Even over unskilled labor, the control given to the USES was not complete. All plants could still hire at the gate. The regulations did not apply to firms with less than one hundred employees and, like skilled labor, farm labor and railroad labor were both exempted.

49. D. M. Reynolds to C. W. Henke, publicity director of Minnesota Public Safety Commission, telegram, July 31, 1917 [1918; typographical error in date], Public Safety Commission Records, box 19, file 279: "USES—D. M. Reynolds," Minnesota Historical Society. For a list of those present at the luncheon, see *USES Bulletin* 1, no. 28 (Aug. 6, 1918), 8.

50. For a detailed report on the publicity received as a direct result of the luncheon and for an overview of the entire advertising campaign, see D. M. Reynolds to the secretary of labor, Aug. 19, 1918, and to A. H. Fleming, chief of State Councils Section, CND, July 25, 1918, Henry Mauris Robinson Papers, box 4, Correspondence, file: "Reynolds, D. M. (2)." See also *USES Bulletin* 1, no. 28 (Aug. 6, 1918), 1, 8. Reynolds himself was surprised at the response. In his letter of August 19, he commented, "I have literally thousands of letters from bank presidents, corporation heads, newspapers, governors, mayors, etc., offering to support the labor employment program to the limit."

51. "Secretary Wilson Completes Organization of War Labor Administration with Cabinet" and "C. T. Clayton, Formerly Asst. Director General, Heads War Badge Board," *USES Bulletin* 1, no. 25 (July 16, 1918), 13. See also "T. V. Powderly Returns to Immigration Bureau," ibid., no. 28 (Aug. 6, 1918), 12.

52. Editorial, *USES Bulletin* 1, no. 29 (Aug. 13, 1918), 6. For descriptions of functions of each division and biographical sketches of the individuals appointed as division heads, see ibid., 1–2.

53. A. H. Young, who was the Illinois employer representative at the meeting of the members of the state organization committees in Washington on July 19, was shown, in confi-

dence, the administrative restructuring plan proposed by Croxton and his group, which embodied the same five divisions announced by Densmore in early August. See A. H. Young to John Glenn, secretary of Illinois Manufacturers Association, July 21, 1918, copy attached to A. H. Young to H. F. Perkins, July 21, 1918, RG 1, WLPB Records, Correspondence of Herbert F. Perkins, file: "Govt. Employment Offices."

54. USES, General Order No. 1, "Purpose and Policy of U.S. Employment Service," reprinted in *USES Bulletin* 1, no. 29 (Aug. 13, 1918), 1.

55. General Order B-1 is reprinted in ibid., 4.

56. "Minutes of Committee Called by Mr. Croxton (Mtg. of Saturday, July 13, at 8.30 P.M.)," p. 2, RG 1, WLPB Records, Correspondence of Chairman and Exec. Secr., file: "Employment Service: Croxton." The matter had been referred to a special committee of the War Labor Policies Board, but that committee was unable to make a unanimous recommendation because of the oppositon of the labor representatives. Frankfurter decided not to press the issue and the matter was not formally discussed again by the War Labor Policies Board.

6. A Federalist U.S. Employment Service

1. After the August reorganization the key individuals in the USES, apart from John B. Densmore, the director general, were Nathan B. Smyth, assistant director general, and the five divisional directors: Luther C. Steward (control); Ferdinand A. Silcox (personnel); William E. Hall (field organization); Sanford H. E. Freund (clearance); A. D. Chiquoine, Jr. (information). Only Steward and Silcox were permanent government employees; Steward had transferred from the Immigration Service in April 1918, and Silcox had transferred from the Forestry Service of the Department of Agriculture in 1917 and had been in charge of the USES office in Seattle. Shortly afterward Silcox was transferred and his place taken by W. H. Winans, a "dollar-a-year man" from the private sector. See *USES Bulletin* 1, no. 29 (Aug. 13, 1918), 2.

2. On Winan's influence on the reorganization of the Cleveland office, see *Proceedings of the Employment Managers' Conference, Rochester, N.Y., May 9, 10, and 11, 1918,* BLS Bulletin No. 247 (1919), 80–81. See also *USES Bulletin* 1, no. 34 (Sept. 17, 1918), 3. Winans replaced F. A. Silcox, who was posted to the field service. Chiquoine contracted typhoid fever at the end of September and spent most of the fall on leave. See ibid., no. 36 (Oct. 1, 1918), 3.

3. See the report of the views of senior USES officials concerning incompetent state representatives in L. K. Lewis to F. J. Warne, memorandum, Oct. 26, 1918, RG 3, U.S. Housing Corporation Records, Industrial Relations Division, box 628, General Correspondence, Subject File, file: "U.S. Employment Service, Washington, D.C."

4. W. E. Hall to director general, USES, memorandum re: "Reporting on the Activities of the Field Organization Division," n.d. [Dec. 1918], RG 183, Bureau of Employment Security, Records of the U.S. Employment Service, 1907–49, box 1516 (among unfiled material). Most of the states that were mentioned (Nebraska, North Dakota, Virginia, West Virginia) did not have their own state employment systems and the state directors were direct appointees of the Department of Labor.

5. E. M. Hopkins to F. Frankfurter, Dec. 21, 1918, Ernest Martin Hopkins Papers, War Department Series, file: "War Labor Policies Board," Dartmouth College, Hanover, New Hampshire.

6. Frankfurter to Densmore, memorandum, Oct. 30, 1918, RG 1, WLPB Records, Correspondence of Chairman and Exec. Secr., file: "Employment Service: Smyth, Nathan A." Frankfurter mentioned that the allegation of excessive union representation in USES appointments had even reached the president. See also chapter 9 below.

7. *USES Bulletin* 1, no. 40 (Nov. 7, 1918), 1–2; ibid. 2, no. 3 (Feb. 28, 1919), 4.

8. See the program headed "Second Session of the first Normal Training Course, State of Illinois, United States Employment Service and Illinois Free Employment Offices, February 19th, 20th and 21st, 1919," copy in War Records Commission: USES, 1918–19, State Headquarters Files, box 7, file: 9-3, Minnesota Historical Society. The conference was held in Chicago.

9. *USES Bulletin* 1, no. 37 (Oct. 15, 1918), 3.

10. Ibid., no. 41 (Nov. 19, 1918), 5.

11. "The Manual of the United States Employment Service," pp. 3–4, mimeo copy in RG 183, Bureau of Employment Security, USES Records, 1907–49, box 1514.

12. D. DeLancey to G. N. Peek, June 18, 1918, RG 61, WIB Records, Technical or Commodity File, 21A-A4, Construction Projects, Labor, box 772 (large unmarked file). The Croxton Committee had urged that action be taken in this area in mid-July 1918 for a different reason: it believed "the lack of such classification and standardization, is at the present time, the most prolific cause of labor turnover." "Minutes of Committee Called by Mr. Croxton (Saturday, July 13, 1918)," p. 2, RG 1, WLPB Records, Correspondence of Chairman and Exec. Secr., file: "Employment Service: Croxton."

13. *USES Bulletin* 1, no. 35 (Sept. 24, 1918), 5.

14. *Iron Age,* May 30, 1918, 1424, clipping in RG 61, WIB Records, Technical or Commodity File, 21-A4, Construction Projects, Labor, box 772, file: "Labor."

15. *USES Bulletin* 1, no. 44 (Dec. 17, 1918), 6.

16. J. B. Densmore, "Instructions Concerning State Advisory Boards, Community Labor Boards, and Organization Committees (July 17, 1918)," *USES Bulletin* 1, no. 26 (July 23, 1918), 2–3. For the initial organization of Community Labor Boards, see chapter 5 above.

17. Editorial, *USES Bulletin* 1, no. 24 (July 9, 1918), 6; Densmore, "Instructions Concerning State Advisory Boards."

18. *USES Bulletin* 1, no. 26 (July 23, 1918), 3. The community labor boards had many similarities to the local draft boards established under the Selective Service System. See John Whiteclay Chambers II, *To Raise an Army,* 182–83. Parallels exist in some other aspects of the wartime mobilization. Compare, for example, the development of community councils of defense that were created under the aegis of the State Councils Section of the Council of National Defense. See William J. Breen, *Uncle Sam at Home: Civilian Mobilization, Wartime Federalism, and the Council of National Defense, 1917–1919* (Westport, Conn.: Greenwood Press, 1984), ch. 9. For an interpretation of the significance of these developments, see Ellis W. Hawley, "The Corporative Component of the American Quest for National Efficiency, 1900–1917" (paper delivered at the Organization of American Historians [OAH] Conference, Apr. 1984).

19. Densmore, "Instructions Concerning State Advisory Boards." Decisions of the community boards could be appealed to the USES State Advisory Board: both boards operated under regulations approved by the WLPB and the Department of Labor.

20. N. A. Smyth to A. H. Fleming, chief of State Councils Section, CND, Aug. 27, 1918, Public Safety Commission Records, 1918–20, Main Subject Files, box 19, file: 279: "U.S. Employment Service—D. M. Reynolds," Minnesota Historical Society.

21. The USES had earlier received general support from the state council of defense system when the central recruiting program was announced in late July. See *USES Bulletin* 1, no. 27 (July 30, 1918), 3. This support extended to preventing the expansion of plants involved in nonessential work and requesting local governments to defer nonessential public works. See N. A. Smyth to A. H. Fleming, Aug. 27, 1918, ibid.

22. For an outline of the proposal, see H. S. Gans to E. B. Parker, Aug. 2, 1918, RG 61, WIB Records, Technical or Commodity File, 21A-A4, Construction Projects, Labor, box 777, file: "Dept. of Labor: Labor Adjustment Service." There was also a good deal of pressure from the states to strengthen the powers of the community labor boards. See, for example, C. A. Munroe to S. Insull, Aug. 20, 1918, and C. A. Munroe to W. E. Hall, Aug. 23, Sept. 6, 1918, Illinois State Council of Defense Papers: Public Service Reserve, file: "USPSR—Letters, etc.—August, 1918," Illinois State Archives, Springfield.

23. W. E. Hall, "Memorandum for the Director General, U.S. Employment Service, Reporting on the Activities of the Field Organization Division," n.d. (c. Dec. 1918), RG 183, Bureau of Employment Security: USES Records, 1907–49, box 1516 (among unfiled material).

24. *USES Bulletin* 1, no. 34 (Sept. 17, 1918), 1–2; ibid., no. 37 (Oct. 15, 1918), 1–2. A large part of the opposition to the inclusion of women on the community labor boards was alleged to come from W. E. Hall. See Felix Morley, "The United States Employment Service," *American Labor Year Book, 1919–20* (New York: Rand School of Social Science, 1920), 73.

25. J. B. Densmore to F. Frankfurter, memorandum, Sept. 9, 1918, RG 1, WLPB Records, Correspondence of Chairman and Exec. Secr.,file: "Employment Service: August–Sept.–October." With the exception of California, all state advisory boards had also been established and were functioning by the end of the first week in September.

26. J. B. Densmore to F. Frankfurter, memorandum, Sept. 9, 1918, ibid; *USES Bulletin* 1, no. 37 (Oct. 15, 1918), 3; *Second Annual Report of the United States Employment Service,* 888.

27. *USES Bulletin* 1, no. 36 (Oct. 1, 1918), 5; ibid., no. 37 (Oct. 15, 1918), 3; "Resume of Annual Reports of Federal Directors for States," addendum to *Second Annual Report of U.S. Employment Service,* 1011 (Ohio), 954 (Conn.), 1048 (Wisc.). For further detail on Ohio, see *How Ohio Mobilized Her Resources,* 89.

28. F. W. Tully to F. Frankfurter, memorandum, Aug. 8, 1918, RG 1, WLPB Records, Correspondence of Chairman and Exec. Secr., file: "Employment Service: Monthly Labor Status Reports, Weekly Reports." See also the complimentary comments on the community labor boards from the chairman of the national committee of drop forge manufacturers. "Memorandum of the conference between Mr. Perkins and Mr. Sivyer, representing the War Labor Policies Board, and certain Drop Forge Manufacturers, at the office of the Board on Thursday, August 8, 1918," p. 2, RG 1, WLPB Records, Correspondence of Herbert F. Perkins, file: "Metal and Building Trades."

29. See report of speech by Charles B. Barnes in *USES Bulletin* 1, no. 47 (Jan. 17, 1919), 5. For the comment on Wisconsin, see "Resume of Annual Reports of Federal Directors for States" (Wisc.), *Second Annual Report of USES,* 1048.
30. On the Negro Division of the USES, see chapter 8 below.
31. See brief report of statement of J. B. Densmore, director general of USES, in "Labor Turnover Meeting of New York Section," *Journal of the American Society of Mechanical Engineers* 40 (Sept. 1918): 768; idem, "Lessons of the War in Shifting Labor," *Annals of the American Academy of Political and Social Science* 81 (Jan. 1919): 35–36. See also *USES Bulletin* 1, no. 16 (May 14, 1918), 1.
32. *USES Bulletin* 1, no. 45 (Dec. 31, 1918), 1–2.
33. *Second Annual Report of USES,* 696.
34. *USES Bulletin* 1, no. 26 (July 23, 1918), 8; ibid., no. 27 (July 30, 1918), 4. For details on the development of the women's organization in the USES in the latter part of 1918, see ibid., no. 37 (Oct. 15, 1918), 5.
35. Darrell H. Smith, *The United States Employment Service: Its History, Activities and Organization* (Baltimore: Johns Hopkins Univ. Press, 1923), 27. The protective orientation of USES policy toward the employment of women is well illustrated in the texts of General Orders B-7 and B-8. See *USES Bulletin* 1, no. 34 (Sept. 17, 1918), 1–2. The standards approved by the War Labor Policies Board to control the work of the Women in Industry Service were to govern the decisions of the community labor boards. See *USES Bulletin* 1, no. 35 (Sept. 24, 1918), 1–2.
36. A copy of the memorandum is reproduced in *USES Bulletin* 1, no. 22 (June 25, 1918), 5. On relations between the Agriculture and Labor departments, see chapters 3 and 5 above.
37. F.C.C. [Croxton] to Frankfurter, memorandum, Aug. 12, 1918, RG 1, WLPB Records, Correspondence of Chairman and Exec. Secr., file: "Agriculture, Dept. of: re Agreement with Labor Dept."
38. F.C.C. [Croxton] to Frankfurter, memorandum, Aug. 21, 1918, ibid.
39. For Frankfurter's proposal, see unheaded, undated, unsigned, 3-page memorandum attached to Frankfurter to C. Ousley, Aug. 22, 1918. This memorandum embodied, virtually verbatim, the memorandum submitted to Frankfurter by Croxton on August 21, 1918. See also Ousley to Frankfurter, Sept. 7, 1918; Frankfurter to Ousley, Sept. 20, 1918; Ousley to Frankfurter, Oct. 5, 1918, RG 16, Department of Agriculture Records, Office of the Secretary, Incoming Correspondence, 1918, Labor, acc. 234, drs. 157, 158. At the end of 1918, as part of this effort to promote its role in providing agricultural labor, the USES reconstituted the Farm Service Section as the Farm Service Division on an equal footing with the five other divisions of the USES. Reduced to a bureau in 1919, it was reconstituted as the Farm Labor Division in 1923.
40. See D. De Lancey, chief of Industrial Furlough Section, AGO, War Department, to B. Baruch, chairman, WIB Records, memorandum re: "Utilization of Manpower," Oct. 19, 1918, RG 61, WIB Records, Consolidated Files/Administrative, Labor Division, 21A-A2, box 115, file: "Labor Divison—Miscellaneous"; D. De Lancey to T. N. Perkins, assistant director of munitions, War Dept., memorandum re: "Utilization of Manpower," Oct. 26, 1918, RG 61, WIB: Technical or Commodity File, 21A-A4, Construction Projects, Labor, box 776, file: "Labor Program." In fact, further conferences were held to strengthen General Crowder's "work or fight" regulations, and a revised version was ready to be

released at the time of the armistice. The revised version had watered down the draconian provisions of the original De Lancey proposal. See Bernard M. Baruch, *American
Industry in the War: A Report of the War Industries Board (March 1921)*, edited by Richard
H. Hippelheuser (New York: Prentice-Hall, 1941), 95. See also John Whiteclay Chambers II, *To Raise an Army*, ch. 7, esp. 199.

41. See "Memorandum for Mr. Frankfurter," unsigned (Smyth or Freund), Nov. 12, 1918,
copy in Felix Frankfurter Papers, box 189, file: "War Department: Correspondence:
October–November, 1918," Manuscript Division, Library of Congress. On relations with
the Navy Department, see *Sundry Civil Bill, 1919: Hearings*, 65th Cong., 2d sess., 1918,
1578 (testimony of J. B. Densmore).

42. C. A. Otis to S. W. Webb, Aug. 27, 1918, RG 61, WIB Records, Technical or Commodity
File, 21A-A4, Construction Projects, Labor, box 771, file: "Labor—General."

43. F. J. Warne, manager of Industrial Relations Division, to general manager of U.S. Hous-
ing Corporation ("Weekly Report of Industrial Relations Division"), Nov. 2, 1918, RG 3,
U.S. Housing Corporation Records, Industrial Relations Division, Subject File, Weekly
Reports.

44. See, for example, WIB Minutes (meetings of Oct. 3, 22, 23, 1918), RG 61, WIB Records,
Chairman's Office, 1-C1, Minutes of WIB Mtgs., box 73. See also "History and Record
of the Labor Section of the Priorities Division of the War Industries Board," 3–4, Bernard M. Baruch Papers, War Industries Board, unit 2, sec. 1, vol. 2, pt. 1, no. 3, Seeley G.
Mudd Manuscript Library, Princeton University.

45. N. A. Smyth to chairman, WLPB, memorandum re: "Extension of Central Labor
Recruiting Program," n.d. (c. Nov. 8, 1918), attached to G. Bell to M. Van Kleeck, Nov.
6, 1918, RG 86, Records of the Women's Bureau: Women in Industry Service, box 2,
Correspondence of Miss Van Kleeck with Members of the War Labor Policies Board.
Another copy of Smyth's memorandum is located in RG 1, WLPB Papers, Correspondence of Chairman and Exec. Secr., file: "Employment Service: Advertising." The memorandum obviously refers to the agreement whereby the WIB was to delegate its priority
powers to the community labor boards to enable them to threaten employers engaged
in nonessential industries with closure unless they agreed to release labor for essential
projects.

46. F. L. Lamson, WIB, to F. B. McLeary, Sept. 14, 1918 (Weekly Progress Report), copy in,
RG 1, WLPB Records, Correspondence of Chairman and Exec. Secr., file: "Lamson, F. L."
See also Lamson to Frankfurter, memorandum re: "Plan for making use of the Community Labor Boards of the U.S. Employment Service as instruments for the securing of
labor data required by the Department of Labor and the War Industries Board," Sept.
18, 1918, RG 1, WLPB Records, Correspondence of Chairman and Exec. Secr., file: "Community Boards." See also *USES Bulletin* 1, no. 39 (Oct. 29, 1918), 8. For the questionnaire
used and the list of industries included in the original survey see *USES Bulletin* 1, no. 36
(Oct. 1, 1918), 1–2.

47. See testimony of Dudley R. Kennedy, wartime manager of industrial labor relations for
the Emergency Fleet Corporation at Hog Island, in U.S. Congress, Joint Committees
on Labor, *National Employment System: Hearings*, 66th Cong., 1st sess., 1919, 472.

48. N. A. Smyth to chairman, WLPB, memorandum re: "Extension of Central Labor Recruiting Program"), n.d. (c. Nov. 8, 1918), RG 86, Records of the Women's Bureau: Women

in Industry Service, box 2, Correspondence of Miss Van Kleeck with Members of the War Labor Policies Board.

49. For the text of the resolution see the 2-page typescript headed "Proposed Resolutions" attached to ibid. Agricultural labor and railroad labor remained outside the scope of the proposed regulations; obviously, USES officials still felt that neither the Department of Agriculture nor the U.S. Railroad Administration were yet prepared to accept such complete reliance on the Department of Labor.

50. See printed newsletter distributed by the Committee on Industrial Relations of the Chamber of Commerce entitled *Liberal Appropriations: United States Employment Service* (June 28, 1918), RG 32, USSB Records, Construction Organization, Industrial Relations Division, General Records, box 64, file 53793-1: "United States Employment Service—General." See also other newsletters: *Organization of Local Labor Administrations,* July 22, 1918, and *A New Service,* Aug. 1, 1918, copies in RG 1, WLPB Records, ser. 7, Information File, box 45, file: "Chamber of Commerce."

51. A formal resolution of support was passed at a National Industrial Conference Board (NICB) meeting on June 20, 1918. In line with that resolution, the NICB then established a Committee on Cooperation to assist. See Magnus Alexander, managing director of NICB, to F. Frankfurter, July 3, 1918, RG 1, WLPB Records, Correspondence of Chairman and Exec. Secr., box 26, file "Conference—Metal Trades Union—Aug. 12." The same file contains a typescript copy of the June 20 resolution.

52. *Report of Proceedings of the Thirty-Eighth Annual Convention of the American Federation of Labor held at St. Paul, Minn., June 10 to 20, Inclusive* (Washington, D.C., 1918), 329.

53. I. W. Litchfield to officers, USES, July 16, 1918, RG 20, Department of Labor: USES, 1917–19, box 14, Correspondence with Director-General, File: "July 15—July 31," Connecticut State Archives, Hartford. For more detail on union cooperation, see report of address by I. W. Litchfield, chief of Clearance Section, USES, in *Proceedings of National War Labor Conference,* 64; *USES Bulletin* 1, no. 22 (June 25, 1918), 1, 5.

54. See, for example, the report of the conference between AFL and USES officials in October 1918, in H. Frayne to K. Ingels, WIB, memorandum, Oct. 24, 1918, RG 61, WIB Records, Technical or Commodity File, 21A-A4, Construction Projects, Labor, box 772, file: "Labor."

55. See the comments of Henry Sterling, legislative representative of the AFL, and Frank Morrison, secretary of the AFL, in U.S. Congress, Joint Committees on Labor, *National Employment System: Hearings,* 66th Cong., 1st sess., 1919, 276, 468. For a general comment on the extent of employment work done within trade unions, see D. P. Smelser, *Unemployment and American Trade Unions* (Baltimore: Johns Hopkins Univ. Press, 1919), chs. 3–4.

7. The Industrial Northeast
Connecticut

1. L. C. Marshall, "The War Labor Program and Its Administration," *Journal of Political Economy* 26 (May 1918): 427–28. See also the graphic map of the distribution of 541 construction projects, worth 817 million dollars, undertaken by the construction divison of the army, in Thomas G. Frothingham, *The American Reinforcement in the World War* (Garden City, N.Y.: Doubleday, Page, 1927), 128. It was not until the fall of 1918 that

government agencies began to contemplate methods to achieve a wider geographical spread of contracts. See J. B. Densmore, "Lessons of the War in Shifting Labor," *Annals of the American Academy of Political and Social Science* 81 (Jan. 1919): 35.

2. The papers of the Connecticut branch of the USES, which have been preserved in the state archives at Hartford, are by far the best and fullest record of any industrial state. That fact helps explain the focus on Connecticut in this chapter. Neighboring New York City was the most important labor market in the country, and that state also had an important industrial base, but virtually all records of the New York USES appear to have been lost.

3. For details cited concerning Connecticut, see David M. Roth, *Connecticut: A Bicentennial History* (New York: W. W. Norton, 1979), 175–77; John W. Jeffries, *Testing the Roosevelt Coalition: Connecticut Society and Politics in the Era of World War II* (Knoxville: Univ. of Tennessee Press, 1979), 5–7.

4. R. M. Bissell to H. K. Smith, May 21, 1917, RG 30, Records of Council of Defense, 1917–19, Classified File, file K.01: "Organization of Man Power and Labor Committee," Connecticut State Archives (CSA), Hartford. On the Connecticut State Council of Defense in World War I, see William J. Breen, *Uncle Sam at Home: Civilian Mobilization, Wartime Federalism, and the Council of National Defense, 1917–1919* (Westport, Conn.: Greenwood Press, 1984), ch. 4.

5. See the comment in E. Shipman Smith, Connecticut Labor Press, New Haven, to H. K. Smith, Nov. 13, 1917, CSA, RG 30, Records of Council of Defense, 1917–19, Classified File, file K.02: "Smith, Herbert Knox. Correspondence File."

6. T. Hewes to W. B. Hale, Aug. 11, 1917, ibid., Classified File, file K.250: "Labor Exchanges—Employment Service."

7. "Report of Committee on Man Power and Labor (December 7, 1918)," pp. 1, 4, 6, 7, CSA, RG 30, Records of Council of Defense, 1917–19, Historical Records Department: "Collected Materials, 1917–19," file: "Manpower and Labor."

8. Henry W. Farnam, chairman, "Report of Community Labor Board, District No. 3, for November (December 5, 1918)," CSA, RG 20, Records of the Labor Department (Part A): United States Employment Service, 1917–19 (hereafter USES 1917–19), Correspondence with the Director-General, file: "Dec. 10–Dec. 14, 1918." The statistics were gathered in late 1918 during a survey of manufacturers by the Community Labor Board, District No. 3, which encompassed the city of New Haven.

9. H. K. Smith to L. C. Marshall, Dec. 18, 1917, CSA, RG 30, Records of Council of Defense, 1917–19, Classified File, file K.230: "H. K. Smith's Correspondence re Labor Supply and Shortage."

10. In addition to the five state employment offices, there were forty-nine private employment agencies in operation that were licensed and inspected by the Connecticut Bureau of Labor. *Twenty-Seventh Report of the Bureau of Labor for the Two Years ended November 30, 1916: State of Connecticut: Public Document No. 23* (Hartford, 1916), 55–56, 79.

11. H. K. Smith to J. A. B. Scherer, Dec. 20, 1917, CSA, RG 30, Records of Council of Defense, 1917–19, Classified File, file K.250: "Labor Exchanges—Employment Service."

12. See "Report of the Connecticut Council of Defense to His Excellency, Governor Marcus H. Holcomb re: The Federal Employment Service (March 6, 1919)," 1–3, CSA, RG 20, Department of Labor: USES, 1917–19, General Correspondence, file: "Reports: Leo A.

Korper, Federal Director." On finances, see L. Korper to director-general (Field Organization Division), memorandum re: "Employment Office Reports," Nov. 30, 1918, box 15, Correspondence with the Director-General, file: "Nov 21–Nov 30." Practically all expenses except salaries were paid out of the state grant. Connecticut spent more than the federal government on the operation of the USES within the state. On relations with the existing state employment offices, see Korper to C. T. Clayton, USES, May 1, 1918, Correspondence with Director General, file: "May 1–May 14."

13. J. W. Alsop to R. M. Bissell, memorandum, Jan. 3, 1918, CSA, RG 30, Council of Defense, 1917–19, Miscellaneous Correspondence, file: "Bissell, Richard M." Alsop was the manager and Bissell was the chairman of the Connecticut State Council of Defense. The appointment of Korper was an unusual step; Pennsylvania was the only other state to appoint a business executive to direct the employment service rather than someone with experience specifically in employment office work.

14. *Report of the Connecticut State Council of Defense, December, 1918* (Hartford, 1919), 107–8.

15. [Leo A. Korper], "Special Report, Committee on Employment Service, Connecticut State Council of Defense, to Dec. 31, 1918," 3–4, in "Report of the Connecticut Council of Defense to His Excellency, Governor Marcus H. Holcomb, re the Federal Employment Service, (March 6, 1919)," CSA, RG 20, Department of Labor: USES, 1917–19, General Correspondence, file: "Reports: Leo A. Korper, Federal Director."

16. Korper to director-general, USES, memorandum re: "Publicity," Oct. 15, 1918, ibid., Correspondence with the Director-General, file: "October 16–October 24." The four superintendents with business backgrounds were C. E. Davenport, Hartford; A. W. Burritt, Bridgeport; Ralph W. Budd, Waterbury; Edwin S. Blodgett, Stamford. The union man was Julius C. Stremlau, the immediate past-president of the Connecticut Federation of Labor and labor's representative on the State Council of Defense. The Yale academic was Henry C. Fairchild, assistant professor of the science of society at Yale University and secretary of the university's Bureau of Appointments, which maintained contact with Yale graduates throughout the country. He was given partial leave from his teaching duties. Burritt was known favorably in labor circles for his recently published book on profit sharing. Arthur W. Burritt, *Profit Sharing: Its Principles and Practice, A Collaboration* (New York: Harper and Brothers, 1918). Korper was careful to select superintendents who were not offensive to labor. See, for example, his comment on Davenport reported in *Hartford Daily Courant,* Apr. 7, 1918, clipping in CSA, RG 20, Department of Labor: USES, 1917–19, box 44, scrapbooks.

17. [Leo A. Korper], "Special Report, Committee on Employment Service, Connecticut State Council of Defense, to Dec. 31, 1918," p. 3, in "Report of the Connecticut Council of Defense to His Excellency, Governor Marcus H. Holcomb (March 6, 1919)." On the regular conferences, see L. Korper to director-general, USES, memorandum re: "General Order A-26," Nov. 19, 1918, CSA, RG 20, Department of Labor: USES, 1917–19, Correspondence with the Director-General, file: "Nov. 15–Nov. 20." Concern over recruiting women for war industry came quite late. The Woman's Division was not established until September 1918.

18. See, for example, Korper's speech reported in *Report of Proceedings of the National War Labor Conference, Washington, June 13–15, 1918* (Washington, D.C.: GPO, 1918), 83. Employment experts also denounced the indiscriminate recruiting methods adopted by the

Department of Labor. See Charles B. Barnes, "Employment and the Labor Market," *American Economic Review* (Supplement) 8 (Mar. 1918): 172–73.

19. See "Convention of the Connecticut Council of Defense, January 17 and 18, 1918," pp. 69–70, CSA, RG 30, Records of Council of Defense, 1917–19, Classified File. Other state branches of the USES had a similar defensive outlook. See, for example, *How Ohio Mobilized Her Resources,* esp. 82–84, 115.

20. *Report of Proceedings of the National War Labor Conference, Washington, June 13–15, 1918,* 83. Korper referred particularly to the difficulty he experienced in overcoming the suspicions of employers in Waterbury. See also *Report of the Connecticut State Council of Defense, December 1918* (Hartford, 1919), 108.

21. L. Korper to director-general, USES, memorandum re: "Recruiting Labor," Oct. 11, 1918, CSA, RG 20, Department of Labor: USES, 1917–19, Correspondence with the Director General, file: "Oct 11–Oct 15."

22. See Breen, *Uncle Sam at Home,* 61–62. See also L. Korper to D. M. Reynolds, July 20, 1918, ibid., Correspondence with the Director-General, file: "July 1–July 14."

23. L. Korper to director-general, Aug. 17, 1918, ibid., box 14, Correspondence with the Director General, file: "Aug 16–Aug 30"; see also L. Korper to USES, Apr. 23, 1918, file: "April," and to I. W. Litchfield, July 8, 1918, file "July 1–July 14."

24. L. Korper to A. W. Burritt, Bridgeport office superintendent, Aug. 22, 1918, ibid., box 23, file: "Branch Office–Bridgeport: July & August." This policy was accepted by the Washington office of the USES. See N. A. Smyth to L. Korper, Aug. 23, 1918, ibid., Correspondence with the Director-General, file: "Aug 16–Aug 30."

25. L. Korper to C. T. Clayton, memorandum re: "Competition for Skilled Labor," June 6, 1918, ibid., Correspondence with the Director-General, file: "June 1–June 15."

26. L. Korper to I. W. Litchfield, July 2, 1918, ibid., file:" July 1–July 14."

27. L. Korper to director-general, Oct. 31, 1918, ibid., Correspondence with the Director-General, file: "Oct 25–Oct 31."

28. Federal director for Connecticut to director-general (Control Division), memorandum re: "Orders for Help—Reports of," Nov. 5, 1918, ibid., file: "Nov 1–Nov 9."

29. L. Korper to director-general, USES, memorandum re: "Forms," Dec. 27, 1918, ibid., Correspondence with the Director-General, file: "Dec 24–Dec 31." On the estimated savings, see [L. Korper], "Special Report, Committee on Employment Service, Connecticut State Council of Defense, to Dec. 31, 1918," p. 5, in "Report of the Connecticut Council of Defense to His Excellency, Governor Marcus H. Holcomb (March 6, 1919)."

30. *USES Bulletin* 1, no. 22 (June 25, 1918), 2.

31. L. Korper to C. T. Clayton, July 20, 1918, CSA, RG 20, Department of Labor: USES, 1917–19, Correspondence with the Director-General, file: "July 15–July 31." The meeting also agreed that workers absent for three consecutive days "with insufficient cause" would be automatically discharged. See *Hartford Times,* July 24, 1918, in CSA, RG 20, Department of Labor: USES, 1917–19, box 44, Scrapbooks. A similar scheme, which may have owed something to the Waterbury example, was subsequently developed in Detroit in October 1918. See Thomas A. Klug, "Employers' Strategies in the Detroit Labor Market, 1900–1929," in Nelson Lichtenstein and Steven Meyer, eds., *On the Line: Essays in the History of Auto Work* (Urbana: Univ. of Illinois Press, 1989). Other localities also began to experiment with the idea. The "stabilization plans" introduced in World War II were very

similar. See Joel Seidman, *American Labor from Defense to Reconversion* (Chicago: Univ. of Chicago Press, 1953), 159–61; George Q. Flynn, *The Mess in Washington: Manpower Mobilization in World War II* (Westport, Conn.: Greenwood Press, 1979), esp. 59–75.

32. The encouragement of centralized hiring practices in Waterbury meshed with a much broader policy of the wartime USES to encourage the development of employment management. The war gave to the recently formed employment management movement substantial recognition and status. Government departments hoped that it would reduce the enormous labor turnover. Reformers hoped that it would lead to a more rational and more sympathetic environment for workers. For an excellent general study, including the World War I period, of what came to be called personnel management, see Sanford M. Jacoby, "The Development of Internal Labor Markets in American Manufacturing Firms," in Paul Osterman, ed., *Internal Labor Markets* (Cambridge, Mass.: MIT Univ. Press, 1984), 23–69.

33. Statement of L. Korper in *Report of Proceedings of the National War Labor Conference, Washington, June 13–15, 1918,* 83–84. See also R. Budd to N. A. Smyth, June 14, 1918, CSA, RG 20, Department of Labor: USES, 1917–19, Correspondence with the Director-General, file: "June 1–June 15."

34. Newspaper clipping, "Disapproval of Waterbury Plan by Laboring Men," c. Aug.–Sept. 1918 (unclear which newspaper), CSA, RG 20, Department of Labor: USES, 1917–19, box 44, scrapbooks. The clipping refers to a recent meeting of delegates to the Central Labor Union, which had expressed "total disapproval" of the Waterbury Plan.

35. R. Beadle, secretary of Waterbury Central Labor Union, to L. Korper, Aug. 17, 1918, and J. B. Densmore to L. Korper, Sept. 10, 1918, ibid., file: "Sept 1–Sept 14."

36. L. Korper to C. T. Clayton, July 20, 1918, ibid., file: "July 15–July 31." Under this arrangement presumably Budd himself had the deciding vote in the event of deadlock.

37. L. Korper to director-general, USES, Sept. 12, 1918, ibid., file: "Sept 1–Sept 14."

38. *Waterbury* (Conn.) *Democrat,* July 29, 1918, clipping in ibid., box 44, scrapbooks.

39. David Elder, federal director for Connecticut, "Annual Report United States Employment Service, State of Connecticut, Fiscal Year Ending June 30, 1919," p. 6, ibid., file: "Reports: Leo A. Korper, Federal Director."

40. R. W. Budd to F. Frankfurter, July 26, 1918, RG 1, War Labor Policies Board Papers, Correspondence of Chairman and Exec. Secr., file: "Employment: A–D." See also R. W. Budd to N. A. Smyth, USES, June 14, 1918, and L. Korper to C. T. Clayton, USES, July 20, 1918, CSA, RG 20, Department of Labor: USES, 1917–19, Correspondence with the Director-General, files: "June 1–June 15" and "July 15–July 31."

41. N. A. Smyth to L. Korper, telegram, Aug. 16, 1918, CSA, RG 20, Department of Labor: USES, 1917–19, Correspondence with the Director-General, file: "Aug 16–Aug 30."

42. War Industries Board, "Memorandum based on statements by Mr. Everett Morss: Brass Rolling and Drawing Mills," n.d. (early Sept. 1918?), RG 61, War Industries Board Records, Technical or Commodity File, 21A-A4, Construction Projects, Labor, box 772, file: "Brass and Copper Industry—Labor."

43. "Resume of Annual Reports of Federal Directors for States" (Connecticut), addendum to *Second Annual Report of U.S. Employment Service for fiscal year ended June 30, 1919,* 66th Cong., 2d sess., H. Doc. 7734, 951.

44. Edwin S. Blodgett, *How Stamford Is Meeting Her War Labor Problems* (Stamford, Conn., 1918), 6–8, 10, 14, 18. Although the film cannot be located, Blodgett's pamphlet contains

some excellent stills from it. The Stamford scheme probably drew on the Waterbury experience. Copies of both the agreement between the Stamford employers and the USES office and of the daily labor entrance, exit, and absence forms to be filled out by employers are reprinted in ibid., 7, 9. Contrasting with the situation in Waterbury, the Stamford Central Labor Union was reasonably cooperative. See *Stamford Bulletin* (Stamford USES Office) 1, no. 3 (Aug. 24, 1918), 1. Copies of Blodgett's pamphlet and the *Stamford Bulletin* found in CSA, RG 20, Department of Labor: USES, 1917–19, box 99, file: "Stamford Office: Clippings and Publicity Material, 1918."

45. J. B. Densmore, director, USES, to L. A. Korper, Feb. 12, 1918, CSA, RG 20, Department of Labor: USES, 1917–19, Correspondence with the Director-General, file: "January–March."

46. L. Korper to J. B. Densmore, Feb. 15, 1918, ibid.

47. C. T. Clayton to L. Korper, Apr. 29, 1918, ibid., file: "April"; L. Korper to C. T. Clayton, May 1, 1918, file: "May 1–May 14"; C. T. Clayton to L. Korper, May 20, 1918, file: "May 15–May 31."

48. S. E. Freund, director of Clearance Section, USES, to federal director [Korper], Connecticut, memo re: "Recruiting of Labor at Bridgeport," Nov. 13, 1918, ibid., Correspondence with Director-General, file: "Nov 15–Nov 20."

49. Federal director for Connecticut to director-general (Clearance Division), memorandum re: "Recruiting of Labor in Bridgeport" Nov. 18, 1918, ibid., Correspondence with Director-General, file: "Nov 15–Nov 20." In September Korper had experienced a similar problem with union officials attempting to recruit plumbers and bricklayers for service in Virginia and had complained bitterly about the practice that was very difficult to detect and control. See L. Korper to director-general, USES, Sept. 21, 1918, ibid., Correspondence with Director-General, file: "Sept 15–Sept 21."

50. Federal director for Connecticut to director-general (Clearance Division), memorandum re: "Recruiting of Labor in Bridgeport," Nov. 18, 1918, ibid., Correspondence with Director-General, file: "Nov 15–Nov 20." For a copy of the letter sent by Korper to the chairman of the Community Labor Board, see L. Korper to W. P. Kirk, chairman of Community Labor Board, District No. 6, Bridgeport, Oct. 19, 1918, ibid., Correspondence with Director-General, file: "Oct 16–Oct 24."

51. S. E. Freund, director of Clearance Division, to federal director, Hartford, memorandum re: "Complaint in connection with recruitment of skilled labor," Nov. 21, 1918; L. Korper to director-general (Clearance Division), memorandum re: "Complaint in connection with recruitment of skilled labor," Nov. 26, 1918, ibid., Correspondence with Director-General, file: "Nov 21–Nov 30."

8. The Midwest and South

1. See chapter 2 above, "Federalist Aspirations in the States."

2. W. M. Leiserson, "Public Employment Offices in the United States," *Proceedings of the American Association of Public Employment Offices: Annual Meetings . . . 1913–1915,* BLS Bulletin No. 192 (1916), 16.

3. W. M. Leiserson, "To the Members and Delegates of the American Association of Public Employment Offices," Buffalo, July 18, 1916, and Charles J. Boyd, general superintendent

of Illinois Free Employment Offices, "Suboffices of Public Employment Bureaus," *Proceedings of the Fourth Annual Meeting of the American Association of Public Employment Offices, Buffalo, N.Y., July 20 and 21, 1916,* BLS Bulletin No. 220 (1917), 7, 90.

4. During the war, some states transferred temporary control of their employment offices to their state councils of defense. This happened, for example, in Ohio. In Minnesota a mixed system developed. Most states retained control of their employment offices, which were usually operated through the state's industrial commission or department of labor.

5. George P. Hambrecht, chairman of Industrial Commission of Wisconsin, "Emergency Employment Situation in Wisconsin: An Open Letter Dated March 21, 1919, addressed to: Hon. E. L. Phillip, Governor of Wisconsin, Members of the Senate, Members of the Assembly," pp. 2, 3, 4, 5, 10, George P. Hambrecht Papers, 1919–35, State Historical Society of Wisconsin; "Resume of Annual Reports of Federal Directors for States" (Minnesota), in *Second Annual Report of the United States Employment Service, for fiscal year ended June 30, 1919,* 991; *How Ohio Mobilized Her Resources,* 86.

6. On the complaints of the Illinois employment service, see Charles J. Boyd to General Advisory Board, Illinois Free Employment Offices, Feb. 24, 1919, State Council of Defense Papers, Public Service Reserve, Illinois State Archives. Although written in early 1919, this letter sums up the various complaints of the state service against the way in which the USES officers conducted the Chicago joint office throughout its year of operation. For further detail, see ibid., file: "Minutes of General Advisory Board of Illinois Free Employment Offices," especially the meetings of Feb. 19, 1917, Sept. 14, 1918, and Mar. 28, 1919. For meeting of Feb. 12, 1918, see ibid., Boys Working Reserve, file: "Reports of Meetings."

7. "National Defense Conference held under the Auspices of the Council of National Defense, Washington, D.C., May 2 and 3, 1917: Transcript of Proceedings," esp. 65–72, RG 62, Council of National Defense Records, Files and Records Division (Post-War), 17-B2, box 1095.

8. See chapter 2 above.

9. Fred C. Croxton, "War Employment Work in Ohio," BLS *Monthly Review* 4 (June 1917): 996. The various forms used are reproduced on pp. 998–1002.

10. W. M. Leiserson, "Mobilizing and Distributing Farm Labor in Ohio," BLS *Monthly Review* 6 (Apr. 1918): 55–56; *How Ohio Mobilized Her Resources,* 77.

11. W. M. Leiserson, "Mobilizing and Distributing Farm Labor in Ohio," 62.

12. "Resume of Annual Reports of Federal Directors for States" (Wisconsin), addendum to *Second Annual Report of the United States Employment Service . . . 1919,* 1045–46.

13. *Report of the Wisconsin State Council of Defense Covering the Period April 12, 1917–June 30, 1919,* 30, copy in Council of Defense Records: State Council of Defense, 1918–19, ser. 1651 (76/1/12), State Historical Society of Wisconsin. For the response in Minnesota, see [Don D. Lescohier?], "Report on the Operation of the Minneapolis office of the Minnesota Public Employment Service (June, 1918)," War Records Commission: U.S. Employment Service, 1918–19, State Headquarters File, box 1, file 1-25, Minnesota Historical Society.

14. See U.S. Congress, House Appropriation Committee, *Sundry Civil Bill, 1919: Hearings,* 65th Cong., 2d sess., 1918, 2:1609 (memorandum submitted by Department of Labor, c. Apr.–May 1918).

15. *How Ohio Mobilized Her Resources,* 83–84. This report reproduces the text of the exchange of telegrams between Ohio and Washington.

16. N. A. Smyth, "The New Labor Recruiting Program," *Report of Proceedings of the National War Labor Conference, Washington, June 13–15, 1918,* 23.

17. See chapter 6 for details.

18. For quotation, see Young to Perkins, n.d. (Aug. 21, 1918?), RG 1, WLPB Records, Correspondence of Chairman and Exec. Secr., file: "Employment: C-1-f:D-K." On labor turnover at Nitro, see W.H. Winans, "Report on Inspection Trip to Nitro, W. Va.," n.d. (c. Aug. 16, 1918 [the inspection trip was carried out Aug. 15–16, 1918]), ibid., file: "Nitro: B-21."

19. See, for example, C. A. Munroe to W. E. Hall, Aug. 23, 1918; C. A. Munroe to S. Insull, Aug. 20, 1918, State Council of Defense Papers: Public Service Reserve, file: "USPSR—Letters, etc.—August, 1918," Illinois State Archives.

20. A. H. Young to S. Insull, n.d. (Aug. 29, 1918?), RG 1, WLPB Records, Correspondence of Herbert F. Perkins, box 40, file: "F. Frankfurter." The delegation was to consist of four, but for various reasons only one of those selected, Arthur H. Young, was able to go to Washington.

21. Ibid. See also J. B. Densmore, "Lessons of the War in Shifting Labor," *Annals of the American Academy of Political and Social Science* 81 (Jan. 1918): 35.

22. David Kennedy, *Over Here: The First World War and American Society,* 281. For further detail on the black migration and on efforts of southern communities to check the migration, see Emmett J. Scott, *Negro Migration During the War,* Carnegie Endowment for International Peace, Preliminary Economic Studies of the War, No. 16 (New York: Oxford Univ. Press, 1920), chs. 6, 7. On the black migration more generally, see William Trotter, Jr., *The Great Migration in Historical Perspective: New Dimensions of Race, Class, and Gender* (Bloomington: Indiana Univ. Press, 1991); Carole Marks, *Farewell--We're Good and Gone: The Great Black Migration* (Bloomington: Indiana Univ. Press, 1989); James R. Grossman, *Land of Hope: Chicago, Black Southerners, and the Great Migration* (Chicago: Univ. of Chicago Press, 1989).

23. J. B. Densmore to secretary of labor, May 21, 1918, RG 174, Department of Labor Records, box 133, file: 129/14-C.

24. H. W. Weir, federal director, Mississippi, to director-general, USES, memorandum re: "Soliciting of Labor," Nov. 12, 1918, copy attached to N. A. Smyth, assistant director-general, USES, to Hugh Frayne, War Industries Board, memorandum re: "Recruiting of Labor at Wiggins, Mississippi," Nov. 16, 1918, RG 61, WIB Records, Labor Division, 8-A1, General Correspondence, file 210: "Labor Recruiting." In this particular instance it seems likely that the USES recruiter had actually overstepped his instructions.

25. U.S. Congress, Joint Committees on Labor, *National Employment Service: Hearings on S. 688, S. 1442, and HR. 4305.* 66th Cong., 1st sess., 1919, 170, 272 (see esp. statements by Miss Grace E. Cooke). The southern states were the only ones to pass laws restricting the activities of labor agents, or "emigrant agents," as they were called. The reaction had begun before U.S. entry into the war. In 1915 Alabama passed legislation forcing "emigrant agents" who solicited labor for interstate projects to pay an annual license fee of $500 in every county where they operated. In the same year North Carolina levied a tax of $100 for a license plus $100 for every county where the agent

operated. In 1916 Virginia raised its license fee from $25 to $500 on itinerant labor agents. In 1917 Georgia insisted on a $1,000 bond plus monthly reports to the commissioner of commerce and labor. See *American Labor Legislation Review* 5 (Dec. 1915): 770; 6 (Sept. 1916): 290; 7 (Sept. 1917): 553.

26. See, for example, S. Gompers to Secretary W. B. Wilson, Aug. 8, 1917, Samuel Gompers Papers, Letterbooks, vol. 235:871–74, Manuscript Division, Library of Congress.

27. See "No Need for the Importation of Chinese and Mexican Labor," *USES Bulletin* 1, no. 2 (Feb. 4, 1918), 3.

28. *First Annual Report of the United States Employment Service (August 1, 1918)*, 692–93. Approximately 17,600 Mexicans entered the United States during 1918 under the relaxed provisions. See also Francis G. Ware, ed., *The American Year Book: A Record of Events and Progress, 1918* (New York, 1919), 471.

29. For details on the appointment of both Haynes and Jackson and the latter's proposals, see William J. Breen, "Sectional Influences on National Policy: The South, the Labor Department, and the Wartime Labor Mobilization, 1917–1918," in Bruce Clayton and John A. Salmond, eds., *The South Is Another Land: Essays on the Twentieth-Century South* (Westport, Conn.: Greenwood Press, 1987), 73–76. See also Henry P. Guzda, "Social Experiment of the Labor Department: The Division of Negro Economics," *Public Historian* 4 (Fall 1982): 7–37.

30. U.S. Congress, House Committee on Appropriations, *Sundry Civil Bill, 1919. Hearings, before a subcommittee of the Committee on Appropriations, House of Representatives, in charge of Sundry Civil Appropriation Bill for 1919*, 65th Cong., 2d sess., 1918, 1577–78 (testimony of J. B. Densmore).

31. J. B. Densmore to F. Frankfurter, "Memorandum Concerning Personnel and Functions of District Superintendents," May 29, 1918, RG 1, WLPB Records, Correspondence of Chairman and Exec. Secr., file: "Employment Service, May–June–July: c-i-f."

32. See unheaded, three-page, carbon typescript ("Submitted by James A. Metcalf, Assistant Superintendent, 6th District, U.S. Employment Service, Meredian, Mississippi, August 26, 1918") attached to Assistant Secretary Post to secretary of labor, memorandum re: "Labor Card System in Sixth District of U.S. Employment Service," Oct. 4, 1918, RG 174, Department of Labor: Chief Clerk's File, box 133, file 129/14-D: "USES: Function & Scope." The scheme proposed by Williams was an extension of the idea behind the "work-or-fight" regulations promulgated by the Selective Service System in March 1918. Instead of covering only those young men subject to the draft, the Williams scheme embraced all able-bodied members of the community, both male and female. On the "work-or-fight" regulations, see John Whiteclay Chambers II, *To Raise an Army*, ch. 7.

33. L. Post to W. B. Wilson, "Report of Western Trip (October 5, 1918)," p. 7, RG 174, Chief Clerk's File, box 89, file 20/746. See also Assistant Secretary Post to secretary of labor, memorandum re: "Letter of October 17, 1918, from Cliff Williams," Oct. 22, 1918, William B. Wilson Papers, box marked "1918," file: "1918," Historical Society of Pennsylvania.

34. *USES Bulletin* 1, no. 47 (Jan. 17, 1919), 7. At each mass meeting a Loyalty League was organized with an executive committee "on which employers, employees, and farmers each had six representatives." There was reported to be a good deal of sympathy within the black community itself for moves to put idlers to work and to encourage, through the formation of special Saturday Service Leagues, a full six days' work on the part of all

agricultural laborers. See, for example, J. F. Duggar, director of Cooperative Extension Work in Agriculture and Home Economics, Auburn, Alabama, to Bradford Knapp, chief of Extension Work in the South, U.S. Department of Agriculture, Apr. 5, 1918, RG 16, Department of Agriculture Records: Office of the Secretary, 1918, Incoming Correspondence, Labor (Apr.), acc. 234, dr. 155.

9. Reconstruction and Political Misjudgment, 1918–1919

1. Burl Noggle, *Into the Twenties: The United States from Armistice to Normalcy* (Urbana: Univ. of Illinois Press, 1974), 68, 75. In the twelve-month period after the armistice, four million servicemen and between two and three million war workers were discharged. See also Edward T. Devine, "The Federal Employment Service: Analysis and Forecast," *Survey* 42 (Apr. 5, 1919): 11, 12.

2. *Second Annual Report of USES,* 935, 899. Regulations governing the centralized recruiting program were immediately canceled, and the Public Service Reserve, the Boys' Working Reserve, the Stevedores and Marine Workers' Division, and the Mining Division were discontinued as separate administrative entities.

3. "Memorandum for Mr. Frankfurter," Nov. 12, 1918, photocopy in Felix Frankfurter Papers, box 189, file: "War Department: Correspondence: Oct–Nov. 1918."

4. *USES Bulletin* 1, no. 43 (Dec. 10, 1918), 1–8; *Second Annual Report of USES,* 911. It was estimated that only 300 of the 2,594 Soldiers and Sailors Bureaus were actually located in USES offices, and the USES itself placed only 474,085 of the millions of soldiers demobilized and civilians changing jobs between December 1, 1918, and September 27, 1919. See Sautter, *Three Cheers for the Unemployed,* 157–58. Sautter fails to appreciate the degree of animosity within the War Department toward the USES.

5. *USES Bulletin,* 1, no. 43 (Dec. 10, 1918), 1–8. See ibid., 8, for list of organizations represented on the Central Board.

6. *Third Annual Report of the Council of National Defense for the Fiscal Year ended June 30, 1919* (Washington, D.C.: GPO, 1919), 107. The existence of this parallel War Department organization is not mentioned in the *Second Annual Report of the USES,* which covered the fiscal year ending June 30, 1919.

7. Dixon Wecter, *When Johnny Comes Marching Home* (Cambridge, Mass.: Houghton Mifflin, 1944), 358. Friction was very pronounced in the Northwest states; some local officers of the USES were even charged with "leftist" or "Bolshevik" tendencies.

8. Resolutions adopted at the annual conventions of the National Association of Manufacturers and the National Industrial Conference Board, held in May 1919, were read into the record of the mid-1919 congressional hearing on the future of the USES. See U.S. Congress, Joint Committee on Labor, *National Employment System: Hearings,* 66th Cong., 1st sess., 1919, 494–96 (testimony of James E. Emery).

9. See speech of Nathan A. Smyth, assistant director-general, USES, in "Minutes of Meeting of U.S. Employment Service held in the Assembly Room, 1 Madison Avenue, New York City, on Tuesday, February 4, 1919, at 10.30 o'clock A.M., Mr. Chiquoine presiding as Chairman," pp. 27–28, CSA, Hartford, RG 20, Department of Labor Records: USES 1917–19, box 10, file: "A. D. Chiquoine, Jr., Editor, *USES Bulletin,* Jan.–March."

10. Ibid.

11. Lombardi, *Labor's Voice*, 311. There had been a vigorous campaign mounted against the Service. See ibid., 309–11.

12. W. B. Wilson to Woodrow Wilson, Feb. 26, 1919, Woodrow Wilson Papers, ser. 4: Executive Office File, 1913–21, case file 19-G, Manuscript Division (microfilm ed., reel 172), Library of Congress.

13. Shelby M. Harrison, et al., *Public Employment Offices: Their Purpose, Structure and Methods* (New York: Russell Sage Foundation, 1924), 132.

14. *Second Annual Report of USES*, 902. Contributions to the support of USES offices averaged $168,000 per month until June 1919. See Udo Sautter, "Unemployment and Government: American Labor Exchanges before the New Deal," *Histoire Sociale—Social History* 18 (Nov. 1985): 343.

15. See A. D. Chiquoine, director of information, USES, to assistants to directors of information (Confidential), Apr. 16, 1919, CSA, Hartford, RG 20, Department of Labor: USES 1917–19, box 17, file: "April 15–April 30." See also "National-State Employment Service: Outline of a Bill Unanimously Adopted by Official National Conference at Washington for Submission to Congress," *American Labor Legislation Review* 9 (June 1919): 195. Secretary Wilson always argued that the organic law creating the department of labor, which specifically stated that one of its purposes was to advance the opportunities for profitable employment of wage earners, was sufficient legal authority for the establishment of the USES in that department and did not require specific congressional authorization. See *National Employment System: Hearings, 1919*, 54.

16. *National Employment System: Hearings, 1919*, 100, 102 (testimony of Nathan A. Smyth).

17. See, for example, A. D. Chiquoine to D. C. Rogers, Jr., Feb. 18, 1919, CSA, Hartford, RG 20, Department of Labor: USES 1917–19, box 10, file: "A. D. Chiquoine, Jr., editor, USES Bulletin, Jan.–Mar." This request, when relayed to employers in the various states, produced a considerable volume of letters of support for the USES. For Connecticut, see correspondence files in box 7 ("Correspondence, 1918–19") and box 40 ("Miscellaneous and Unfiled Material, 1917–19"). For Wisconsin, see War History Commission: Emergency Employment Situation in Wisconsin, 1918–19, ser. 83/0/11, box 1, State Historical Society of Wisconsin.

18. Secretary Wilson to Hon. Edward Keating, Feb. 21, 1919, copy attached to J. B. Densmore to George P. Hambrecht, USES federal director, Wisconsin, Apr. 3, 1919, Industrial Commission, Administration, Numerical Subject File, 1911–60, ser. 29/1/3, box 91, file C597: "Employment Offices—General, 1918–1919/A," State Historical Society of Wisconsin.

19. John B. Andrews, "Report of Work, 1919," *American Labor Legislation Review* 10 (Mar. 1920): 77. See also Felix Morley, "The United States Employment Service," *American Labor Year Book, 1919–1920* (New York: Rand School of Social Science, 1920), 70. Morley, who had been the assistant editor of the *USES Bulletin* in 1918, referred to the "inexcusable failure" of the secretary of labor over this issue.

20. See chapter 3 above.

21. See draft headed "A Bill to provide for the establishment in the Department of Labor of a Bureau to be known as the U.S. Employment Service," attached to N. A. Smyth to F. Frankfurter, memorandum, Jan. 2, 1919, RG 1, WLPB Records, Correspondence of Chairman and Exec. Secr., file: "Employment—1919." For Post's criticisms, see Post to Secretary Wilson, memorandum re: "Proposed bill to provide for the establishment in the

Department of a U.S. Employment Service," Jan. 23, 1919, RG 174, Department of Labor Records, Chief Clerk's File, box 133, file 129/14E.

22. See "Minutes of the conference on employment called by W. B. Wilson, Secretary of Labor, to meet in Washington April 23, 24, and 25, 1919," reprinted in *National Employment System: Hearings, 1919,* 71–72. For Densmore's recognition of the seriousness of the situation, see ibid., 633–34. For a discussion of the conference, see Sautter, *Three Cheers for the Unemployed,* 160–63. Sautter's belief that the wartime USES always represented a centralized structure causes him to misunderstand the motives behind much of the political maneuvering in the postwar period.

23. "Minutes of the conference on employment called by W. B. Wilson . . . April 23, 24 and 25, 1919," 71–83. The minutes included the texts of the various bills proposed. For Nathan Smyth's comments on the conference, see ibid., 83–85. Note especially his comment that delegates felt that a cooperative service would avoid "any possibility of the building up of a great Federal office-holding machine," which might "build up a great big political department." On the conference, see also "National-State Employment Service," *American Labor Legislation Review* 9 (June 1919): 196–97. For an abbreviated version, see BLS *Monthly Review* 8 (May 1919): 1404–5.

24. For the text of both the bill approved by the April conference and the one introduced in Congress by Nolan/Kenyon, see *Second Annual Report of the U.S. Employment Service (August 15, 1919),* 903–6. On the reasons for Secretary Wilson's deletion of the reference to an advisory council, see *National Employment System: Hearings, 1919,* 52–53 (testimony of Secretary of Labor William B. Wilson). Note that the *American Labor Legislation Review,* in its article supporting the measure, printed the bill as adopted by the conference, which included the optional advisory board. See "National-State Employment Service," *American Labor Legislation Review* 9 (June 1919): 195–98.

25. Members of the AAPEO, at the second annual conference of the association in September 1914, had voted in favor of the elimination of "all private employment offices operating for a profit" via federal and state legislation. At the annual meeting of the AAPEO, in September 1917, a draft bill had been unanimously approved that specifically gave to the USES the power to regulate private agencies. However, the Department of Labor was more cautious. The bill recommended to Congress by the department in its annual report issued in November 1917 did not mention private agencies.

26. The full texts of the three bills are published in *National Employment System: Hearings, 1919,* 6–11.

27. For quotation, see testimony of Secretary W. B. Wilson, *National Employment System: Hearings, 1919,* 32–33. See also the supportive testimonies of Nathan A. Smyth and Dr. George W. Kirchwey (who was former dean of the Columbia Law School and the federal director of the USES for New York State), ibid., 107, 430. For Densmore's comments, see ibid., 249. The USES had been exempted from the civil service regulations during the war.

28. For the Secretary Wilson quotation, see *National Employment System: Hearings, 1919,* 13–14. For the list of federal directors, see ibid., 113–14. See also the list printed in the *Congressional Record,* 65th Cong., 3d sess. (Feb. 22, 1919), 4069–70. A three-page, undated typescript of this list, headed "Personnel U.S. Employment Service," was found in RG 183, Bureau of Employment Security: USES 1907–49, box 1516 (among unfiled

material). On that list only five of the forty-eight state directors of the USES were actually union members, and approximately twelve were, or had been, members of state labor departments or industrial commissions.

29. *National Employment Service: Hearings, 1919,* 636–38. The examiner was immediately cautioned and reassigned to Maryland, but the memory of the incident was kept alive by critics of the USES. Densmore was exaggerating somewhat in saying that the Muskegon incident was the only point of criticism. For those within the wartime administration, the situation in Seattle had raised suspicions of a prounion bias in the operation of the USES. See chapter 4 above. For details on the Muskegon incident from the employers' viewpoint, see the testimony and supporting evidence of Harris E. Galpin in *National Employment Service: Hearings, 1919,* 384–403.

30. *National Employment Service: Hearings, 1919,* 494–95 (testimony of James A. Emery).

31. Ibid., 406, 414–15 (testimony of Mark M. Jones).

32. Ibid., 469–72 (testimony of Dudley R. Kennedy).

33. Ibid., 624 (testimony of William E. Hall).

34. Ibid., 18, 20–21, 49 (testimony of Secretary W. B. Wilson). See also ibid., 619 (testimony of William E. Hall). A table of fees charged by private agencies is in ibid., 621–22. On the opposition of private employment agencies to the USES, see ibid., 255–72 (testimony of Miss Grace E. Cooke, secretary of the Massachusetts Technical and Employment Association).

35. Ibid., 53 (testimony of Secretary W. B. Wilson). See also W. B. Wilson to Sen. W. S. Kenyon, May 26, 1919, p. 4, RG 174, Department of Labor Records, Chief Clerk's File, box 134, file 129/14G.

36. See *National Employment System: Hearings, 1919,* 331 (testimony of Royal Meeker), 306, 314 (testimony of Louis T. Bryant), 343, 347 (testimony of Don. D. Lescohier).

37. Ibid., 31 (testimony of Secretary W. B. Wilson).

38. See, for example, the testimony of Nathan A. Smyth and Royal Meeker in *National Employment System: Hearings, 1919,* 109, 331.

39. Ibid., 306 (testimony of Louis T. Bryant), 468 (testimony of Frank Morrison).

40. Ibid., esp. 330 (testimony of Royal Meeker).

41. Ibid., 276 (testimony of Henry Sterling), 467 (testimony of Frank Morrison). The June 1919 annual convention of the AFL had passed a resolution in favor of the Nolan bill.

42. *National Employment System: Hearings, 1919,* 494–95 (testimony of James A. Emery).

43. W. E. Hall to C. A. Munroe, June 20, 1919, State Council of Defense: Public Service Records, File: "U.S.P.S.R.—Letters: Feb–Oct, 1919," Illinois State Archives.

44. See J. B. Densmore to Joseph P. Tumulty, June 25, 1919, Woodrow Wilson Papers, ser. 4, case file 19G, Department of Labor, USES (reel 172).

45. Director-general and assistant director-general, USES, to secretary of labor, memorandum re: "Reorganization of the U.S. Employment Service," Sept. 27, 1919, RG 183, Bureau of Employment Security: USES Records, box 1515, Junior Division Personnel, file: "USES (misc.), Dec., 1918–April, 1924."

46. Densmore to all federal directors, telegram, Sept. 30, 1919, ibid.

47. D. M. Reynolds to H. M. Robinson, July 3, 1918, Henry Mauris Robinson Papers, file: "Reynolds, D. M. (1)," Hoover Institution Archives. Reynolds was a publicity man who was assisting the Department of Labor at the time.

48. For Densmore's view of the tactics of the "organized opposition," see director-general and assistant director-general, USES, to secretary of labor, memorandum re: "Reorganization of the U.S. Employment Service," Sept. 27, 1919, p. 2, RG 183, Bureau of Employment Security: USES Records, box 1515, Junior Division Personnel, file: "USES (misc.), Dec., 1918–April, 1924."

10. Postwar Reckoning

1. *Second Annual Report of the U.S. Employment Service (August 15, 1919)*, 935. However, almost half that activity took place after the armistice.

2. *Annual Report of the Secretary of War (November 11, 1919)*, vol. 1, pt. 1:18–19. U.S. Congress, 66th Cong., 2d Sess., H. Doc. 426. The War Department estimated that during the war the total number of men engaged in war work (excluding those in the armed services) was around 7.1 million, with another 18.6 million employed in nonwar work; approximately 2.2 million women were engaged in war work, with 25.7 million in nonwar work. These estimates are, of course, an inadequate indication of actual labor market demand because of the inflationary effect of labor turnover.

3. *Second Annual Report of the U.S. Employment Service (August 15, 1919)*, 898, 909, 925. Unfortunately, these figures on USES placements cannot be expressed as a proportion of the total number of placements throughout the nation for that period because no such statistics exist. Labor turnover, which probably averaged around 100 percent in the immediate prewar period, skyrocketed during the war to reach figures of 2,000 percent in certain plants. By late 1918, with the central recruiting program in effect, the USES statistics covered all large plants engaged in war contracts and employing over one hundred workers.

4. U.S. Congress, Joint Committees on Labor, *National Employment System: Hearings, 1919*, (testimony of Don D. Lescohier, July 14), 338. On labor turnover in this period, see Slichter, *The Turnover of Factory Labor*.

5. Don D. Lescohier, *The Labor Market* (New York: Macmillan, 1918), 198.

6. Ibid., 192.

7. Ibid., 193–94. See also Sautter, *Three Cheers for the Unemployed*, 165–67.

8. *Second Annual Report of the U.S. Employment Service (August 15, 1919)*, 888.

9. Lescohier, *Labor Market*, 195–96.

10. J. B. Densmore to secretary of labor, memorandum, Jan. 7, 1920 (note at bottom says "Approved January 24, 1920. W.B.W."), RG 174, Department of Labor Records, Chief Clerk's File, file 129/14-I. The same file contains a copy of USES General Order No. 16, headed "Policy of Department in re Labor Troubles (January 22, 1919)."

11. On the problems facing WIB administrators, see Robert D. Cuff, *The War Industries Board: Business-Government Relations during World War I* (Baltimore: Johns Hopkins Univ. Press, 1973), 3–6.

12. Sautter, *Three Cheers for the Unemployed*, 158–59.

13. Harrison, *Public Employment Offices*, 2.

14. Sautter, "Unemployment and Government," 346–47.

15. "Outline of Permanent Employment System," *Report of the President's Conference on Unemployment, September 26 to October 13, 1921*, 77 (resolution adopted on Oct. 11, 1921),

reprinted in Harrison, *Public Employment Offices,* 2–3n.2. See also Charles J. Boyd, Seaman F. Northrup, Louis H. Sullivan, Lewis T. Bryant, Fred C. Croxton, Fred Kleinsmith, Harry Lippart, and Robert J. Peters to Hon. Francis I. Jones, director-general, USES, Oct. 22, 1921, RG 174, Department of Labor Records, Chief Clerk's File, file 129/14J.

16. Sautter, "Unemployment and Government," 346.

17. *Twelfth Annual Report of the Secretary of Labor for the Fiscal Year ended June 30, 1924* (Washington, D.C.: GPO, 1924), 37. By 1930 the number of participating states had dropped from twenty-eight to twenty-three.

18. Darrell H. Smith, *The United States Employment Service: Its History, Activities and Organization* (Baltimore: Johns Hopkins Univ. Press, 1923), 59.

19. See the table of estimated federal expenses for 1924 and, for details on the individual states, the table of cooperating state employment offices in ibid., 60, 71–75.

20. For a breakdown of federal funding to the states in 1930, see Ruth M. Kellogg, *The United States Employment Service* (Chicago: Univ. of Chicago Press, 1933), 28 (table 4), which lists twenty-three cooperating states.

21. *Tenth Annual Report of the Secretary of Labor for the Fiscal Year ended June 30, 1922* (Washington, D.C.: GPO, 1922), 30. In 1923, following some criticism of the methods used, the scope of the survey was expanded somewhat and was integrated with the work of the Bureau of Labor Statistics.

22. Ralph G. Hurlin, "The Employment Statistics of the United States Employment Service," *American Statistical Association Quarterly* (Dec. 1922), 497; reprint found in, RG 183, Bureau of Employment Security: USES Records, box 1515, Junior Division Personnel, file: "USES, Dec. 1918–April 1919: misc."

23. See, for example, the very favorable comments of Frank S. Deibler, professor of economics at Northwestern University, in his "The Measurement of Unemployment—The Need for Additional Information," *Proceedings of the Ninth Annual Meeting of the International Association of Public Employment Services held at Buffalo, New York, September 7–9, 1921,* BLS Bulletin No. 311 (Aug. 1922), 64

24. In 1930, President Hoover became involved in an embarrassing political row when he quoted the unemployment figures collected by the USES, and Frances Perkins, who was at that time the industrial commissioner of New York, declared publicly that they were inaccurate and misleading. See Frances Perkins, *The Roosevelt I Knew* (New York: Viking Press, 1946), 96–97.

25. *Ninth Annual Report of the Secretary of Labor for the Fiscal Year ended June 30, 1921* (Washington: GPO, 1921), 17.

26. For a list of the cities, see *Thirteenth Annual Report of the Secretary of Labor for the Fiscal Year ended June 30, 1925* (Washington, D.C.: GPO, 1925), 38–39.

27. There was some criticism of the use of posters on the ground that "experience has shown that more desirable workers may be found in comparatively restricted areas adjoining the wheat belt and in the smaller localities, rather than in the larger industrial centers." See Harrison, *Public Employment Offices,* 540. This comment echoed similar criticism of the USES made by employment experts during the war years.

28. H. Paul Douglass, "Migratory Labor in the Wheat Harvest," report to the Interchurch World Movement, n.d. (1919?), quoted in Harrison, *Public Employment Offices,* 542.

29. See, for example, *Fifteenth Annual Report of the Secretary of Labor for the Fiscal Year ended June 30, 1927* (Washington, D.C.: GPO, 1927), 31, 34.

30. *Nineteenth Annual Report of the Secretary of Labor for the Fiscal Year ended June 30, 1931* (Washington, D.C.: GPO, 1931), quoted in Kellogg, *The United States Employment Service,* 56–57. Kellogg goes on to point out the difficulty of assessing the accuracy of the numbers quoted and the imprecise nature of the term "directed to employment." The figures quoted were undoubtedly impressionistic and included all the placement work done by state and local offices with no real assistance from the skeletal USES offices. As it had done in the war period, the USES was inflating the amount of work it had done by including the work of the state employment offices as its own.

Epilogue
Keeping the Federalist Faith, 1920–1933

1. Harrison, *Public Employment Offices.* For details on the organization of the project, see Shelby M. Harrison, "A Study of Public Employment Service—A Statement of Scope and Status," *International Association of Public Employment Services, Proceedings of Eighth Annual Meeting, Ottawa, Canada, September 20–22, 1920* (Ottawa: Department of Labour, 1921), 57–59.
2. See Harrison, *Public Employment Offices.* See also Harrison to Leiserson, Oct. 18, 1924 (and attached news release), William M. Leiserson Papers, Professional Correspondence, file: "Russell Sage Foundation, 1915–1941," State Historical Society of Wisconsin.
3. William M. Leiserson, *Adjusting Immigrant and Industry* (New York: Harper and Brothers, 1924), chs. 1–3, esp. 63, 64.
4. Sautter, "Unemployment and Government," 347–50. This is the best brief description. See also J. Joseph Huthmacher, *Senator Robert F. Wagner and the Rise of Urban Liberalism* (New York: Atheneum, 1968), 62, 78–80, 84. See also Kellogg, *The United States Employment Service,* 62–69.
5. Kellogg, *The United States Employment Service,* ch. 4, esp. 71. See also the detailed discussion of the Doak reorganization in Sautter, *Three Cheers for the Unemployed,* 257–68.
6. ? [signature indecipherable] to D. Lescohier, May 25, 1931. State Industrial Commission, Administration, Numerical Subject File, 1911–1960, ser. 29/1/3, file C.597, State Historical Society of Wisconsin. Lescohier, who had been involved in the Minnesota USES during the war and had subsequently taken a position at the University of Wisconsin, had wired friends in Washington asking for information on what was happening.
7. B. M. Squires (BMS) to D. Lescohier, May 13, 1931, and ? to Lescohier, May 25, 1931, State Industrial Commission, Administration, Numerical Subject File, 1911–1960, ser. 29/1/3, file C.597, State Historical Society of Wisconsin.
8. R. G. Knudsen to Robert M. La Follette, June 4, 1932, ibid.
9. Kellogg, *The United States Employment Service,* 30–33, 60–61, 74, 83–87.
10. Ibid., 54–55, 86, 96–104. The Kellogg investigation had also pointed to the shortcomings of existing state employment offices. Barely half of the forty-eight states operated even one employment office. Most of those in operation were inadequately financed, staffed, and housed and were dominated by politics and the spoils system. The Wagner proposal to integrate all public employment offices into a nationwide system policed by the federal government via the matching grant mechanism seemed the obvious solution.

11. "State Employment Service Officials Condemn Doak 'Reorganization,'" *American Labor Legislation Review* 21 (Dec. 1931): 393. Unfortunately, the formal proceedings of the 1931 IAPES conference were never printed. In the midst of this controversy, Senator Wagner reintroduced his bill in January 1932. Again it was favorably reported out of committee but nothing further happened.

12. "An Act to provide for the establishment of a national employment system and for cooperation with the States in the promotion of such system, and for other purposes, June 6, 1933" (Wagner-Peyser Act), *Statutes at Large, 1933,* 113–17.

13. Fred C. Croxton, "Development of a Federal Public Employment System in the United States," *International Association of Public Employment Services (IAPES), Proceedings of the Eighteenth Annual Meeting, Toronto, Canada, September 9–12, 1930,* BLS Bulletin No. 538 (May 1931), 162–66.

14. William M. Leiserson, "What Constitutes a Good Employment Service," IAPES, *Proceedings of Sixteenth Annual Meeting held at Cleveland, Ohio, September 18–21, 1928,* BLS Bulletin No. 501 (Oct. 1929), 21–29. There had been moments of pessimism and doubt. For a brief period, in the mid-1920s, Leiserson had wondered whether government-sponsored employment offices would ever be really effective. See Leiserson to P. U. Kellogg, Mar. 18, 1925, William M. Leiserson Papers, Professional Correspondence, file: "Survey Associates, Inc., 1911–1932," State Historical Society of Wisconsin.

Essay on Sources

The records of the first U.S. Employment Service were destroyed in a warehouse fire in Virginia in the early 1930s, prior to the establishment of the National Archives. Dixon Wecter, in *When Johnny Comes Marching Home* (Cambridge, Mass.: Houghton, Mifflin, 1944), alleges that William Nuckles Doak, secretary of labor in the Hoover administration, was responsible for their deliberate destruction (p. 574). Whether the allegation is true or not, the destruction of the records no doubt accounts for the absence of serious historical work dealing with the first USES and, indeed, its virtual disappearance from historical memory. My own interest in the workings of the labor market during World War I was aroused when doing research for an earlier study on the work of the state councils of defense, some of which had active committees on labor that cooperated with the USES. Trying to find out something about the USES made me realize how little had been written about the labor mobilization in World War I and the central importance of the USES to that story.

The research for the study of the state councils of defense not only piqued my interest in the first USES but, by chance, also alerted me to the existence of a considerable quantity of forgotten USES records. As part of my research for the earlier project, I had worked with state council of defense records located in a number of state archives. Working in those state archives (often, I suspect, the first person to look at the World War I records since they were deposited) made me aware that a few of the states not only had excellent collections of state council of defense material but also housed the complete papers of the state branch of the USES. After an extensive correspondence with state archivists in an endeavor to locate all surviving USES records, I visited nine states that seemed to have promising collections. I felt that those state branch records, if used in conjunction with other related material, might overcome the handicap of the destruction of the central records and enable me to reconstruct the history of the USES. Other important collections of primary sources included the surviving records of the Department of Labor itself, the federal departments and wartime agencies that interacted with the USES, and the personal papers of individuals who were in some way connected with the activities of the USES. It was later, as I began to work with the records, that I realized the need to research the prewar and the postwar history in order to understand the full story of the first USES.

As far as I am able to judge, the best collections of USES materials in state archives are held in Connecticut, Illinois, Minnesota, Wisconsin, Indiana, Ohio, and New York. The records held in the Connecticut state archives in Hartford (RG 20, Records of the Connecticut Labor Department [Part A]: United States Employment Service, 1917–19) constituted a very large, well-organized, and extremely valuable collection. It is the most detailed collection of the workings of a state branch of the USES that has survived, and it includes what appears to be a complete set of the almost daily correspondence between the state office in Hartford and the central office in Washington, as well as material sent between the Hartford office and the various local offices within the state. I also consulted the Connecticut State Council of Defense records (RG 30, Records of the Connecticut State Council of Defense, 1917–19), because the State Council was involved in labor issues within the state from the beginning of the war and conducted the negotiations with the federal Department of Labor concerning the establishment of the USES in Connecticut. Again, it is a very large and extremely valuable collection.

The only other collection of USES material that matched the Connecticut collection in volume was held at the Illinois state archives in Springfield (Illinois State Council of Defense Records, U.S. Department of Labor, USES Records). This is an immense collection and, although there is an inventory, the collection itself is not well organized, and specific material is very difficult to locate. As a consequence, the collection was (as of February 1982) fairly impenetrable. The Springfield collection also contains two related collections that are much smaller and easier to use: the papers of the state branches of both the U.S. Public Service Reserve (Illinois State Council of Defense Records, U.S. Department of Labor, USES, U.S. Public Service Records) and the U.S. Boys' Working Reserve (Illinois State Council of Defense Records, U.S. Department of Labor, USES, U.S. Boys' Working Reserve Records). These are very valuable collections and undoubtedly contain the best material that has survived on how both organizations actually operated at the state level.

At the Minnesota Historical Society, in St. Paul, I consulted three collections (War Records Commission, USES, 1918–19; Public Safety Commission Records, 1918–20; Minnesota Department of Labor and Industry, Bureau of Labor Records). The most valuable was the USES collection, which comprised eighteen cartons of densely packed and very relevant material. The papers are in the original numerical file order, but, unfortunately, the index is missing; in effect, therefore, the collection is uncataloged. Nonetheless, it is a very useful collection that details the work of the USES in Minnesota and has a helpful collection of material relating to the Boys' Working Reserve. The Public Safety Commission records contain a good file of material on the employment office it operated during the war, which was supervised by Don D. Lescohier. The records of the Department of Labor and Industry, unfortunately, were not helpful.

At the State Historical Society of Wisconsin I was able to consult three relevant collections (War History Commission, Emergency Employment Situation in Wisconsin, 1918–19; Wisconsin State Council of Defense Papers, 1917–18; Wisconsin Industrial Commission Papers). The Emergency Employment Situation papers relate to the publicity drive in February 1919 aimed at influencing Congress to support the USES. The collection does indicate the impressive support that the USES was able to command throughout Wisconsin. In the other collections, the semi-verbatim minutes of the State Council of Defense contain a good deal of information about labor problems in the state, and the Industrial Commission papers have a lot of useful material on employment offices in Wisconsin both during and after the war.

The 184 bound volumes of the papers of the Indiana State Council of Defense (Archives Division, Indiana Commission on Public Records, Indiana State Library, Indianapolis) contain four volumes relating to labor (Series 14) and one relating to the Public Service Reserve. Unfortunately, these collections are mainly confined to the official mimeo bulletins, general orders, and similar material; there is virtually no correspondence from the officials in charge of labor matters in Indiana, which limits the value of the collection. In neighboring Ohio, the State Council of Defense papers (Ohio Branch, Council of National Defense Papers, Series 1135) are held in the

Ohio Historical Society's archives in Columbus. The collection contains considerable material relating to the organization of the state employment offices, particularly during 1917, but very little on relations with the USES and the Department of Labor. The papers of the Ohio Industrial Commission (Series 757, Ohio Historical Society) contained only some scattered fragments of information relating to the USES.

Other state archives that I visited contained very little of relevance. The collection of New York State Defense Council Papers (State Archives, Albany) is well organized and easy to use, but it did not contain very much of value to this project apart from the section dealing with the Public Service Reserve. Most of the early state Department of Labor records, which probably included those relating to the USES, were apparently destroyed prior to the formal organization of the New York State Archives in the 1970s. In Pennsylvania, no records relating to the employment work in the state during World War I appear to have survived. Given the importance of that state during the war, this was a great disappointment. The state archives in Harrisburg do, however, contain the records of the State Council of Defense (RG 10, Records of the Office of the Governor, Council of National Defense and Committee of Public Safety), which were not of much value for this project, although the detailed "Minutes of the Executive Committee" contained some fragments of information relating to the USES. That collection does contain a seven-volume set of scrapbooks, containing clippings from the state newspapers depicting the home-front mobilization in Pennsylvania, which is probably the best collection of its kind for World War I. In Massachusetts the story was similar: I was unable to locate any records relating to the state employment service or to the USES in that state. The papers of the State Council of Defense (Massachusetts Committee on Public Safety Records) have been microfilmed and are held in the Massachusetts State Library vault, Boston. Unfortunately, they contained nothing of relevance, as far as I could determine.

At the National Archives, Washington, D.C., I consulted the surviving records of the Department of Labor (RG 174, Department of Labor Records), which contain a scattering of relevant material in the William B. Wilson and the Hugh Kerwin papers, but the most important section was the Chief Clerk's file. The National Archives also contains a collection directly related to the USES (RG 183, Bureau of Employment Security, Records of the U.S. Employment Service, 1907–49). However, this proved to be a disappointment because, apart from some limited material relating to the Omaha office of the USES for the World War I period, most of the collection was

concerned with the post-1930 period. However, the records of the War Labor Policies Board (RG 1), which exercised a general supervision over the
USES in the second half of 1918, were very helpful.

The Emergency Fleet Corporation of the U.S. Shipping Board had an
extensive connection with the USES, and its papers were extremely valuable (RG 32, U.S. Shipping Board Records, Construction Organization).
Of particular value were the Records of the Industrial Relations Division
and the General Records relating to Ship Construction, which include the
Charles M. Schwab, Charles Piez, and J. L. Ackerson papers. The papers of
the Committee on Labor of the Council of National Defense (RG 62, Council of National Defense Records), which was chaired by Samuel Gompers,
helped clarify a good deal about the internal, political maneuvering that
went on in the second half of 1917. The papers of the U.S. Housing Corporation (RG 3, U.S. Housing Corporation, Industrial Relations Division)
contained the weekly reports of its Industrial Relations Division and included comments on the assistance given by the USES. The well-organized
records of the Office of the Secretary of Agriculture (RG 16, Department of
Agriculture, Office of the Secretary, Incoming Correspondence) contained
a good deal of very useful material on the cordial but rather distrustful
relations between that department and the USES.

The records of the Railroad Administration (RG 14, U.S. Railroad Administration, Records of the Office of the Director General and Records of
the Division of Labor) contained nothing of relevance that I could locate.
My greatest disappointment among the institutional records was my failure (in spite of the assistance of three different archivists) to find material of
much consequence relating to the USES in the voluminous records of the
War Department. I checked three separate collections without success (RG
165, Records of the War Department General and Special Staffs; RG 92,
Records of the Office of the Quartermaster General, General Correspondence; RG 77, Office of the Chief of Engineers, Construction Division,
1890–1945). This last collection (RG 77) did contain the records of the War
Department's Construction Division for World War I, which had been
transferred there in 1941. Unfortunately, it was not particularly helpful for
my purposes. Given the importance of the War Department's construction
program, and the strained relations between the War Department and the
Department of Labor throughout the war, the dearth of documentation
was an unexpected setback. Nor were the records of the Navy Department
that I consulted of very much assistance (RG 181, Records of Naval Districts and Shore Establishments).

The papers of the War Industries Board (RG 61, Records of the War Industries Board) contained little of relevance in the Labor Division or the Chairman's Office files, although the WIB *Minutes* clearly indicate the increasing concern about the shortage of labor in the summer and fall of 1918. The most directly useful section of the WIB papers related to labor on construction sites (Technical or Commodity File, Construction Projects, Labor).

I consulted the personal papers of a large number of individuals. The Woodrow Wilson Papers (Library of Congress, Manuscript Division [microfilm]) contained valuable material, particularly in Series 4, Executive Office Files, 1913–21, Case file 19-19G (reels 171 and 172). This file also contains the best collection that I found of the weekly reports prepared by the USES on labor conditions in the United States. The collection covers March 20 through August 10, 1918. The papers of Secretary of Labor William Bauchop Wilson (Historical Society of Pennsylvania, Philadelphia), although voluminous, contain very little of direct relevance to the USES. One folder of material, headed "Employment Service, 1917," was helpful. That collection supplemented but was not as useful for my purposes as the W. B. Wilson papers included in the official Department of Labor Records (RG 174) in the National Archives. The papers of Secretary of War Newton Diehl Baker (Library of Congress, Manuscript Division [microfilm]) are also voluminous but, again, contain little specifically relevant to the USES. There is a sprinkling of material dealing with wider labor policy issues affecting the War Department, but I could not locate much material specifically on relations between the Department of Labor and the War Department.

Senior wartime administrators left little of value relating to the USES in their papers. Felix Frankfurter's papers (Library of Congress, Manuscript Division), although containing the best organized collection of WLPB minutes and related papers and reports, contained little else that was helpful. Most of the collection relates to his later career. Fortunately, the War Labor Policies Board papers in the National Archives (RG 1) contain a good deal of relevant Frankfurter material. The small collection of the papers of Louis Freeland Post, assistant secretary of labor (Library of Congress, Manuscript Division), was, like the Frankfurter Papers, very disappointing. The collection does contain a lengthy unpublished autobiography, which, unfortunately, says very little about the USES. That omission may be related to Post's defeat in this area. Post does make clear the personal animosities and factions within the Department of Labor and his own obsessive mistrust of businessmen who offered their services to the government during the war. The Terence Vincent Powderly Papers (Catholic University of America, Washington, D.C.; microfilm edition available from Microfilming Corporation of America) contain some useful information on the prewar period but nothing of substance on the wartime experience. Powderly, sixty-eight years old in 1917, was in charge of the Division of Information in the Bureau of Immigration, which, in the prewar period, had been responsible for the employment service work of the Department of Labor. The Division was switched to the USES at the end of 1917 and remained there until August 1918.

The papers of the two key advisers to the secretary of war on labor matters, Stanley King (Amherst College, Amherst, Massachusetts) and Ernest Martin Hopkins (Dartmouth College, Hanover, New Hampshire), contain a good deal on general labor issues but very little directly related to the USES. The desk diaries for 1918–19 of Major General George W. Goethals (George Washington Goethals Papers, Library of Congress, Manuscript Division), who was responsible for consolidating the War Department's supply functions, contain some brief references to labor conditions, particularly to Hopkins's active promotion of greater centralization of the government's labor supply machinery.

Other personal collections yielded some insights. The William Morris Leiserson Papers (State Historical Society of Wisconsin, Madison), although mainly concerned with his later career, contain some helpful material on his prewar and wartime activies. Perhaps the most valuable item in that collection for this study was the copy of an unpublished paper he read to a meeting of the Ohio Academy of Social Sciences on March 29, 1918, in which he vented his frustration at the actions of the Department of Labor and was bitterly critical of the manner in which the USES was being conducted. Leiserson also published a number of articles relating to employment work. Unfortunately, the Fred C. Croxton Papers in the Herbert Hoover Presidential Library, West Branch, Iowa, do not relate to his World War I activities. The small collection of the papers of George P. Hambrecht (State Historical Society of Wisconsin, Madison), who was chairman of the Wisconsin Industrial Commission and in charge of the USES offices, contains useful material on the activities of the USES in Wisconsin during and immediately after the war. Some of this material is duplicated in the Wisconsin Industrial Commission records. The Donald Reed Cotton Papers (Minnesota Historical Society, St. Paul) also contained some relevant material.

The Records of the American Association for Labor Legislation (John Bertram Andrews Papers), Labor-Management Documentation Center, Catherwood Library, Cornell University, Ithaca, New York (available on microfilm), although mainly concerned with other issues being promoted by the American Association for Labor Legislation, particularly workers' compensation, did contain some material (reels 18 and 19) relating to the lobbying efforts undertaken by Andrews in order to get USES legislation and appropriations through Congress during the war. By contrast, the huge collection of Samuel Gompers Papers (American Federation of Labor Records: The Samuel Gompers Era) located in the State Historical Society of Wisconsin, Madison (also available on microfilm), proved to be mainly routine matters and contained virtually nothing of consequence concerning the USES. The papers of Frank Morrison, the long-time secretary of the AFL (Duke University, Durham, North Carolina), were similarly disappointing. This paucity of references to the USES is probably an accurate reflection of the low priority that organized labor placed on its work. The Henry Mauris Robinson Papers (Hoover Institution Archives, Stanford University, Palo Alto, California), although mainly reflecting Robinson's work in the State Councils Section of the Council of National Defense, did contain some USES-related material, including an interesting set of correspondence with D. M. Reynolds, the publicity man invited by Secretary of Labor Wilson to take charge of the USES publicity campaigns in 1918.

If the unpublished records relating to the USES are fairly sketchy and uneven, some of the contemporary published sources offer a great deal of information on the organization and operation of the service. Among material published by the Department of Labor itself there are some outstanding items. The weekly *United States Employment Service Bulletin* (vol. 1, nos. 1–49 [Jan. 28, 1918–Jan. 31, 1919]; vol. 2, nos. 1–3 [Feb. 3–28, 1919]) contains a great deal of detail about the workings of the USES. It needs to be used with some caution, however, because it is written very much from the viewpoint of the USES. The monthly official bulletin of the U.S. Boys' Working Reserve, *Boypower* (vol. 1, nos. 1–12 [Nov. 15, 1917–Dec. 15, 1918]; vol. 2, nos. 1–5 [Jan. 15–June 15, 1918]), is more exhortative and contains less detailed information on the work of the Reserve. A more useful printed work on the Boys' Working Reserve is the thirty-page report titled *Report of National Conference of Directors of United States Boys' Working Reserve, Department of Labor, Washington, D.C., Friday and Saturday, June 29 and 30, 1917* (n.d.).

The Department of Labor also published the verbatim proceedings of a national conference of USES officials, including all the state representatives, held in Washington in June 1918. It is a splendid source and contains a great deal of very frank statements about the labor problem and about the shortcomings of the USES (Department of Labor, USES, *Report of Proceedings of the National War Labor Conference, Washington, June 13–15, 1918* (Washington, D.C.: Government Printing Office, 1918). The department's Bureau of Labor Statistics published the *Monthly Review,* which contains quite useful articles and digests of current developments relating to labor. The annual reports of the Department of Labor and the two detailed, published reports of the U.S. Employment Service (Aug. 1, 1918, and Aug. 15, 1919) by John Densmore, the director-general, surveyed the activities of the USES, although, naturally, they reflected the department's views. They need to be read with care; one gets little sense, for instance, of the long struggle over the administrative structure of the USES or of the importance of the reorganization in the summer of 1918 and no indication of the complete defeat of the ambitions of the Department of Labor.

The various congressional hearings relating to the USES proved to be an unparalleled contemporary source of detailed information. The most important single hearing was held in mid-1919 (Joint Committees on Labor, *National Employment System: Hearings on S 688, S 1442 and HR 4305,* 66th Cong., 1st sess.). The hearings stretched over five weeks and included a large number of witnesses. Another important hearing was held before the House Committee on Appropriations in May 1918 (*Sundry Civil Bill, 1919: Hearings Before Subcommittee of House Committee on Appropriations on Sundry Civil Appropriations Bill, 1919,* 65th Cong., 2d sess.). For the prewar period, the most useful hearing was held in February 1916 (House Committee on Labor, *National Employment Bureau: Hearings on HR 5783,* 64th Cong., 1st sess.).

The Emergency Fleet Corporation published the verbatim proceedings of a number of special conferences it organized during the war. These conferences usually included representatives of the USES who spoke on the role of that organization in supplying shipbuilding labor. Some of these are quite illuminating. See, especially, U.S. Shipping Board, Emergency Fleet Corporation, *Report of New England Shipbuilding Conference held under the auspices of the Industrial Service Department, Division of Construction, Emergency Fleet Corporation, at Chamber of Commerce Building, Boston, Mass., October 1, 1917* (Washington, D.C.: Government Printing Office, 1917), and *Report of the Shipyard Employment Managers' Conference Held under the*

Auspices of the Industrial Service Department of the Division of Construction, Emergency Fleet Corporation, Washington, D.C., November 9 and 10, 1917 (Washington, D.C.: Government Printing Office, 1917).

The best nongovernmental contemporary source is provided by the proceedings of the annual meetings of the American Association of Public Employment Offices (AAPEO) between 1913 and 1933. The name of this association was changed to the International Association of Public Employment Services (IAPES) in September 1920, when the meeting was held in Ottawa, Canada. The proceedings contain all the papers read at the annual conferences, including those given by various Department of Labor and USES officials, by a large number of state employment service representatives, and by a number of other employment experts. The papers were published by the Bureau of Labor Statistics (except for the 1920 and 1930 volumes, which were published by the Canadian government). Unfortunately, the proceedings of the annual meetings covering the war years and reconstruction, 1917–19, were not published. The proceedings of the meetings of a related, newly organized, quasi-professional group, the employment managers, also contained some material on wartime problems that involved the USES. See, especially, *Proceedings of Employment Managers' Conference, Rochester, N.Y., May 9, 10, and 11, 1918,* Bureau of Labor Statistics (BLS) Bulletin No. 247 (Washington, D.C.: Government Printing Office, 1919).

Some other professional societies devoted part of their annual conferences during the war to labor and employment issues. The December 1917 meeting of the American Association for Labor Legislation in Philadelphia included an important joint session with the American Economic Association and the American Farm Management Association on "Mobilizing the Labor Supply." It also included an important additional session on "Labor Conservation in War Time." The general discussion following the joint session is recorded somewhat differently by both associations. See reports in *American Labor Legislation Review* 8 (Mar. 1918) and *American Economic Review* [supplement] 8 (Mar. 1918). The *Annals of the American Academy of Political and Social Science, 1917–1919* also contained some relevant material, particularly the special session titled "A Reconstruction Labor Policy," published in vol. 81 (Jan. 1919).

The most helpful contemporary journal was probably the *Survey,* which contained particularly useful articles by Leiserson, March and April 1918, on the wartime labor market and the shortcomings of the USES, and by Edward T. Devine, February and April 1919, analyzing the postwar attack on the USES and reviewing the accomplishments of the wartime service. The *American Labor Legislation Review* was probably the next most helpful journal. The *New Republic* had some useful articles, as did the *Journal of Political Economy*. The major journals published by employer and union organizations were not very helpful. The *American Federationist,* the journal of the American Federation of Labor, and the *Nation's Business,* published by the U.S. Chamber of Commerce, did not publish much of value to this study. *Industrial Mangement,* which was aimed at industrial executives, particularly employment managers, and mechanical engineers, contained some useful material relating to the labor problem. Newspapers tended to reprint the publicity material sent out by the USES without exercising much independent judgment.

Secondary literature on the USES is sparse. This is reflected vividly in the almost complete absence of any reference to the USES in two recent surveys of American involvement in World War I: David Kennedy, *Over Here: The First World War and American Society* (New York: Oxford University Press, 1980), and Robert H. Ferrell, *Woodrow Wilson and World War I* (New York: Harper and Row, 1985). Immediately after World War I, Don D. Lescohier published *The Labor Market* (New York: Macmillan, 1919), drawing, in part, on his own wartime experiences as the superintendent of the Minnesota employment office. In Part 2, "The Machinery of the Labor Market," Lescohier deals directly with the prewar development of public employment offices as well as with the development and operation of the USES. It remains an excellent short study of the USES. Lescohier also covered the topic, taking it up to 1933, in volume 3 of John R. Commons et al., *History of Labor in the United States, 1896–1932,* 4 vols. (New York: Macmillan, 1918–35). Other early work included Darrell H. Smith, *The United States Employment Service: Its History, Activities and Organization* (Baltimore: Johns Hopkins University Press, 1923), which was part of a series of descriptive studies in administration published for the Institute for Government Research. It relied entirely on Department of Labor published reports and congressional reports and hearings. Although a quite useful surface summary, it completely lacks any depth or analysis.

The following year Shelby M. Harrison et al. published *Public Employment Offices: Their Purpose, Structure and Methods* (New York: Russell Sage Foundation, 1924), which was financed by the Russell Sage Foundation and based on a 1919–20 investigation of what lessons could be learned from the wartime experience concerning employment work. Initially, a series of questionnaires was mailed to various groups and individuals; then, in the second half of 1919, a team of experienced researchers did extensive field work, visiting employment offices across the nation and in Canada. The book assumes that increased government activity in employment work is necessary and, indeed, inevitable. The introduction states that the study "was planned with a view to assisting . . . those who, both inside and outside the Service, are already seeking to lift it to an increasingly higher plane of accomplishment" (p. 19). The book contains a good deal of information on the operation of the USES. Fred Croxton's views are quoted favorably and extensively, and the book is, in fact, a detailed and reasonably convincing argument in favor of a federal rather than a national USES. In the same year William M. Leiserson published *Adjusting Immigrant and Industry* (New York: Harper and Brothers, 1924), which was also a plea for a federal rather than a national USES.

In 1933 Ruth M. Kellogg published *The United States Employment Service* (Chicago: University of Chicago Press, 1933), which was based on field research in sixteen different states during the late summer and fall of 1932. Coming in the wake of the Doak reorganization of the USES in 1931, the object of the survey was declared to be "primarily for the purpose of gathering reliable data and evaluating the reorganized United States Employment Service" (p. x). The aim of the book was to provide material that "may be used constructively in building up and improving our free employment service in the United States" (p. xi). The book pointed to the fairly deplorable situation of public employment offices in the majority of states and to the need for a national body to integrate these disparate efforts. In fact, the book is a sustained argument in favor of a genuinely federal USES as embodied in the proposed Wagner bill, which did eventually become law in 1933.

All of the early secondary works on the USES endorsed the general principle that the federal government, through the USES, should have some role in organizing the nation's labor market. However, it was to be a limited role reflecting a USES that was organized on federalist, not nationalist, assumptions. The federalists, not the nationalists, won the battle of the books in the interwar era. In 1942, John Lombardi's useful study of the early history of the Department of Labor—*Labor's Voice in the Cabinet: A History of the Department of Labor from Its Origin to 1921* (New York: Columbia University Press, 1942)—upset the pattern. That part of the study that deals with the USES is quite laudatory and tends to blame most of its shortcomings on the difficulties of trying to function through a federal-state arrangement. In this respect it was a muted revival of the argument for a national, rather than a federal, USES.

In the 1960s and 1970s there was a revival of interest in the wider issue of unemployment in American history. Paul T. Ringenbach's study of unemployment in New York—*Tramps and Reformers, 1873–1916: The Discovery of Unemployment in New York* (Westport, Conn.: Greenwood Press, 1973)—contains some useful chapters on the development of interest in the problem and the early steps to establish public employment offices in that state. He has a good section on the role of William Leiserson with the Wainwright Commission between 1909 and 1911 and the work of the American Association for Labor Legislation in this area. In 1968, an article by Irwin Yellowitz, "The Origins of Unemployment Reform in the United States" (*Labor History* 9 [Fall 1968]: 338–60), helped place the development of public employment offices in the early twentieth century in the wider context of the drive for unemployment insurance and analyzed the reasons for the lukewarm attitude of organized labor. Roy Lubove's *The Struggle for Social Security 1900–1935* (Cambridge, Mass.: Harvard University Press, 1968) has a brief section dealing with the development of state public employment offices and the USES that emphasizes their overall failure: Lubove attributes this mainly to the indifference of both employers and workers to labor market organization under public auspices (pp. 147–59). Two superb recent studies of employment and unemployment that should be mentioned, although neither deals specifically with the USES, are Alex Keyssar, *Out of Work: The First Century of Unemployment in Massachusetts* (Cambridge: Cambridge University Press, 1986), and Walter Licht, *Getting Work: Philadelphia, 1840–1950* (Cambridge, Mass.: Harvard University Press, 1992).

In 1980 Robert D. Cuff's article on bureaucratic politics in the wartime labor administration, "The Politics of Labor Administration during World War I" (*Labor History* 21 [Fall 1980]: 546–69), opened a new dimension on the study of the USES by placing its development within the context of the overall bureaucratic struggle between different groups within the wartime labor administration. The article emphasized the role of Louis Post, the assistant secretary of labor, and his efforts to use the USES as a weapon in his struggle to enhance the position of the Department of Labor in the wartime administrative hierarchy. Two of my own articles, "Administrative Politics and Labor Policy in the First World War: The U.S. Employment Service and the Seattle Labor Market Experiment" (*Business History Review* 61 [Winter 1967]: 582–605) and "The Mobilization of Skilled Labor in World War I: 'Voluntarism,' the U.S. Public Service Reserve, and the Department of Labor, 1917–1918" (*Labor History* 32 [Spring 1991]: 253–72), enlarge on this general theme of bureaucratic politics and on the related theme of voluntarism. A third article, "The Labor Market, the Reform Impetus, and the Great War: The Reorganization of the State-City Employment Exchanges in Ohio, 1914–1918" (*Labor History* 29 [Fall 1988]: 475–97), is a case study of the motivation of employment office reformers and the employment methods they adopted. For more detail on the role of the USES in the effort to collect usable statistics on the operation of the labor market in the World War I era, see my "Labor Market Statistics and the State: The United States in the Era of the Great War, 1914–1930," *Journal of Policy History* 8, no. 3 (1996).

Over the past decade or so, Udo Sautter has published a number of detailed articles on the pre–New Deal development of public employment offices in North America. He has recently published a major study, *Three Cheers for the Unemployed: Government and Unemployment Before the New Deal* (Cambridge: Cambridge University Press, 1991), which covers the development of three governmental responses to the problem of unemployment in the late nineteenth and early twentieth centuries: public employment offices, public works, and unemployment insurance. The section dealing with the pre–World War I development of public employment offices in the states and the beginnings of the USES are good surveys of the material. Sautter makes the sensible point that public employment offices in the prewar period had very little impact on the overall labor market. The very brief overview chapter on World War I is dependent on existing printed sources, particularly the *Annual Reports* of the Department of Labor, and hence fails to emphasize the critical importance of the federalist-centralist struggle in explaining why the USES developed as it did. Similarly, the discussion of the political maneuvering in 1919 associated with the demise of the USES is weakened by the failure to understand the way in which the wartime experience had shaped the attitudes and expectations of the participants. Sautter's discussion of the 1920s is a good detailed study that complements the epilogue in this book. Overall, *Three Cheers for the Unemployed* offers an excellent synthesis of the available material on public employment office developments in the prewar period and in the 1920s. The sections on World War I and the postwar reconstruction reflect the absence of detailed historical research on the first USES during the wartime crisis; that gap in our knowledge is undoubtedly related to the lack of accessible sources mentioned at the beginning of this essay.

Most of the general studies of labor policy in the World War I era have told a relatively straightforward story of a slow and hesitant evolution of policy and administration from a very decentralized to a relatively centralized model. In that interpretation, most of the pressures for change are associated with the direct effects of the war on society. However, as this study of the first USES suggests, the process of administrative evolution was, in practice, more complex than a simple decentralized/centralized model suggests. The forces pushing for change were not all associated with the larger, wartime pressures in American society, and the process of defining exactly what the proposed centralization actually meant in practice proved to be more ambiguous and elusive than the model suggests.

Index

LABOR MARKET POLITICS AND THE GREAT WAR

was composed in 11/13 Adobe Garamond
on a Power Macintosh using PageMaker 6.0
at The Kent State University Press
printed by sheet-fed offset
on 50-pound Glatfelter Supple Opaque Natural stock
(an acid-free recycled paper),
notch case bound over binder's boards
in Kingston natural cloth,
and wrapped with dust jackets printed in two colors
on 100-pound enamel stock finished with film lamination
by Thomson-Shore, Inc.;
designed by Diana Gordy
and published by

The Kent State University Press
Kent, Ohio 44242